OZ: THE MARVELOUS LAND OF OZ. Contains material originally published in magazine form as THE MARVELOUS LAND OF OZ #1-8. First printing 2010. ISBN# 978-0-7851-4028-3. Published by MARVEL WORLDWIDE, INC., a subsidiary of MARVEL ENTERTAINMENT, LLC. OFFICE OF PUBLICATION: 417 5th Avenue, New York, NY 10016. Copyright © 2009 and 2010 Marvel Characters, Inc. All rights reserved. $29.99 per copy in the U.S. and $34.99 in Canada (GST #R127032852); Canadian Agreement #40668537. All characters featured in this issue and the distinctive names and likenesses thereof, and all related indicia are trademarks of Marvel Characters, Inc. No similarity between any of the names, characters, persons, and/or institutions in this magazine with those of any living or dead person or institution is intended, and any such similarity which may exist is purely coincidental. **Printed in the U.S.A.** ALAN FINE, EVP - Office of the President, Marvel Worldwide, Inc. and EVP & CMO Marvel Characters B.V.; DAN BUCKLEY, Chief Executive Officer and Publisher - Print, Animation & Digital Media; JIM SOKOLOWSKI, Chief Operating Officer; DAVID GABRIEL, SVP of Publishing Sales & Circulation; DAVID BOGART, SVP of Business Affairs & Talent Management; MICHAEL PASCIULLO, VP Merchandising & Communications; JIM O'KEEFE, VP of Operations & Logistics; DAN CARR, Executive Director of Publishing Technology; JUSTIN F. GABRIE, Director of Publishing & Editorial Operations; SUSAN CRESPI, Editorial Operations Manager; ALEX MORALES, Publishing Operations Manager; STAN LEE, Chairman Emeritus. For information regarding advertising in Marvel Comics or on Marvel.com, please contact Ron Stern, VP of Business Development, at rstern@marvel.com. For Marvel subscription inquiries, please call 800-217-9158. **Manufactured between 8/2/10 and 9/1/10 by R.R. DONNELLEY, INC., SALEM, VA, USA.**

10 9 8 7 6 5 4 3 2 1

THE MARVELOUS LAND OF OZ

ADAPTED FROM THE NOVEL BY L. FRANK BAUM

Writer: ERIC SHANOWER
Artist: SKOTTIE YOUNG
Colorist: JEAN-FRANCOIS BEAULIEU
Letterer: JEFF ECKLEBERRY

Assistant Editor: MICHAEL HORWITZ
Editor: NATE COSBY

Collection Editor: MARK D. BEAZLEY
Editorial Assistants: JAMES EMMETT & JOE HOCHSTEIN
Assistant Editors: ALEX STARBUCK & NELSON RIBEIRO
Editor, Special Projects: JENNIFER GRÜNWALD
Senior Editor, Special Projects: JEFF YOUNGQUIST
Senior Vice President of Sales: DAVID GABRIEL
Production: JERRY KALINOWSKI
Book Design: ARLENE SO

Editor in Chief: JOE QUESADA
Publisher: DAN BUCKLEY
Executive Producer: ALAN FINE

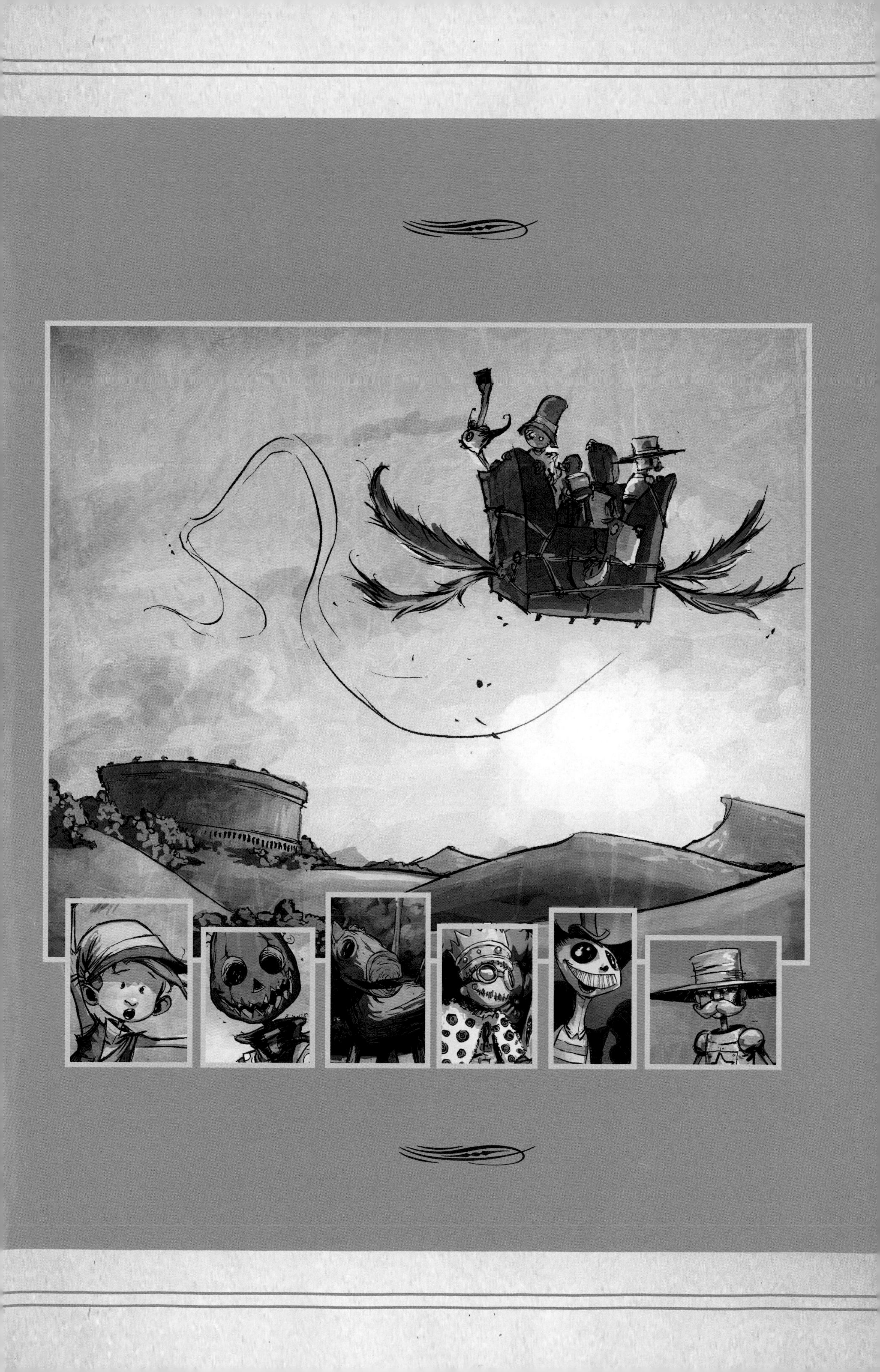

COUNTING BY TWOS

For anyone who ever wanted to know what happened to the characters after the end of *The Wonderful Wizard of Oz*, I bring good news—here are more adventures in *The Marvelous Land of Oz*. And the good news continues—this is only the beginning. Oz author L. Frank Baum wrote fourteen full-length Oz books as well as a slew of shorter Oz stories. Other writers continued the series after Baum's death until there were forty Oz books in the official series.

In this sequel to *The Wonderful Wizard of Oz*, the Scarecrow and the Tin Woodman are back. Dorothy Gale and the Cowardly Lion, however, aren't in *The Marvelous Land of Oz*. You'll have to wait for the next Oz story to find out what happens to them.

Instead of Dorothy from Kansas, *The Marvelous Land of Oz* features a boy named Tippetarius, who's usually called Tip. Tip isn't from Kansas or anywhere else in our Great Outside World. He's lived all his life in the Land of Oz. You might think Tip is lucky to live in Oz, but he's actually unlucky enough to live with an old woman named Mombi. Mombi looks like a witch, acts like a witch, and has enough magical powers for a dozen witches. But she refuses to call herself a witch. The reason Tip lives with Mombi is one of the most surprising secrets in all of American children's literature. Don't worry, I wouldn't dream of revealing the secret here. You'll have to read the story to discover it.

At the end of *The Wonderful Wizard of Oz*, the Scarecrow was declared the ruler of the Emerald City. As *The Marvelous Land of Oz* begins, he's doing his best to rule his people using the brains given to him by the Wizard. Likewise, the Tin Woodman rules the Winkies, a position he accepted after Dorothy destroyed the Wicked Witch of the West. Other familiar characters from the previous Oz story return here, such as Glinda the Good. Like Mombi, Glinda doesn't call herself a witch, although that's how she was introduced in the first Oz book. Instead, Glinda has become a sorceress, and that's what she'll be from now on. The Queen of the Field Mice also comes back to offer valuable assistance to Tip and his friends. Other returning characters—the Soldier with the Green Whiskers, the Guardian of the Gate, and the Emerald City maid with green hair—play small but important parts too.

You can be sure though that this Oz story is no rehash of the first. For instance, there are plenty of new magical items. Instead of Silver Shoes and Golden Cap, you'll see the incredible Powder of Life as well as Dr. Nikidik's problematic Wishing Pills at work. New characters fill the panels almost to bursting. Meet fragile, innocent Jack Pumpkinhead and a Sawhorse made all of wood. Then there are the pompous, human-sized insect named Prof. H. M. Woggle-bug, T. E.; a flying contraption known as the Gump; and General Jinjur, leader of the Army of Revolt.

Jinjur's rather absurd female army seems to be author L. Frank Baum's attempt to poke gentle fun at the women's rights movement of his day. Today the idea of women as soldiers is no longer unusual. In fact, these days the author's portrayal of women soldiers as silly airheads could seem offensive if it weren't for three things. First, the other all-female army of the story, the one led by Glinda the Good, is capable, formidable, and never played for laughs. Second, L. Frank Baum was the son-in-law of prominent suffragist and women's rights leader Matilda Joslyn Gage, with whom he enjoyed a close relationship. All evidence suggests that Baum was familiar with and sympathetic to Matilda Gage's views. Gage was even a major early influence on Baum's writings when she strongly encouraged him to write down his stories for children. Because of this, Gage's current biographer has gone so far as to dub Gage the "mother of Oz." And third, the many strong females in Baum's fantasy stories, such as Dorothy Gale, Glinda the Good, and—well, I won't go farther because I don't want to spoil any surprises.

When L. Frank Baum wrote *The Wonderful Wizard of Oz*, he never intended to write a sequel to that book, much less create a series that would be continued for decades after he was gone. So why did *The Marvelous Land of Oz* come into existence?

Baum loved the stage. In fact, he'd been a successful actor, director, and playwright long before *The Wonderful Wizard of Oz* was published. When that book became a bestseller, it was only natural for Baum to adapt his popular story for the stage.

The resulting musical extravaganza of *The Wizard of Oz* was the runaway hit of New York's Broadway in 1903. It made stars of the comedy team that played the Scarecrow and Tin Woodman. It made L. Frank Baum a wealthy man. And it made Oz a household word. Baum hoped to recreate this amazing success, so he sat down to write another Oz book and turn it into a musical extravaganza, too. *The Marvelous Land of Oz* was published in 1904. Baum made sure that his story prominently featured the star characters of the *Wizard* stage musical, the Scarecrow and Tin Woodman, and dedicated the book to the actors who played those characters, Fred Stone and David Montgomery. The endpaper illustration of the book even featured a photograph of the two actors in their Oz costumes.

The stage version of *The Wizard of Oz* contained many features that couldn't be found in the original Oz book. Some of those features made it into *The Marvelous Land of Oz*. For instance, we learn the Tin Woodman's real name, Nick Chopper. In the stage version of *Wizard*, Nick is short for Niccolo—in order to rhyme with piccolo, an instrument the character often played. *The Marvelous Land of Oz* also reveals that the Emerald City was once ruled by a king named Pastoria, a major character in the stage musical who was trying to recover his throne from the Wizard of Oz.

In his attempt to duplicate the riches and popularity brought by *The Wizard of Oz* musical extravaganza, Baum turned *The Marvelous Land of Oz* into a musical extravaganza called *The Woggle-Bug*. Unfortunately for Baum, *The Woggle-Bug* flopped in Chicago and never reached Broadway.

I'll let you in on a secret, though. If you compare this comics version of *The Marvelous Land of Oz* to L. Frank Baum's original book, you might notice some differences, especially in speeches by Mombi and General Jinjur's Army of Revolt. Where did these differences come from? Did I just make them up because I thought L. Frank Baum had fallen down on the job? No. Those differences were written by L. Frank Baum himself—in his script for *The Woggle-Bug*, his stage version of this story. I simply inserted bits of Baum's script into this version wherever I saw that they would enhance the story.

But enough explanation. Get ready—get set—to experience a second journey through *The Marvelous Land of Oz* as seen through the generous eyes of artist Skottie Young and colorist Jean-Francois Beaulieu. Let's go!

Eric Shanower
San Diego, July 2010

Folklore, legends, myths and fairy tales have followed childhood through the ages, for every healthy youngster has a wholesome and instinctive love for stories fantastic, marvelous and manifestly unreal.

The story of "The Wonderful Wizard of Oz" was written solely to please children of today. It aspires to being a modernized fairy tale, in which the wonderment and joy are retained and the heartaches and nightmares are left out.

L. FRANK BAUM CHICAGO, APRIL, 1900.

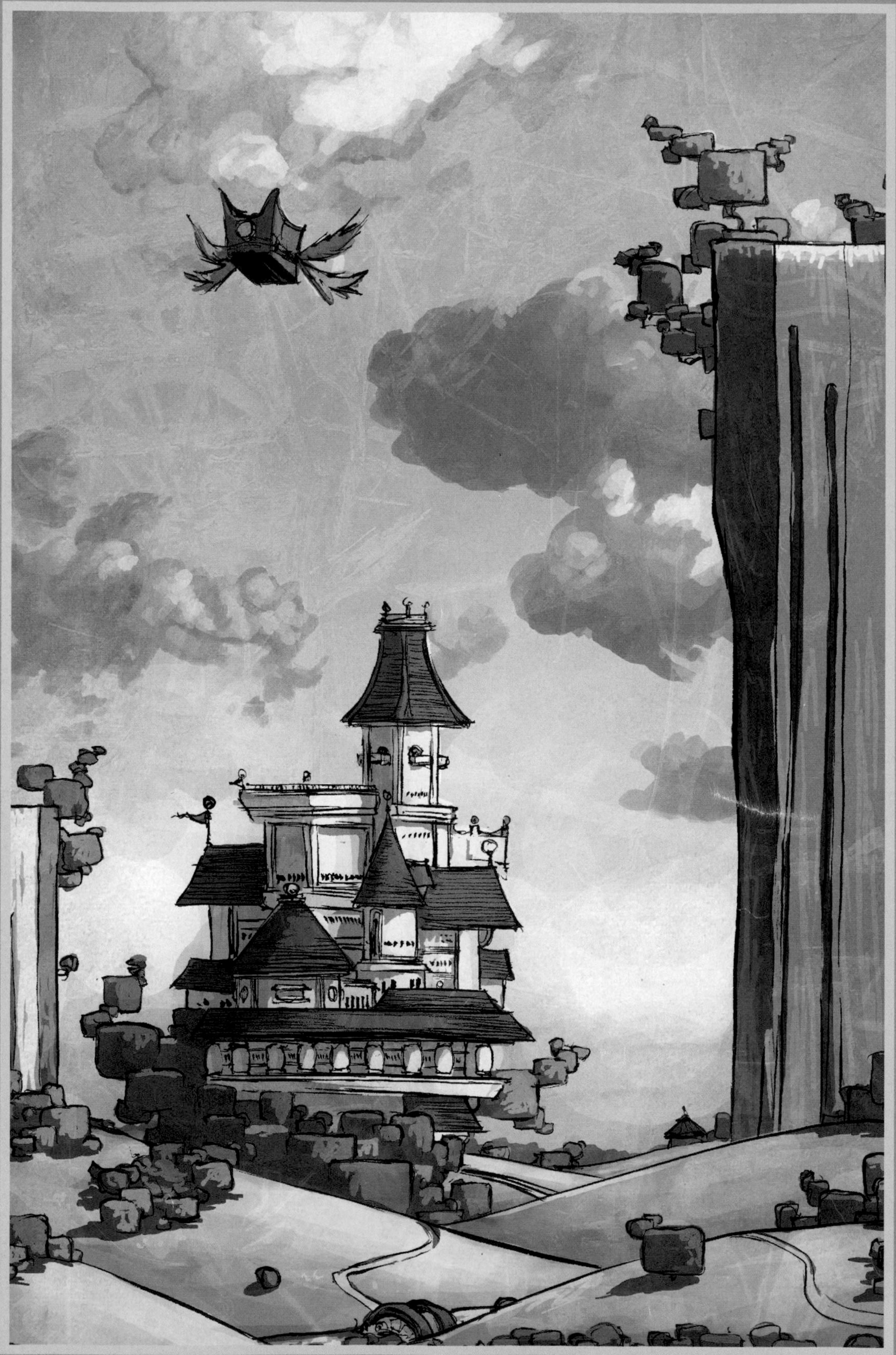

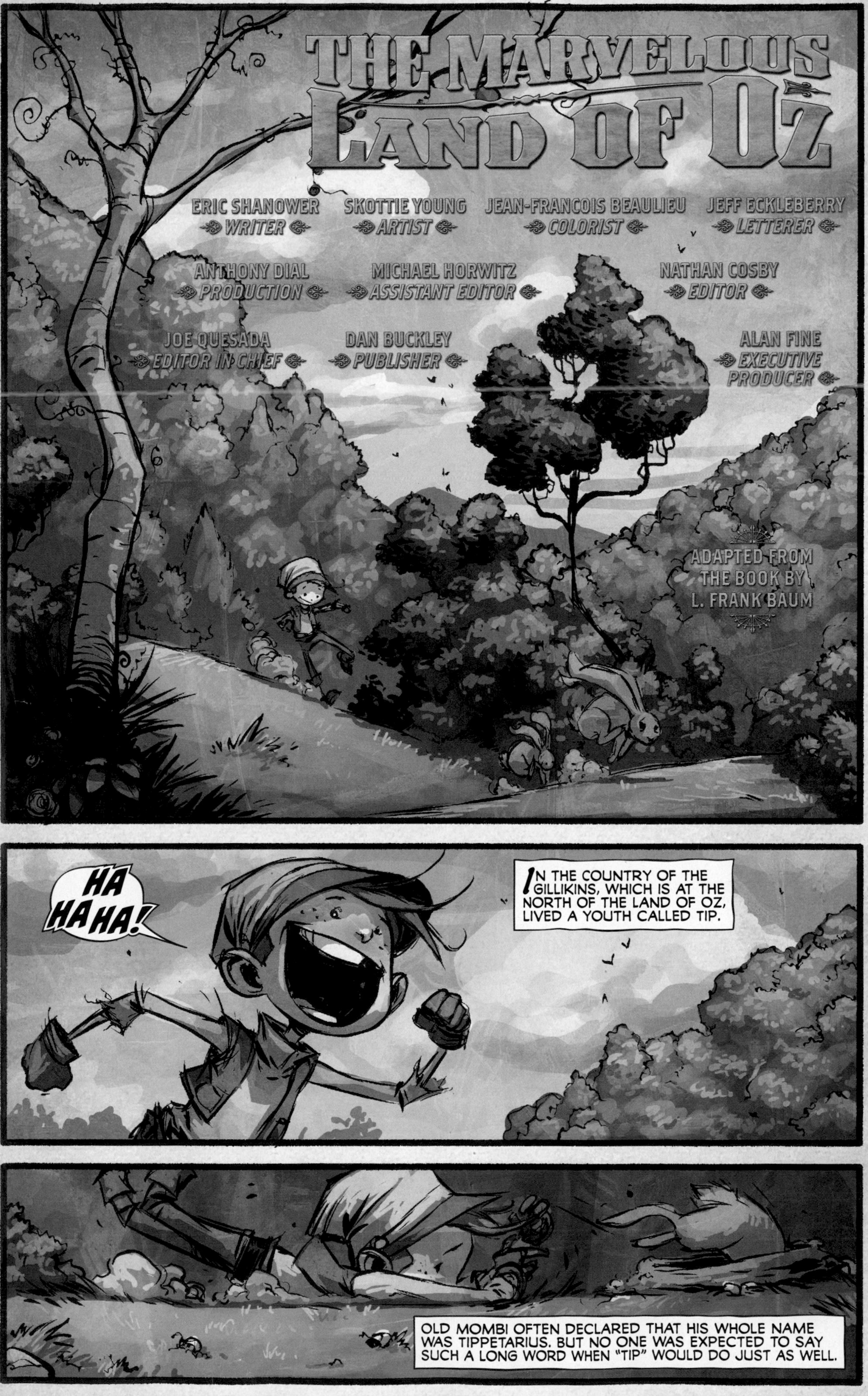
THE MARVELOUS LAND OF OZ
ERIC SHANOWER WRITER
SKOTTIE YOUNG ARTIST
JEAN-FRANCOIS BEAULIEU COLORIST
JEFF ECKLEBERRY LETTERER
ANTHONY DIAL PRODUCTION
MICHAEL HORWITZ ASSISTANT EDITOR
NATHAN COSBY EDITOR
JOE QUESADA EDITOR IN CHIEF
DAN BUCKLEY PUBLISHER
ALAN FINE EXECUTIVE PRODUCER
ADAPTED FROM THE BOOK BY L. FRANK BAUM
IN THE COUNTRY OF THE GILLIKINS, WHICH IS AT THE NORTH OF THE LAND OF OZ, LIVED A YOUTH CALLED TIP.
HA HA HA!
OLD MOMBI OFTEN DECLARED THAT HIS WHOLE NAME WAS TIPPETARIUS. BUT NO ONE WAS EXPECTED TO SAY SUCH A LONG WORD WHEN "TIP" WOULD DO JUST AS WELL.

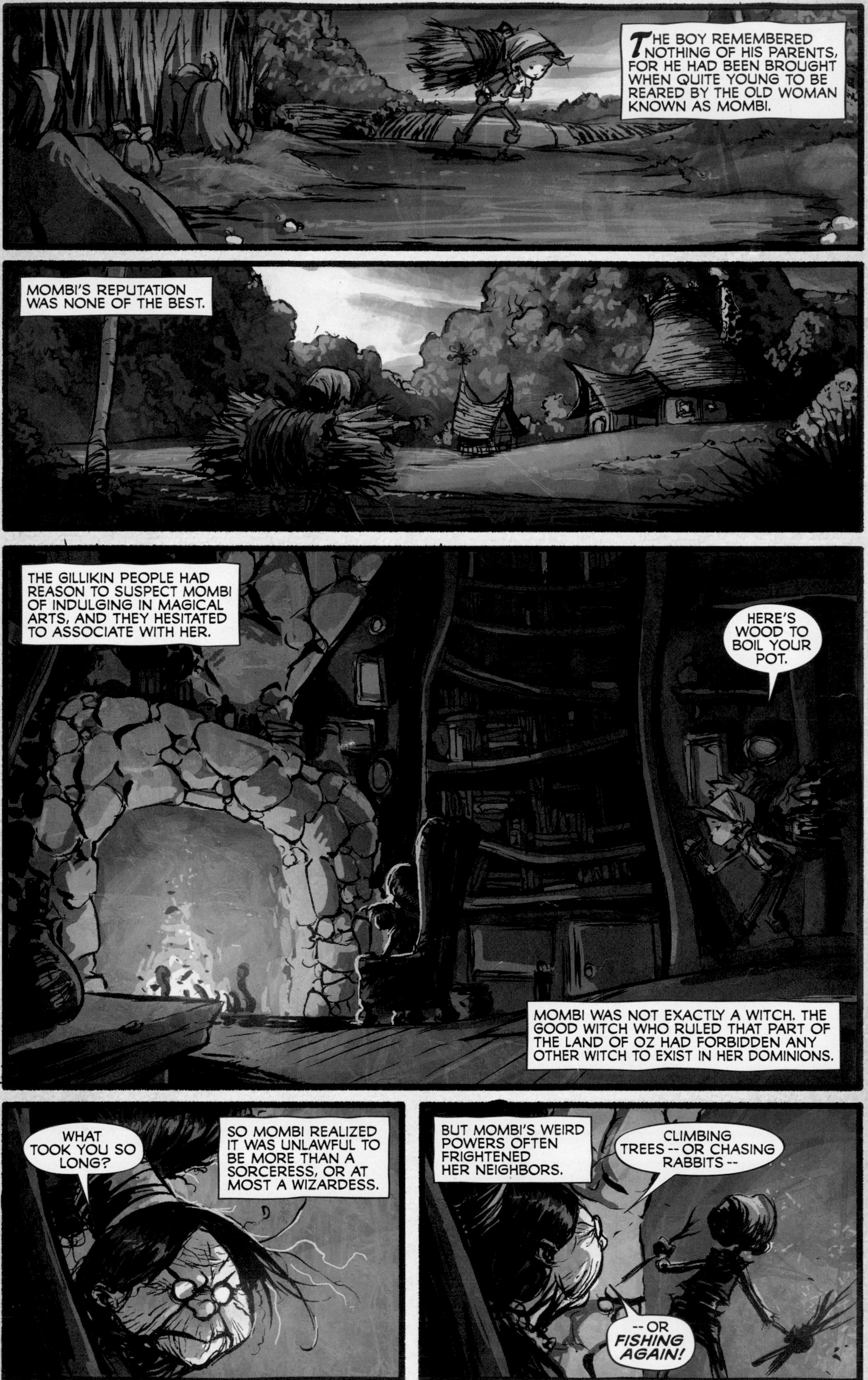
THE BOY REMEMBERED NOTHING OF HIS PARENTS, FOR HE HAD BEEN BROUGHT WHEN QUITE YOUNG TO BE REARED BY THE OLD WOMAN KNOWN AS MOMBI.
MOMBI'S REPUTATION WAS NONE OF THE BEST.
THE GILLIKIN PEOPLE HAD REASON TO SUSPECT MOMBI OF INDULGING IN MAGICAL ARTS, AND THEY HESITATED TO ASSOCIATE WITH HER.
HERE'S WOOD TO BOIL YOUR POT.
MOMBI WAS NOT EXACTLY A WITCH. THE GOOD WITCH WHO RULED THAT PART OF THE LAND OF OZ HAD FORBIDDEN ANY OTHER WITCH TO EXIST IN HER DOMINIONS.
WHAT TOOK YOU SO LONG?
SO MOMBI REALIZED IT WAS UNLAWFUL TO BE MORE THAN A SORCERESS, OR AT MOST A WIZARDESS.
BUT MOMBI'S WEIRD POWERS OFTEN FRIGHTENED HER NEIGHBORS.
CLIMBING TREES -- OR CHASING RABBITS --
-- OR *FISHING AGAIN!*

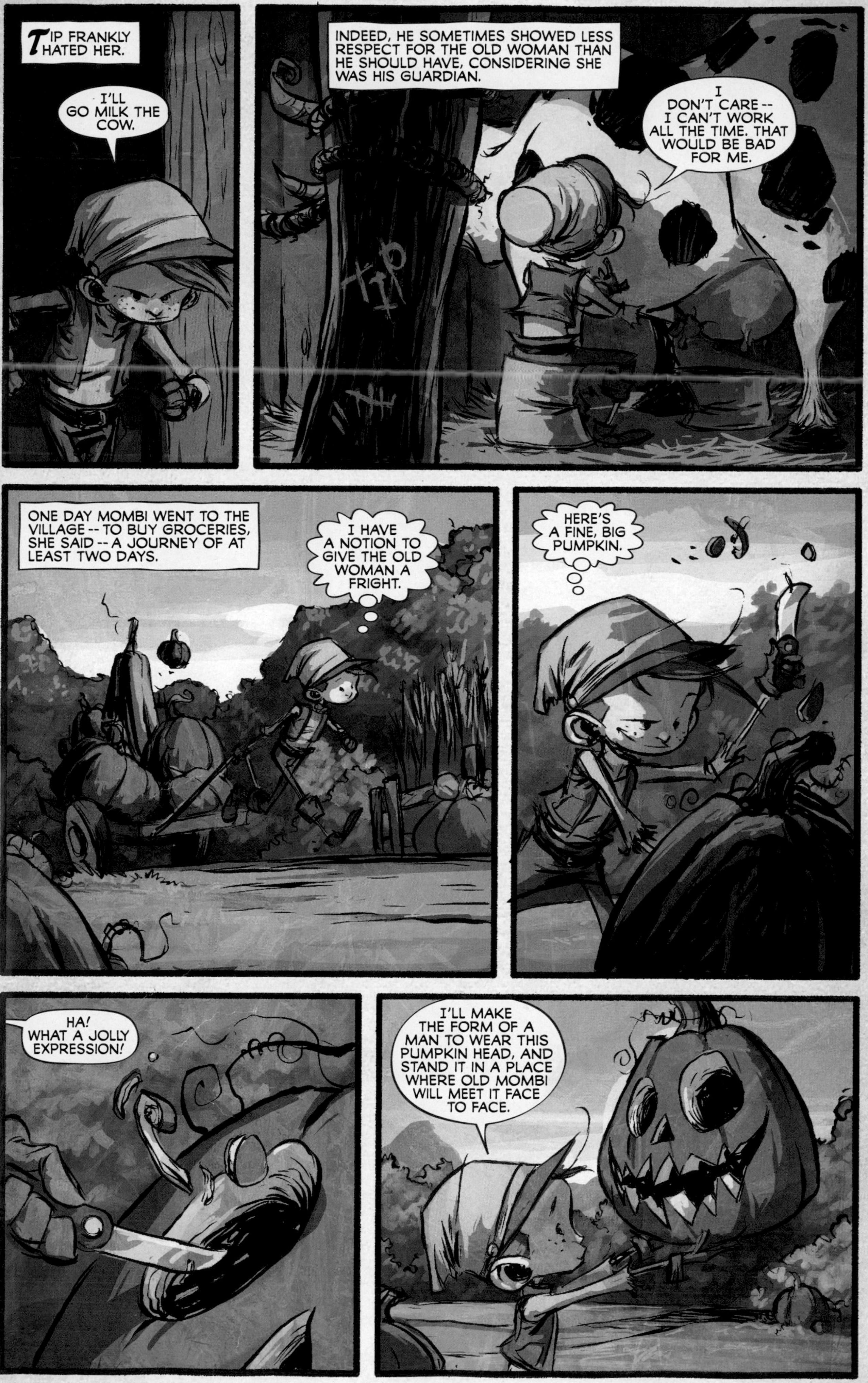
TIP FRANKLY HATED HER.
I'LL GO MILK THE COW.
INDEED, HE SOMETIMES SHOWED LESS RESPECT FOR THE OLD WOMAN THAN HE SHOULD HAVE, CONSIDERING SHE WAS HIS GUARDIAN.
I DON'T CARE -- I CAN'T WORK ALL THE TIME. THAT WOULD BE BAD FOR ME.
ONE DAY MOMBI WENT TO THE VILLAGE -- TO BUY GROCERIES, SHE SAID -- A JOURNEY OF AT LEAST TWO DAYS.
I HAVE A NOTION TO GIVE THE OLD WOMAN A FRIGHT.
HERE'S A FINE, BIG PUMPKIN.
HA! WHAT A JOLLY EXPRESSION!
I'LL MAKE THE FORM OF A MAN TO WEAR THIS PUMPKIN HEAD, AND STAND IT IN A PLACE WHERE OLD MOMBI WILL MEET IT FACE TO FACE.

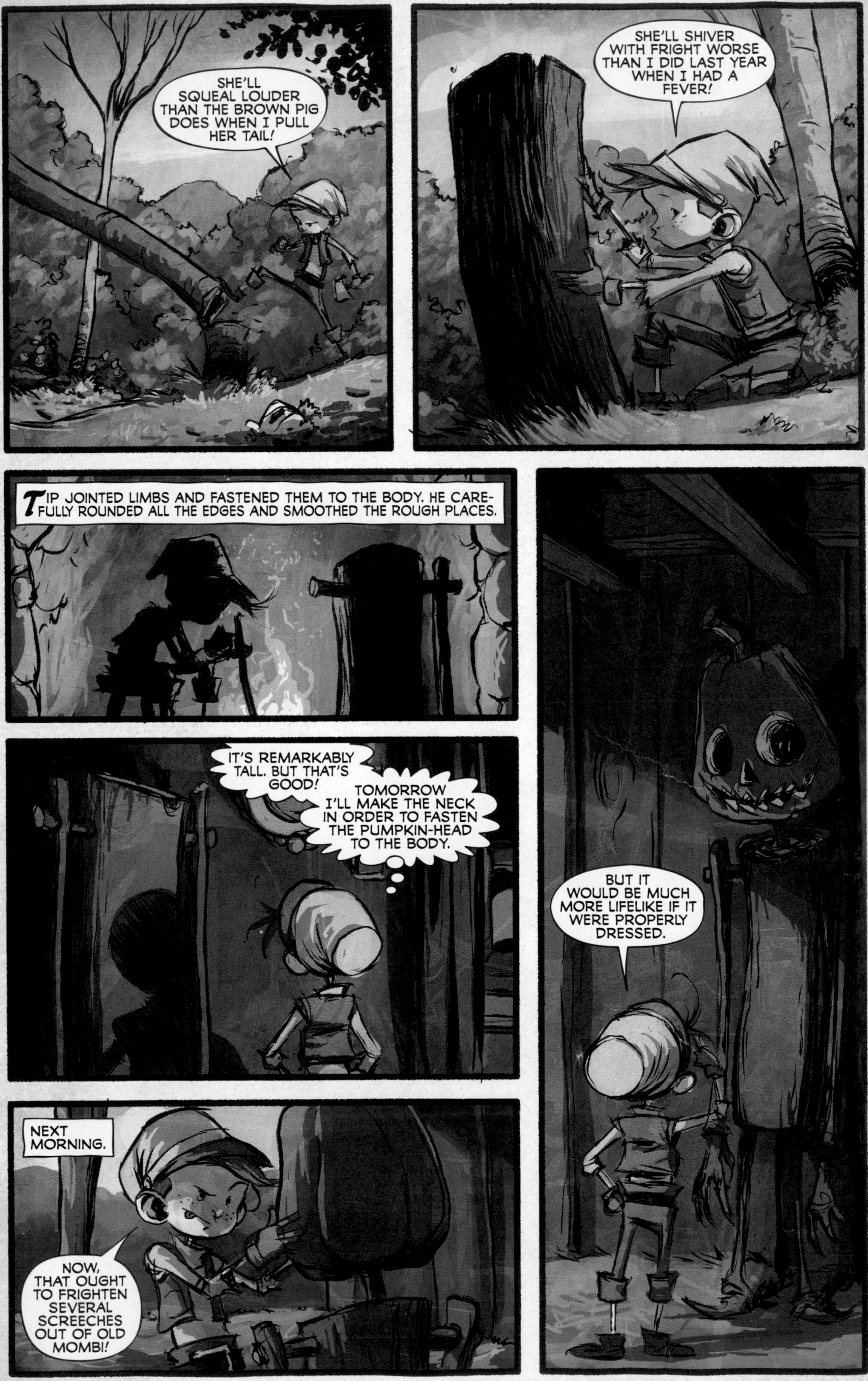
SHE'LL SQUEAL LOUDER THAN THE BROWN PIG DOES WHEN I PULL HER TAIL!
SHE'LL SHIVER WITH FRIGHT WORSE THAN I DID LAST YEAR WHEN I HAD A FEVER!
TIP JOINTED LIMBS AND FASTENED THEM TO THE BODY. HE CAREFULLY ROUNDED ALL THE EDGES AND SMOOTHED THE ROUGH PLACES.
IT'S REMARKABLY TALL. BUT THAT'S GOOD!
TOMORROW I'LL MAKE THE NECK IN ORDER TO FASTEN THE PUMPKIN-HEAD TO THE BODY.
NEXT MORNING.
NOW, THAT OUGHT TO FRIGHTEN SEVERAL SCREECHES OUT OF OLD MOMBI!
BUT IT WOULD BE MUCH MORE LIFELIKE IF IT WERE PROPERLY DRESSED.

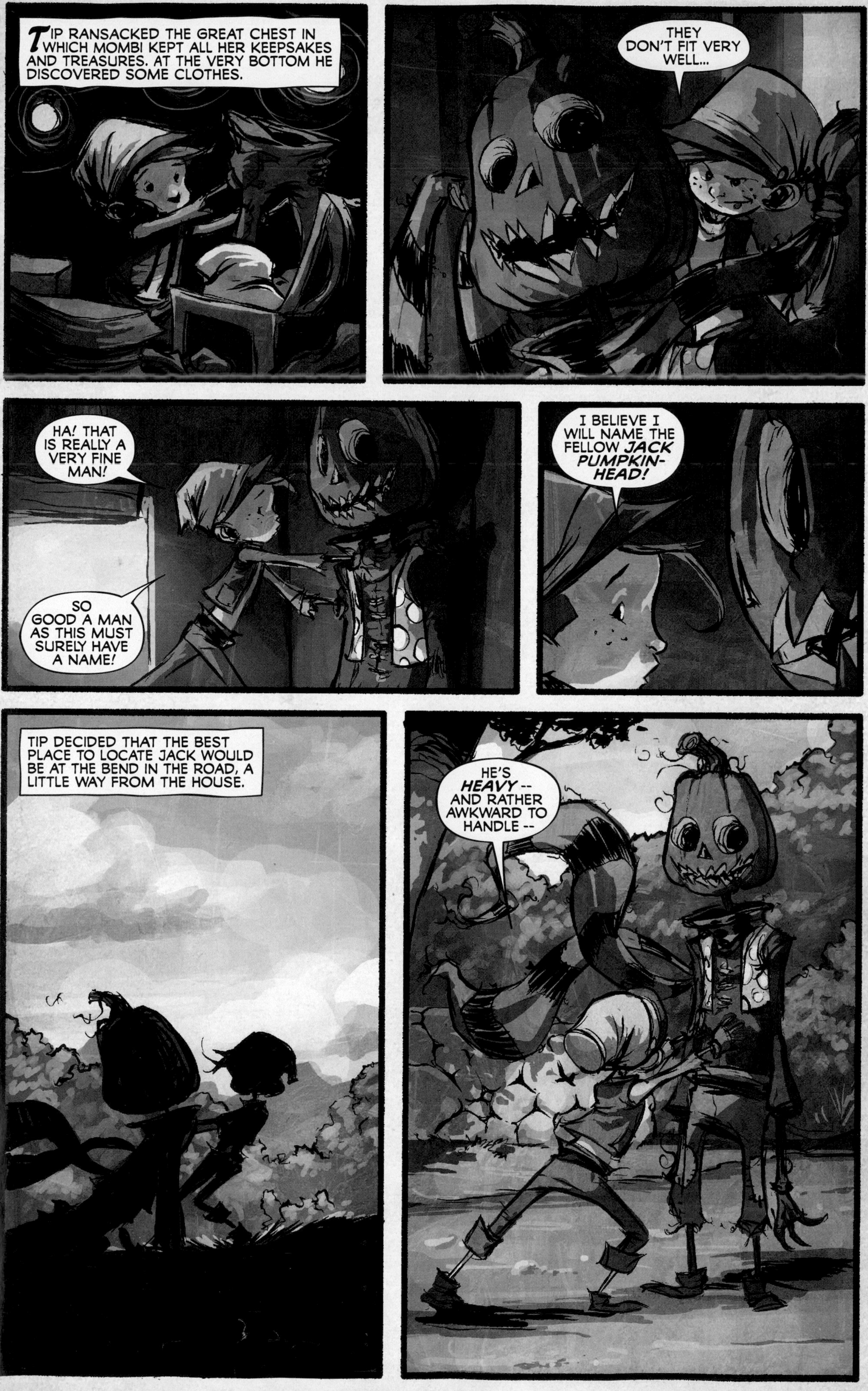
TIP RANSACKED THE GREAT CHEST IN WHICH MOMBI KEPT ALL HER KEEPSAKES AND TREASURES. AT THE VERY BOTTOM HE DISCOVERED SOME CLOTHES.
THEY DON'T FIT VERY WELL...
HA! THAT IS REALLY A VERY FINE MAN!
SO GOOD A MAN AS THIS MUST SURELY HAVE A NAME!
I BELIEVE I WILL NAME THE FELLOW JACK PUMPKIN-HEAD!
TIP DECIDED THAT THE BEST PLACE TO LOCATE JACK WOULD BE AT THE BEND IN THE ROAD, A LITTLE WAY FROM THE HOUSE.
HE'S HEAVY -- AND RATHER AWKWARD TO HANDLE --

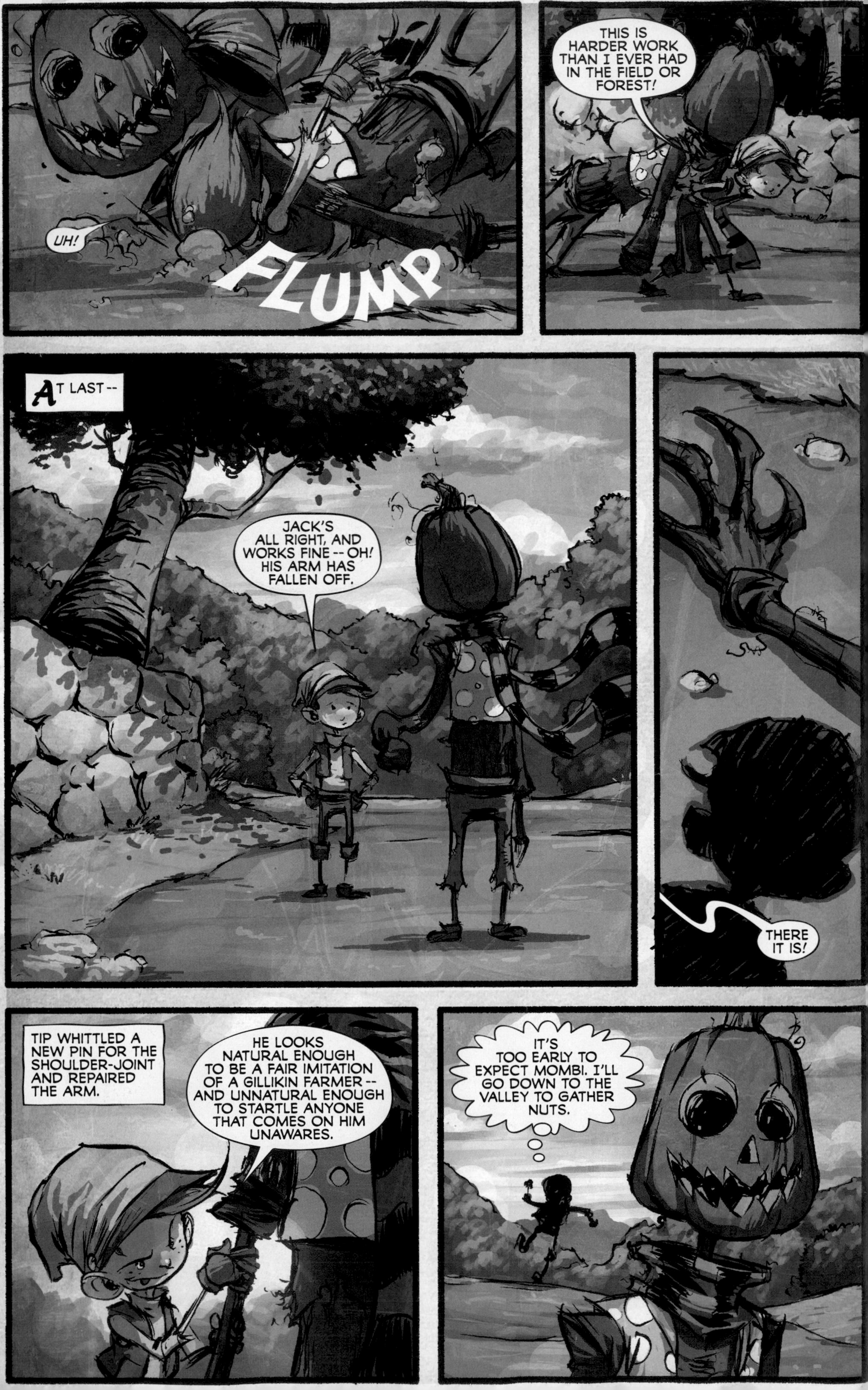
UH!
FLUMP
THIS IS HARDER WORK THAN I EVER HAD IN THE FIELD OR FOREST!
AT LAST --
JACK'S ALL RIGHT, AND WORKS FINE -- OH! HIS ARM HAS FALLEN OFF.
THERE IT IS!
TIP WHITTLED A NEW PIN FOR THE SHOULDER-JOINT AND REPAIRED THE ARM.
HE LOOKS NATURAL ENOUGH TO BE A FAIR IMITATION OF A GILLIKIN FARMER -- AND UNNATURAL ENOUGH TO STARTLE ANYONE THAT COMES ON HIM UNAWARES.
IT'S TOO EARLY TO EXPECT MOMBI. I'LL GO DOWN TO THE VALLEY TO GATHER NUTS.

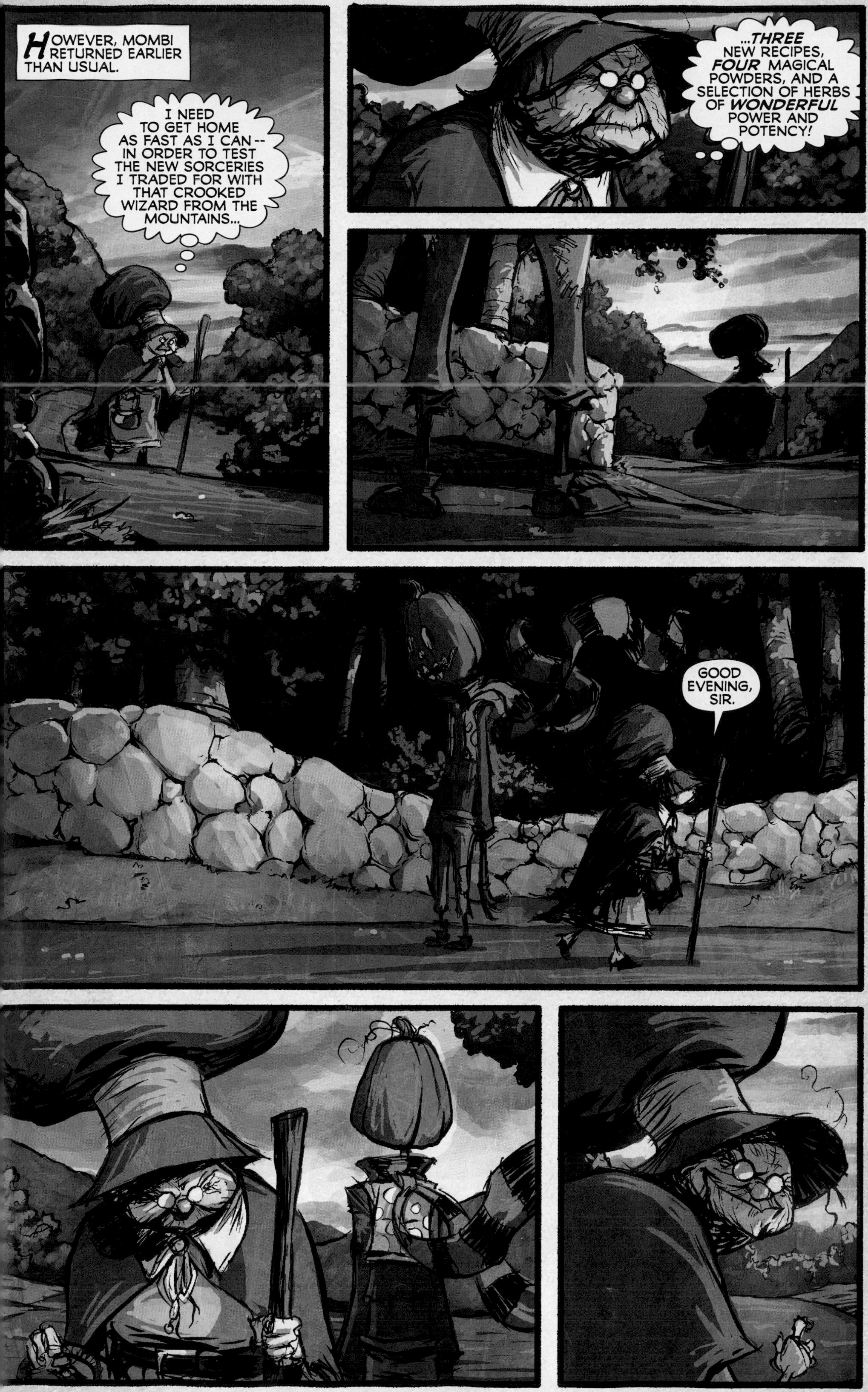
HOWEVER, MOMBI RETURNED EARLIER THAN USUAL.
I NEED TO GET HOME AS FAST AS I CAN -- IN ORDER TO TEST THE NEW SORCERIES I TRADED FOR WITH THAT CROOKED WIZARD FROM THE MOUNTAINS...
...THREE NEW RECIPES, FOUR MAGICAL POWDERS, AND A SELECTION OF HERBS OF WONDERFUL POWER AND POTENCY!
GOOD EVENING, SIR.

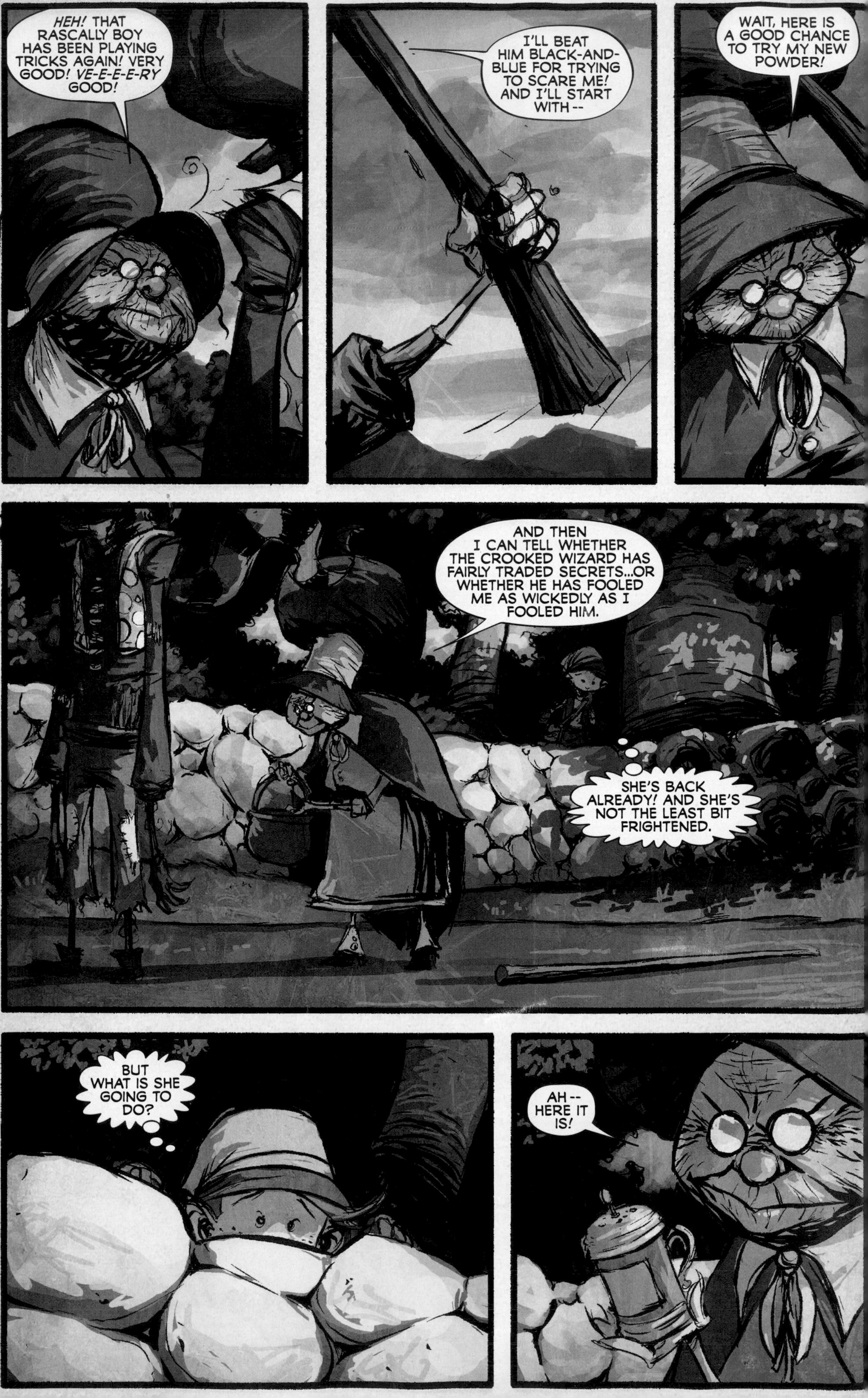
HEH! THAT RASCALLY BOY HAS BEEN PLAYING TRICKS AGAIN! VERY GOOD! VE-E-E-RY GOOD!
I'LL BEAT HIM BLACK-AND-BLUE FOR TRYING TO SCARE ME! AND I'LL START WITH --
WAIT, HERE IS A GOOD CHANCE TO TRY MY NEW POWDER!
AND THEN I CAN TELL WHETHER THE CROOKED WIZARD HAS FAIRLY TRADED SECRETS...OR WHETHER HE HAS FOOLED ME AS WICKEDLY AS I FOOLED HIM.
SHE'S BACK ALREADY! AND SHE'S NOT THE LEAST BIT FRIGHTENED.
BUT WHAT IS SHE GOING TO DO?
AH -- HERE IT IS!

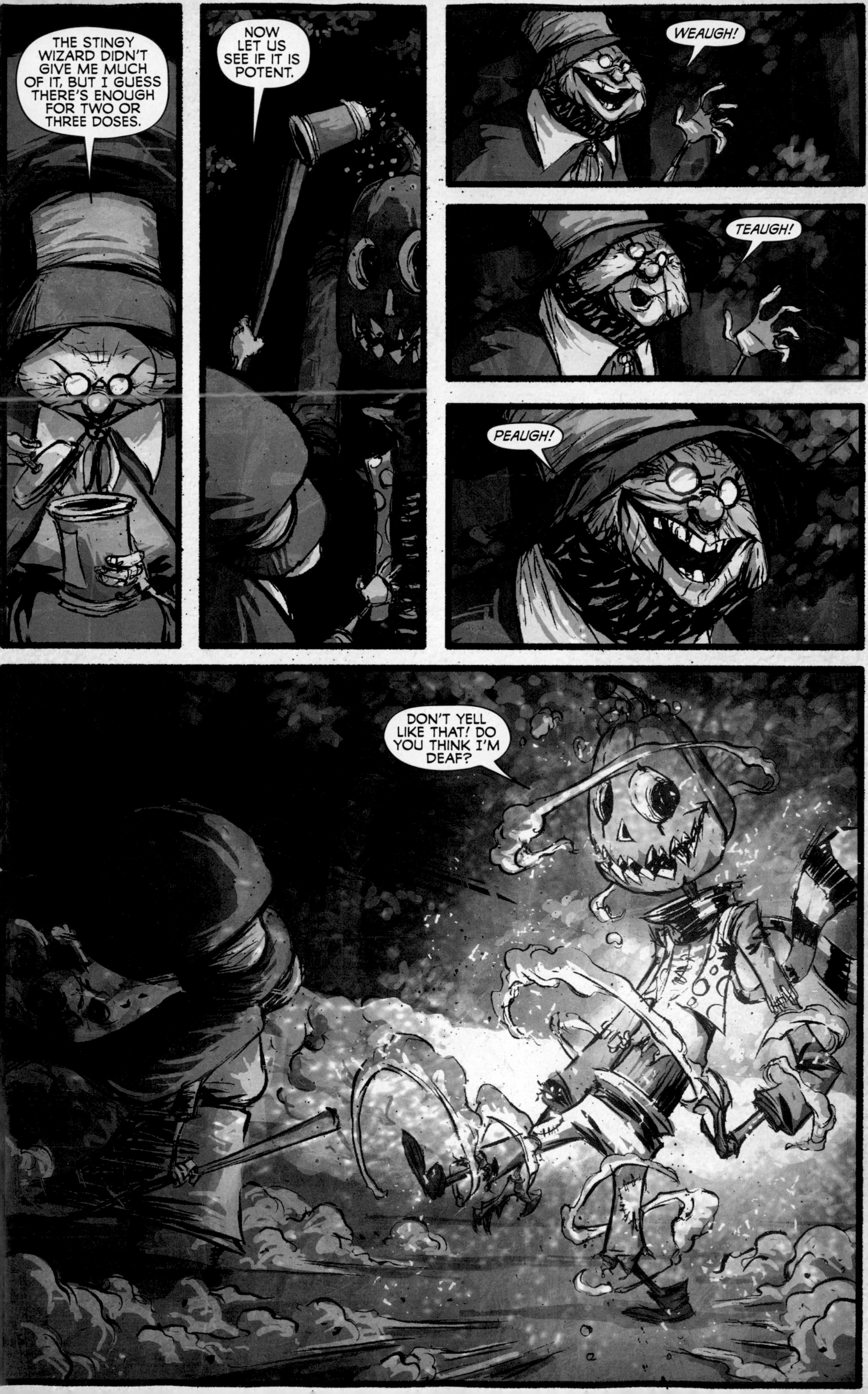
THE STINGY WIZARD DIDN'T GIVE ME MUCH OF IT, BUT I GUESS THERE'S ENOUGH FOR TWO OR THREE DOSES.
NOW LET US SEE IF IT IS POTENT.
WEAUGH!
TEAUGH!
PEAUGH!
DON'T YELL LIKE THAT! DO YOU THINK I'M DEAF?

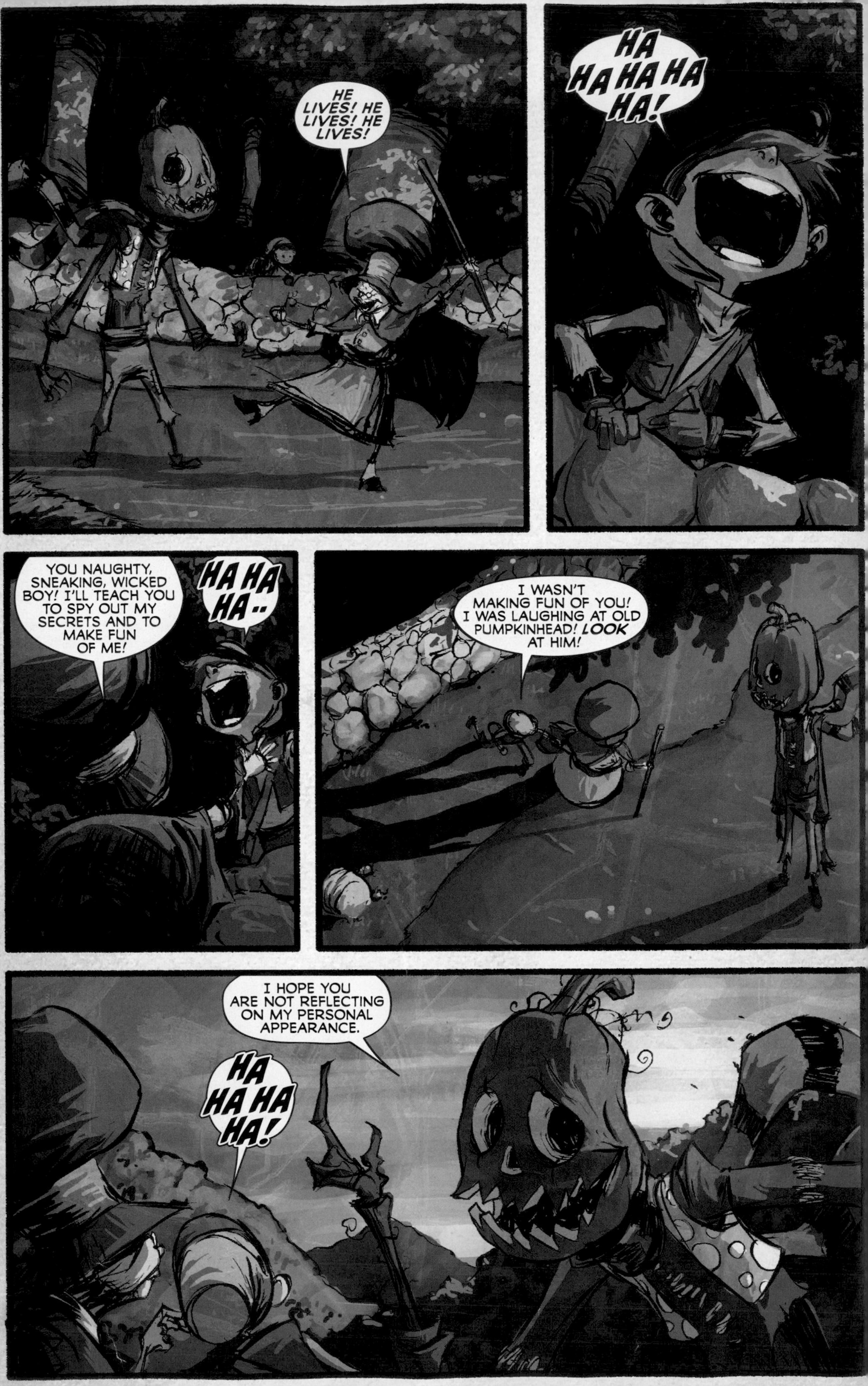
HE LIVES! HE LIVES! HE LIVES!
HA HA HA HA HA!
YOU NAUGHTY, SNEAKING, WICKED BOY! I'LL TEACH YOU TO SPY OUT MY SECRETS AND TO MAKE FUN OF ME!
HA HA HA..
I WASN'T MAKING FUN OF YOU! I WAS LAUGHING AT OLD PUMPKINHEAD! LOOK AT HIM!
I HOPE YOU ARE NOT REFLECTING ON MY PERSONAL APPEARANCE.
HA HA HA HA!

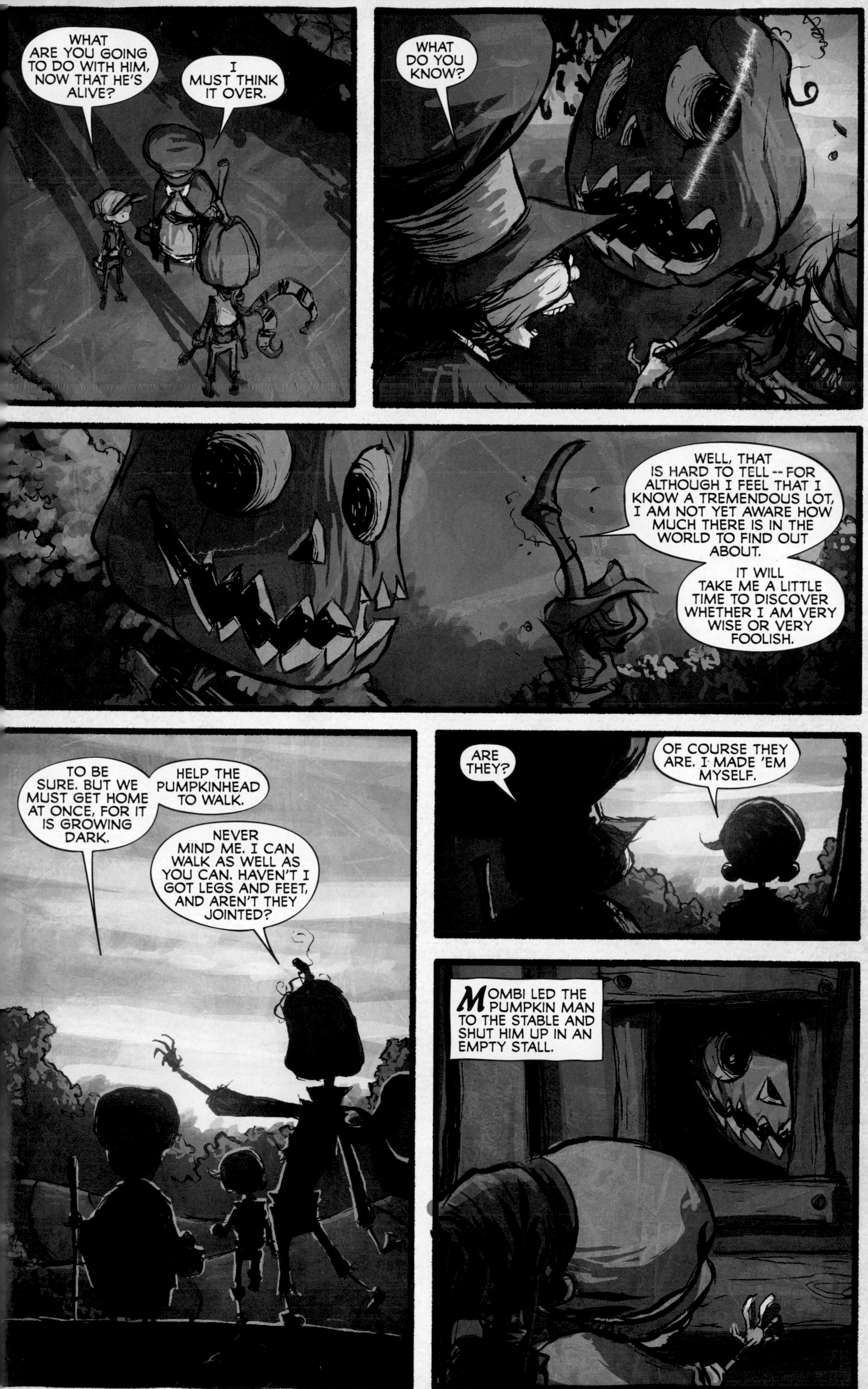
WHAT ARE YOU GOING TO DO WITH HIM, NOW THAT HE'S ALIVE?
I MUST THINK IT OVER.
WHAT DO YOU KNOW?
WELL, THAT IS HARD TO TELL -- FOR ALTHOUGH I FEEL THAT I KNOW A TREMENDOUS LOT, I AM NOT YET AWARE HOW MUCH THERE IS IN THE WORLD TO FIND OUT ABOUT.
IT WILL TAKE ME A LITTLE TIME TO DISCOVER WHETHER I AM VERY WISE OR VERY FOOLISH.
HELP THE PUMPKINHEAD TO WALK.
TO BE SURE. BUT WE MUST GET HOME AT ONCE, FOR IT IS GROWING DARK.
NEVER MIND ME. I CAN WALK AS WELL AS YOU CAN. HAVEN'T I GOT LEGS AND FEET, AND AREN'T THEY JOINTED?
ARE THEY?
OF COURSE THEY ARE. I MADE 'EM MYSELF.
MOMBI LED THE PUMPKIN MAN TO THE STABLE AND SHUT HIM UP IN AN EMPTY STALL.

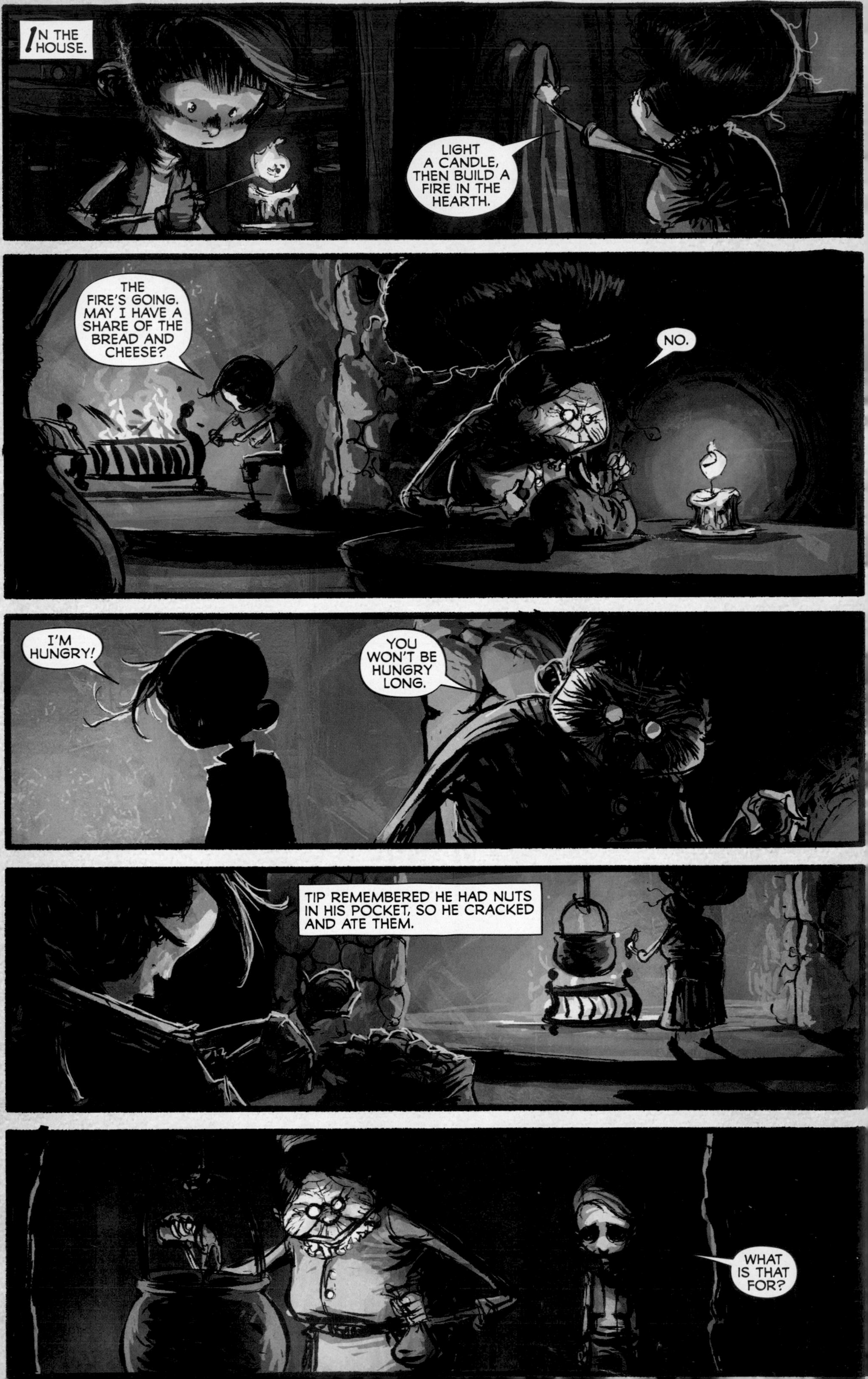

IN THE HOUSE.
LIGHT A CANDLE, THEN BUILD A FIRE IN THE HEARTH.
THE FIRE'S GOING. MAY I HAVE A SHARE OF THE BREAD AND CHEESE?
NO.
I'M HUNGRY!
YOU WON'T BE HUNGRY LONG.
TIP REMEMBERED HE HAD NUTS IN HIS POCKET, SO HE CRACKED AND ATE THEM.
WHAT IS THAT FOR?

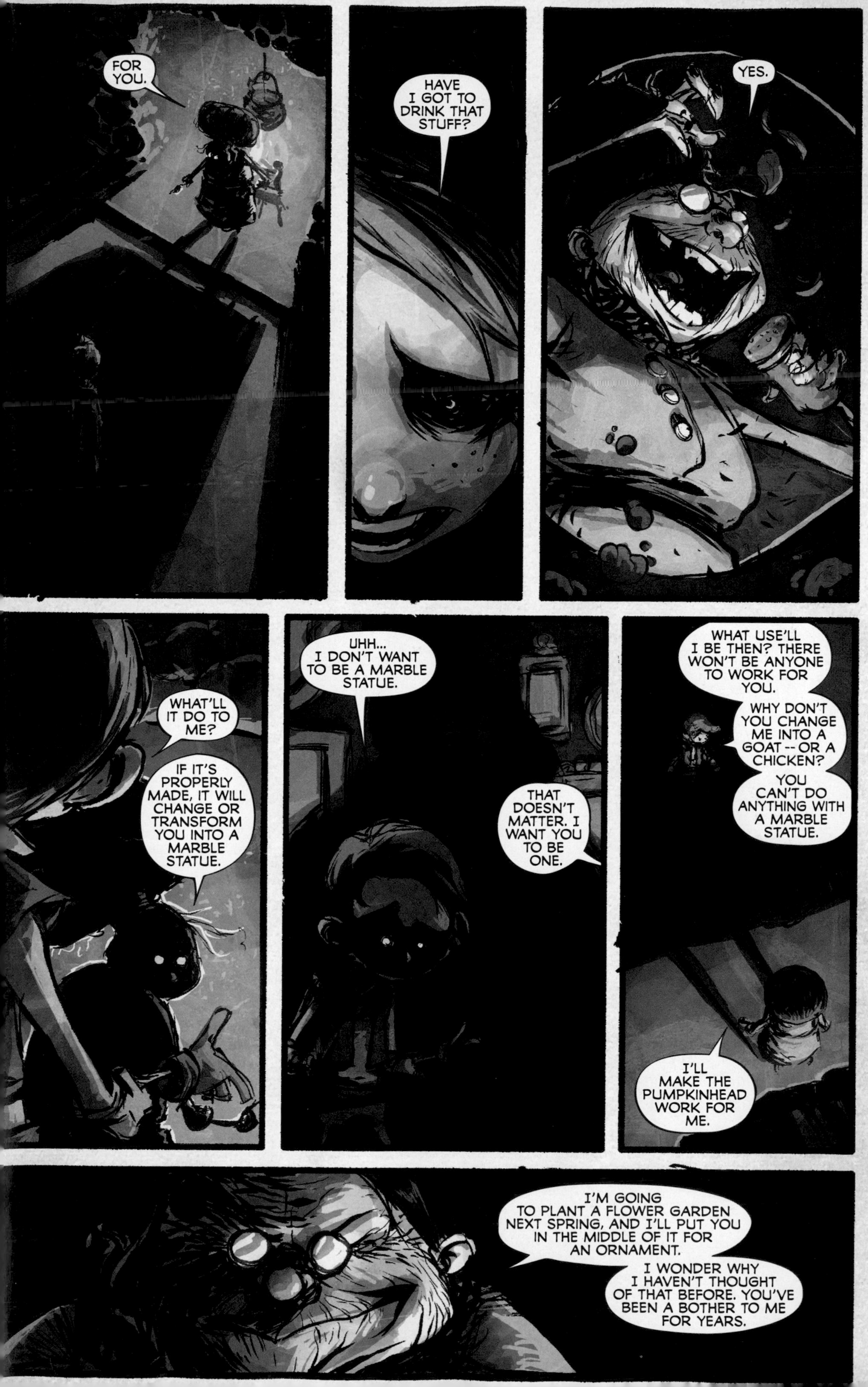
FOR YOU.
HAVE I GOT TO DRINK THAT STUFF?
YES.
WHAT'LL IT DO TO ME?
IF IT'S PROPERLY MADE, IT WILL CHANGE OR TRANSFORM YOU INTO A MARBLE STATUE.
UHH... I DON'T WANT TO BE A MARBLE STATUE.
THAT DOESN'T MATTER. I WANT YOU TO BE ONE.
WHAT USE'LL I BE THEN? THERE WON'T BE ANYONE TO WORK FOR YOU.
WHY DON'T YOU CHANGE ME INTO A GOAT -- OR A CHICKEN?
YOU CAN'T DO ANYTHING WITH A MARBLE STATUE.
I'LL MAKE THE PUMPKINHEAD WORK FOR ME.
I'M GOING TO PLANT A FLOWER GARDEN NEXT SPRING, AND I'LL PUT YOU IN THE MIDDLE OF IT FOR AN ORNAMENT.
I WONDER WHY I HAVEN'T THOUGHT OF THAT BEFORE. YOU'VE BEEN A BOTHER TO ME FOR YEARS.

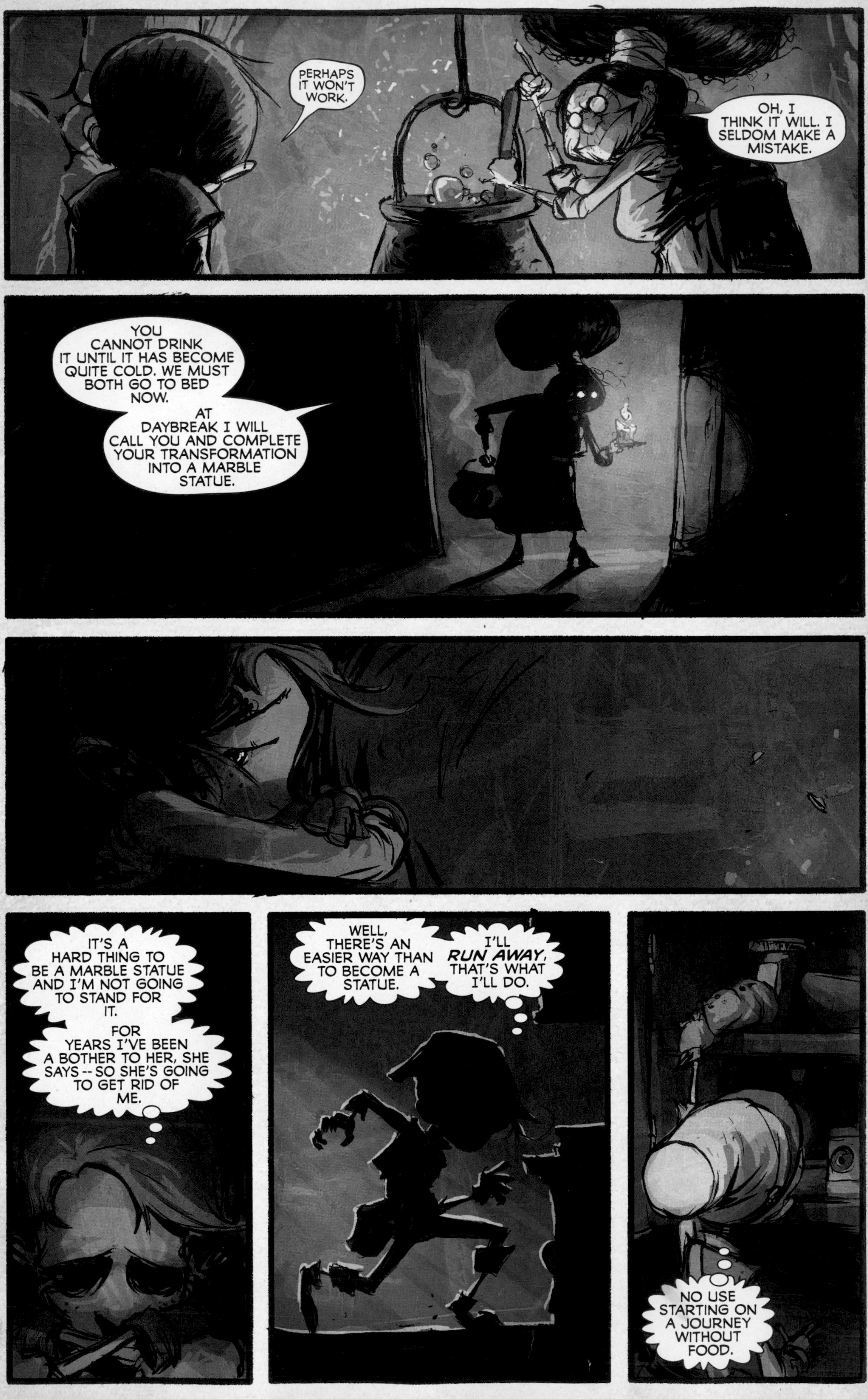
PERHAPS IT WON'T WORK.
OH, I THINK IT WILL. I SELDOM MAKE A MISTAKE.
YOU CANNOT DRINK IT UNTIL IT HAS BECOME QUITE COLD. WE MUST BOTH GO TO BED NOW.
AT DAYBREAK I WILL CALL YOU AND COMPLETE YOUR TRANSFORMATION INTO A MARBLE STATUE.
IT'S A HARD THING TO BE A MARBLE STATUE AND I'M NOT GOING TO STAND FOR IT.
FOR YEARS I'VE BEEN A BOTHER TO HER, SHE SAYS -- SO SHE'S GOING TO GET RID OF ME.
WELL, THERE'S AN EASIER WAY THAN TO BECOME A STATUE.
I'LL RUN AWAY, THAT'S WHAT I'LL DO.
NO USE STARTING ON A JOURNEY WITHOUT FOOD.

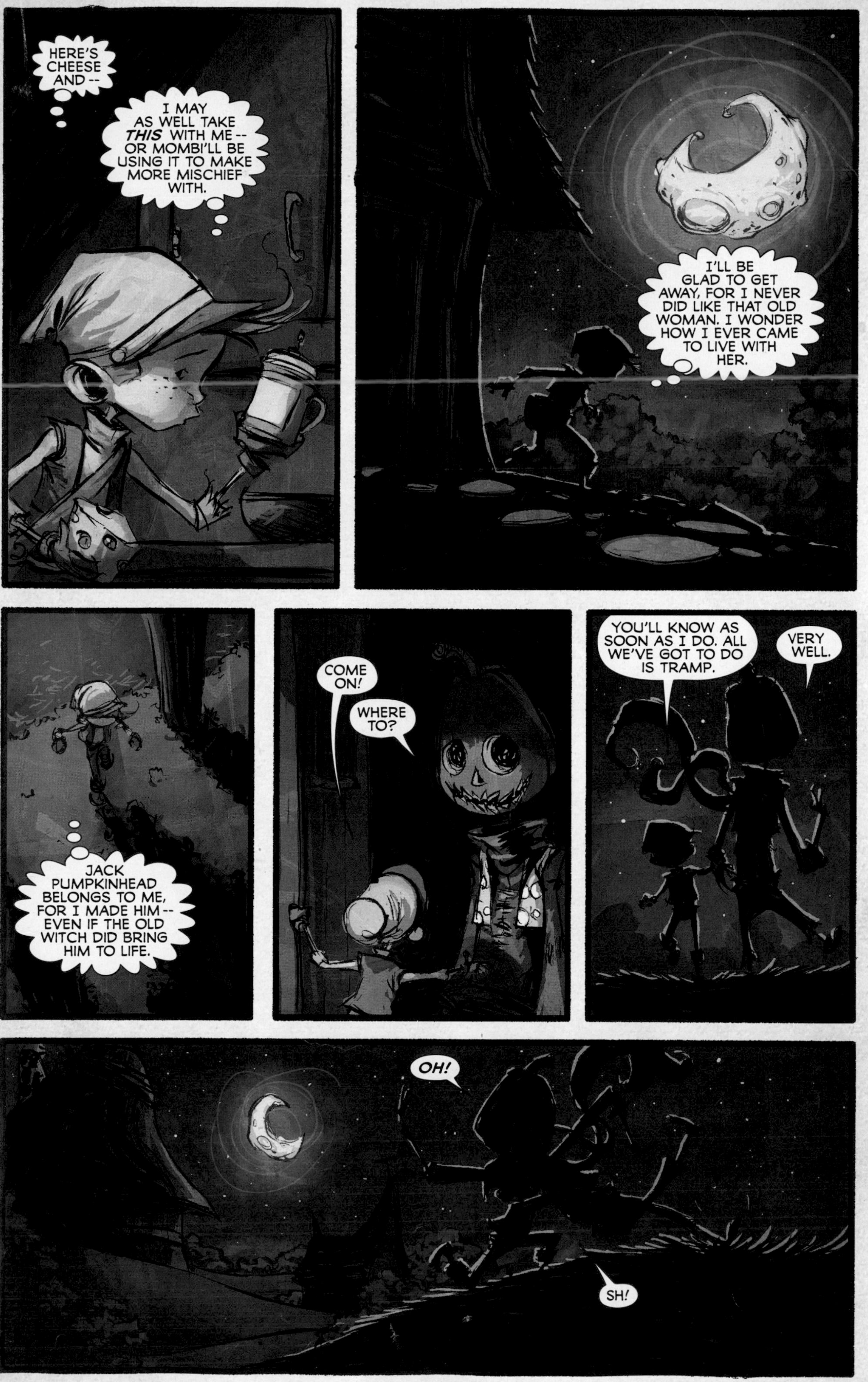
HERE'S CHEESE AND --
I MAY AS WELL TAKE *THIS* WITH ME -- OR MOMBI'LL BE USING IT TO MAKE MORE MISCHIEF WITH.
I'LL BE GLAD TO GET AWAY, FOR I NEVER DID LIKE THAT OLD WOMAN. I WONDER HOW I EVER CAME TO LIVE WITH HER.
JACK PUMPKINHEAD BELONGS TO ME, FOR I MADE HIM -- EVEN IF THE OLD WITCH DID BRING HIM TO LIFE.
COME ON!
WHERE TO?
YOU'LL KNOW AS SOON AS I DO. ALL WE'VE GOT TO DO IS TRAMP.
VERY WELL.
OH!
SH!

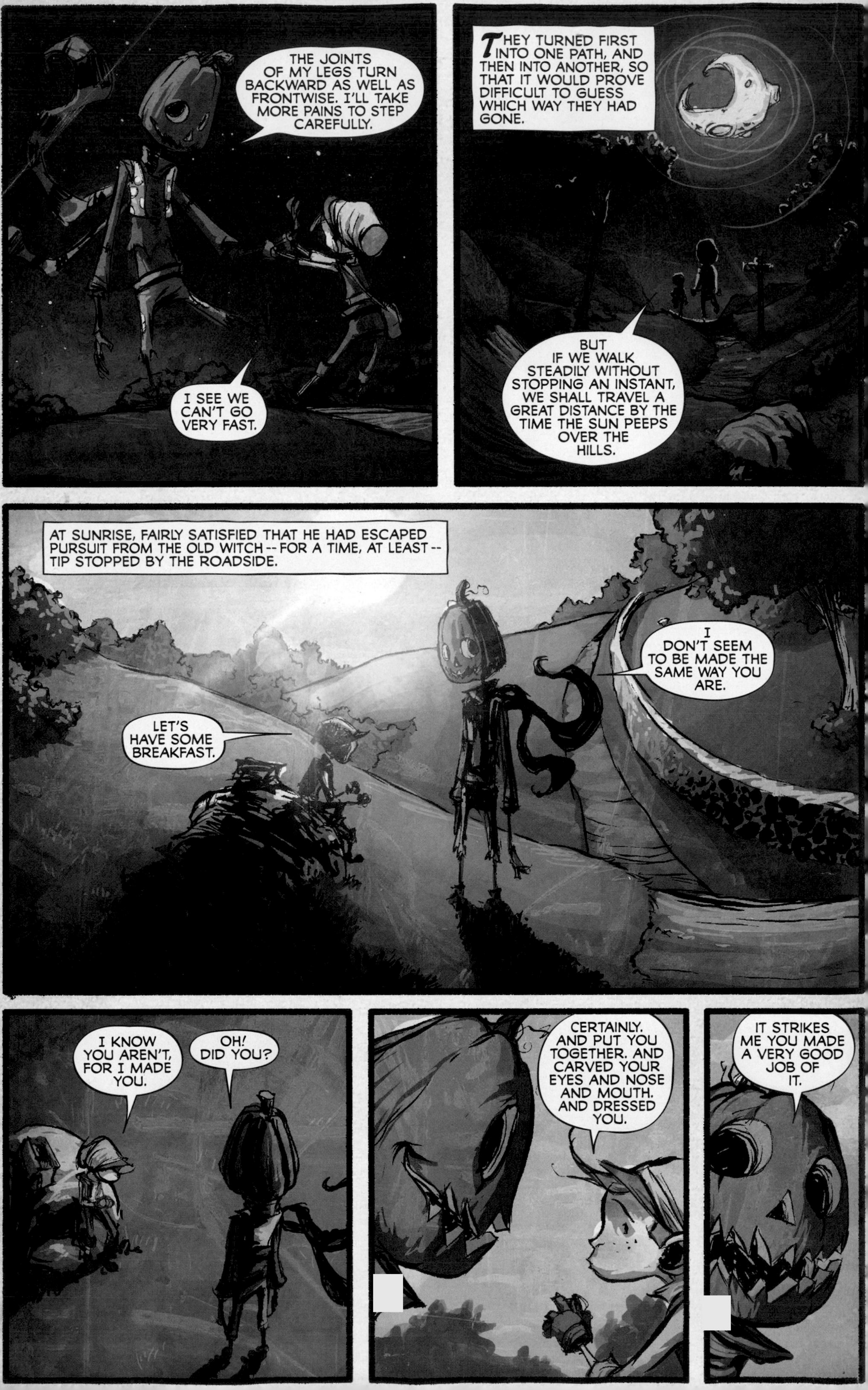

THE JOINTS OF MY LEGS TURN BACKWARD AS WELL AS FRONTWISE. I'LL TAKE MORE PAINS TO STEP CAREFULLY.
I SEE WE CAN'T GO VERY FAST.
THEY TURNED FIRST INTO ONE PATH, AND THEN INTO ANOTHER, SO THAT IT WOULD PROVE DIFFICULT TO GUESS WHICH WAY THEY HAD GONE.
BUT IF WE WALK STEADILY WITHOUT STOPPING AN INSTANT, WE SHALL TRAVEL A GREAT DISTANCE BY THE TIME THE SUN PEEPS OVER THE HILLS.
AT SUNRISE, FAIRLY SATISFIED THAT HE HAD ESCAPED PURSUIT FROM THE OLD WITCH -- FOR A TIME, AT LEAST -- TIP STOPPED BY THE ROADSIDE.
LET'S HAVE SOME BREAKFAST.
I DON'T SEEM TO BE MADE THE SAME WAY YOU ARE.
I KNOW YOU AREN'T, FOR I MADE YOU.
OH! DID YOU?
CERTAINLY. AND PUT YOU TOGETHER. AND CARVED YOUR EYES AND NOSE AND MOUTH. AND DRESSED YOU.
IT STRIKES ME YOU MADE A VERY GOOD JOB OF IT.

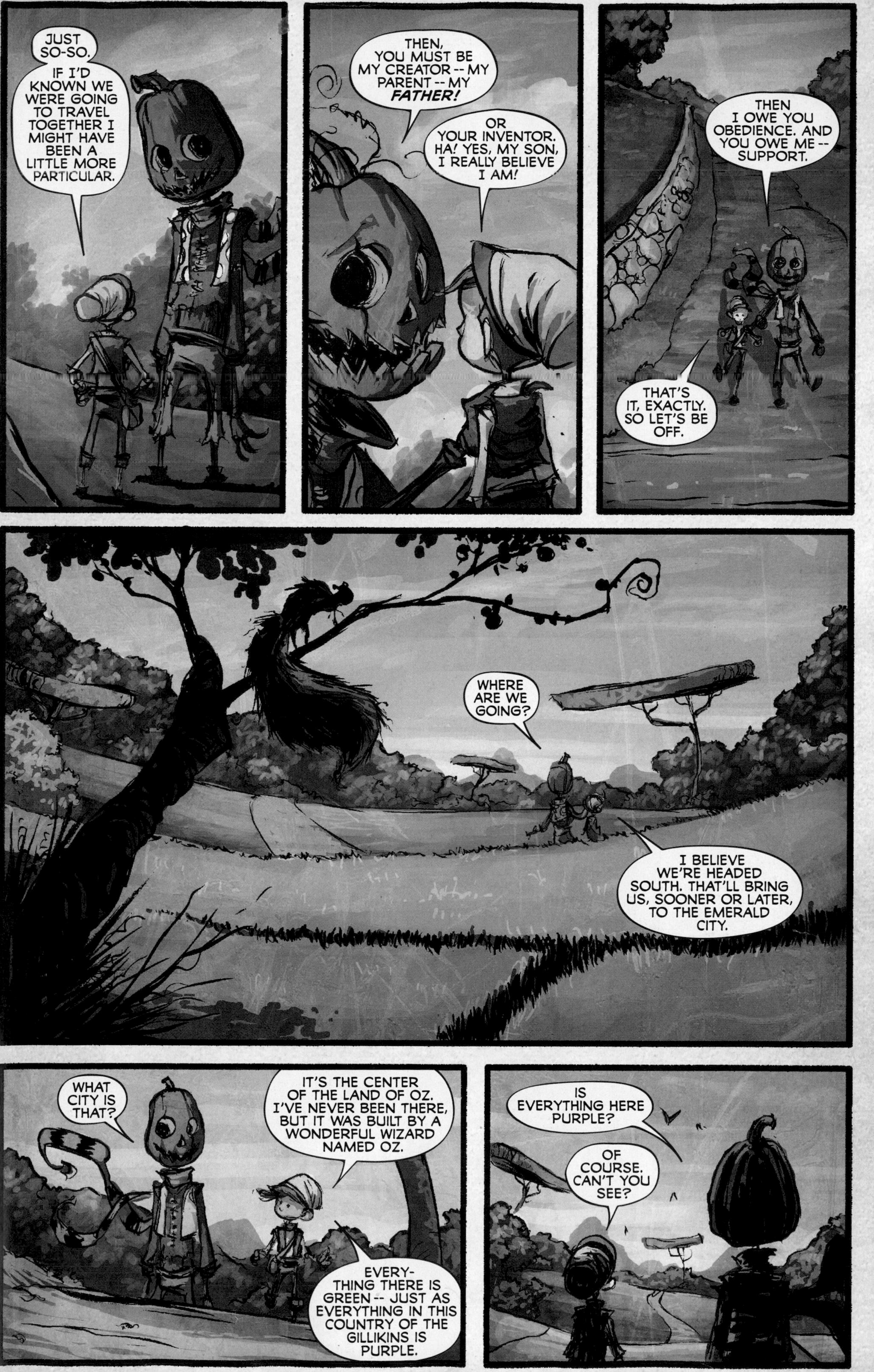
JUST SO-SO.
IF I'D KNOWN WE WERE GOING TO TRAVEL TOGETHER I MIGHT HAVE BEEN A LITTLE MORE PARTICULAR.
THEN, YOU MUST BE MY CREATOR -- MY PARENT -- MY *FATHER!*
OR YOUR INVENTOR. HA! YES, MY SON, I REALLY BELIEVE I AM!
THEN I OWE YOU OBEDIENCE. AND YOU OWE ME -- SUPPORT.
THAT'S IT, EXACTLY. SO LET'S BE OFF.
WHERE ARE WE GOING?
I BELIEVE WE'RE HEADED SOUTH. THAT'LL BRING US, SOONER OR LATER, TO THE EMERALD CITY.
WHAT CITY IS THAT?
IT'S THE CENTER OF THE LAND OF OZ. I'VE NEVER BEEN THERE, BUT IT WAS BUILT BY A WONDERFUL WIZARD NAMED OZ.
EVERY-THING THERE IS GREEN -- JUST AS EVERYTHING IN THIS COUNTRY OF THE GILLIKINS IS PURPLE.
IS EVERYTHING HERE PURPLE?
OF COURSE. CAN'T YOU SEE?

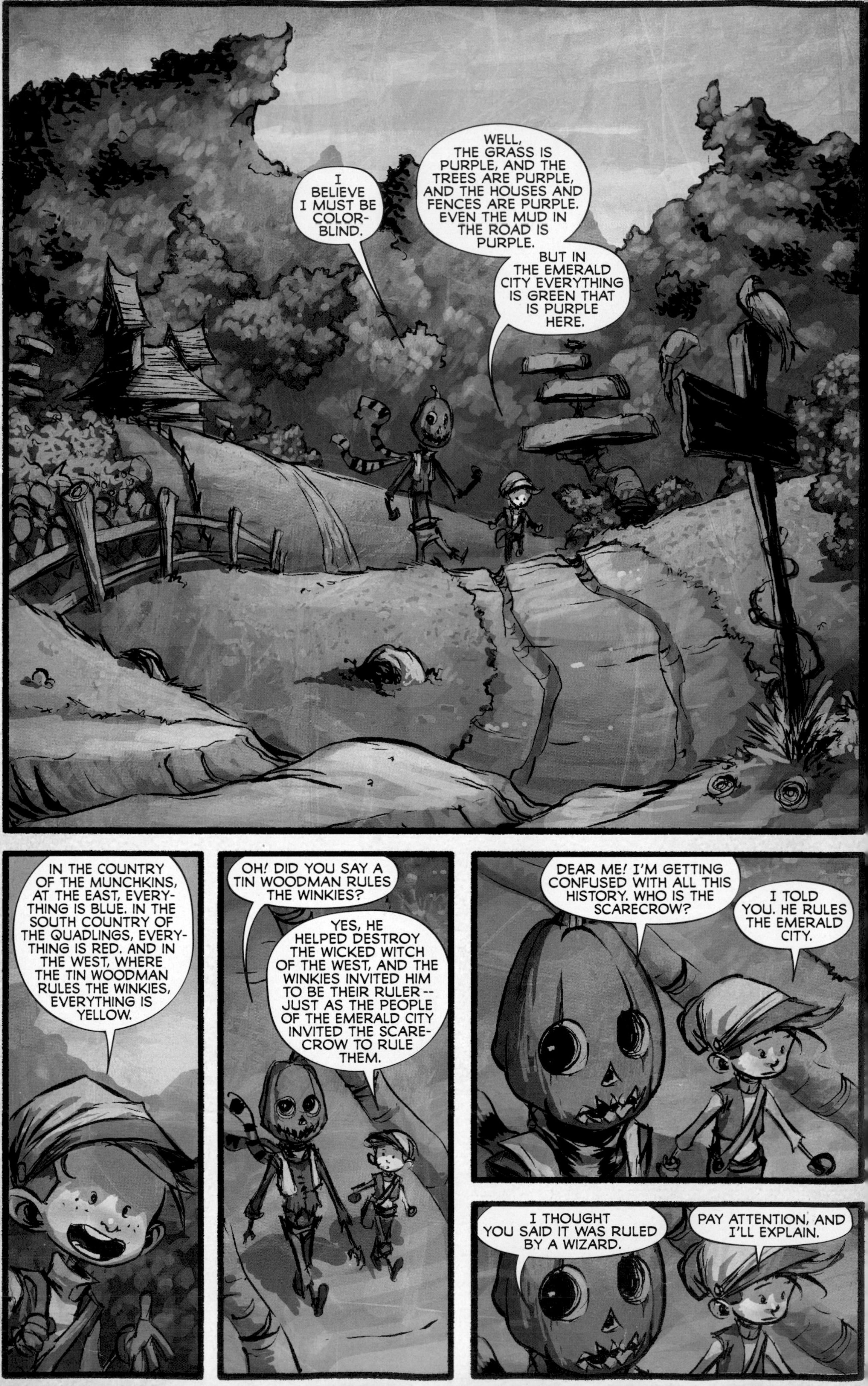

I BELIEVE I MUST BE COLOR-BLIND.
WELL, THE GRASS IS PURPLE, AND THE TREES ARE PURPLE, AND THE HOUSES AND FENCES ARE PURPLE. EVEN THE MUD IN THE ROAD IS PURPLE.
BUT IN THE EMERALD CITY EVERYTHING IS GREEN THAT IS PURPLE HERE.
IN THE COUNTRY OF THE MUNCHKINS, AT THE EAST, EVERYTHING IS BLUE. IN THE SOUTH COUNTRY OF THE QUADLINGS, EVERYTHING IS RED. AND IN THE WEST, WHERE THE TIN WOODMAN RULES THE WINKIES, EVERYTHING IS YELLOW.
OH! DID YOU SAY A TIN WOODMAN RULES THE WINKIES?
YES, HE HELPED DESTROY THE WICKED WITCH OF THE WEST, AND THE WINKIES INVITED HIM TO BE THEIR RULER -- JUST AS THE PEOPLE OF THE EMERALD CITY INVITED THE SCARECROW TO RULE THEM.
DEAR ME! I'M GETTING CONFUSED WITH ALL THIS HISTORY. WHO IS THE SCARECROW?
I TOLD YOU. HE RULES THE EMERALD CITY.
I THOUGHT YOU SAID IT WAS RULED BY A WIZARD.
PAY ATTENTION, AND I'LL EXPLAIN.

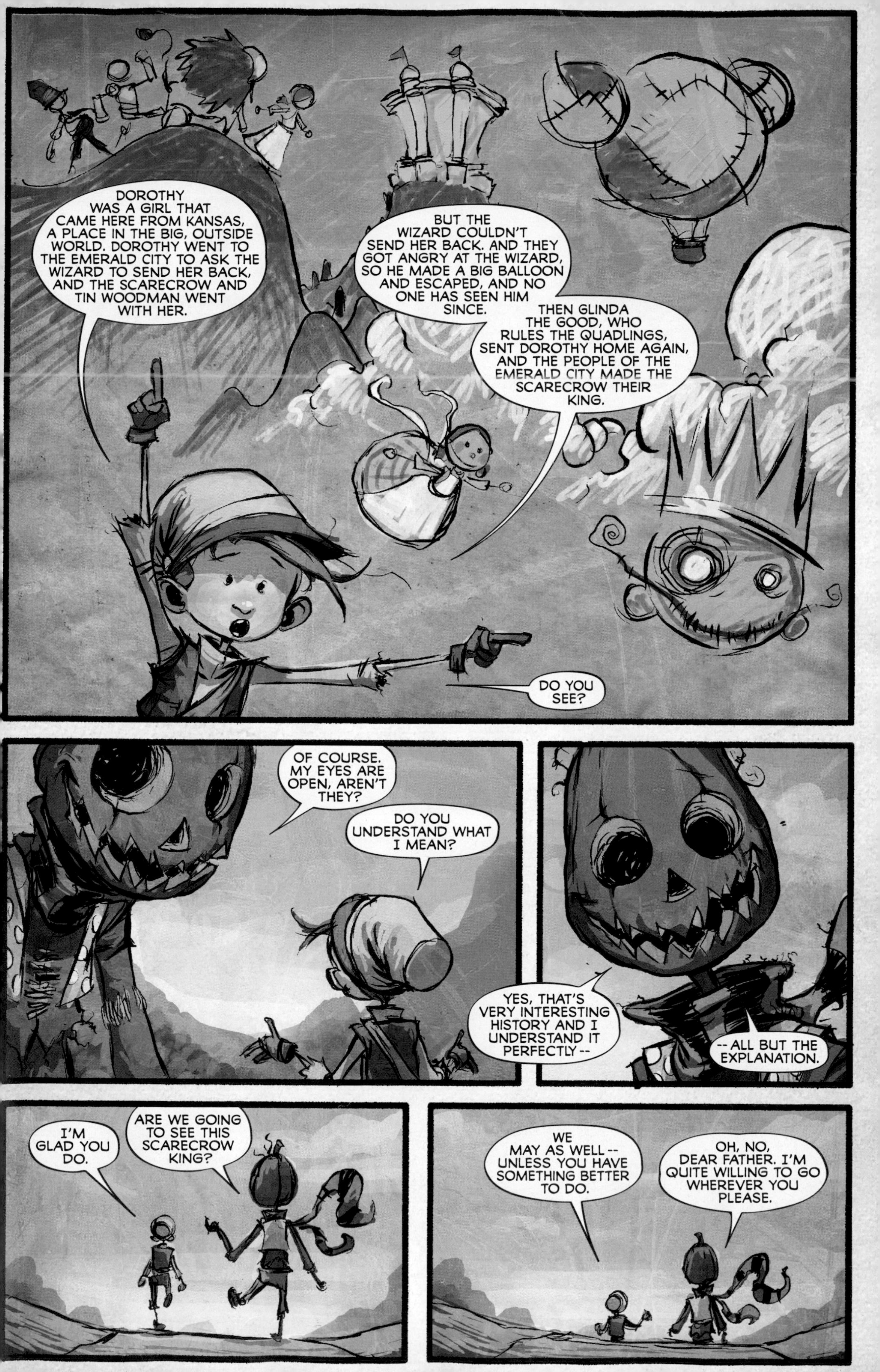
DOROTHY WAS A GIRL THAT CAME HERE FROM KANSAS, A PLACE IN THE BIG, OUTSIDE WORLD. DOROTHY WENT TO THE EMERALD CITY TO ASK THE WIZARD TO SEND HER BACK, AND THE SCARECROW AND TIN WOODMAN WENT WITH HER.
BUT THE WIZARD COULDN'T SEND HER BACK. AND THEY GOT ANGRY AT THE WIZARD, SO HE MADE A BIG BALLOON AND ESCAPED, AND NO ONE HAS SEEN HIM SINCE.
THEN GLINDA THE GOOD, WHO RULES THE QUADLINGS, SENT DOROTHY HOME AGAIN, AND THE PEOPLE OF THE EMERALD CITY MADE THE SCARECROW THEIR KING.
DO YOU SEE?
OF COURSE. MY EYES ARE OPEN, AREN'T THEY?
DO YOU UNDERSTAND WHAT I MEAN?
YES, THAT'S VERY INTERESTING HISTORY AND I UNDERSTAND IT PERFECTLY --
-- ALL BUT THE EXPLANATION.
I'M GLAD YOU DO.
ARE WE GOING TO SEE THIS SCARECROW KING?
WE MAY AS WELL -- UNLESS YOU HAVE SOMETHING BETTER TO DO.
OH, NO, DEAR FATHER. I'M QUITE WILLING TO GO WHEREVER YOU PLEASE.

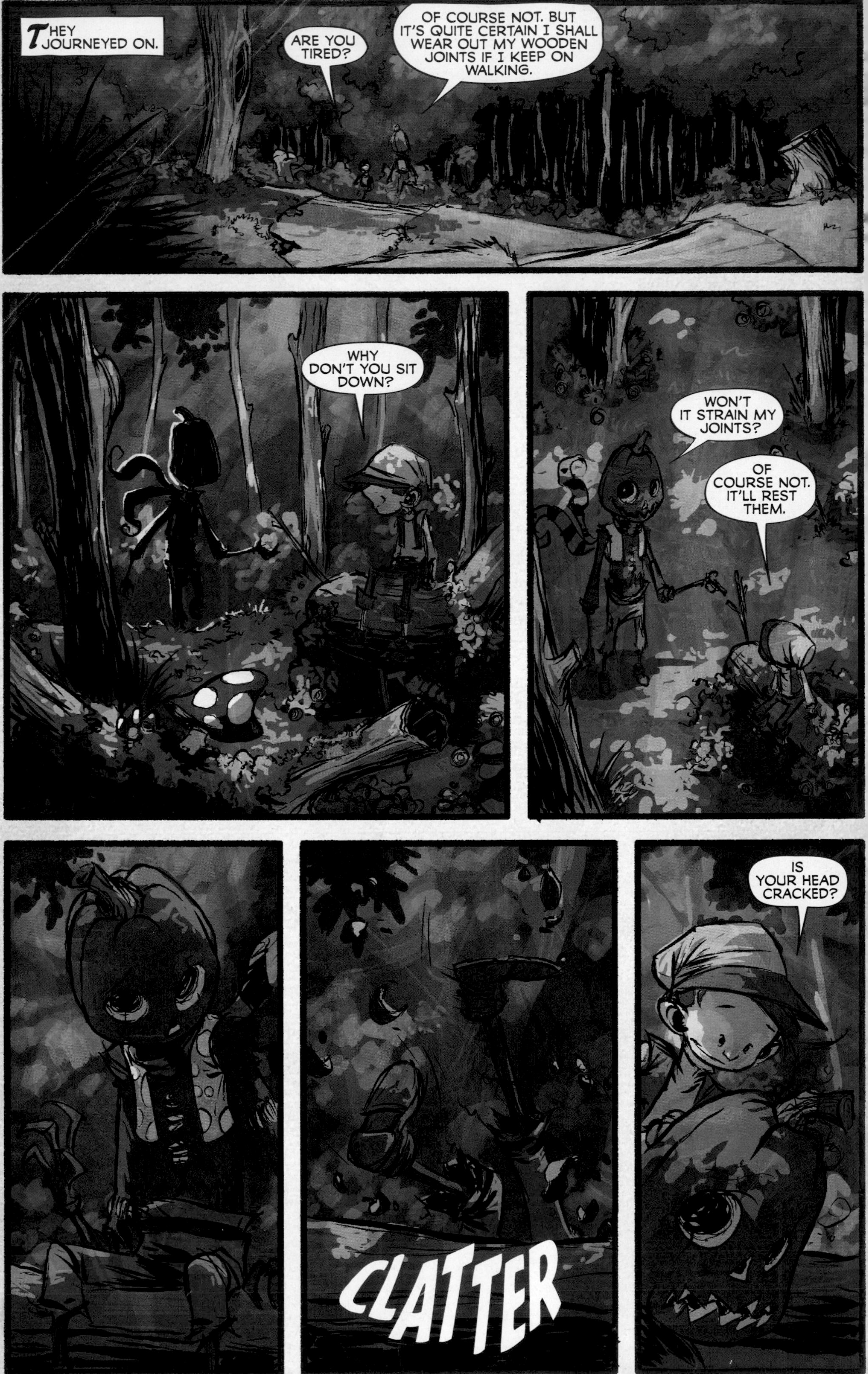
THEY JOURNEYED ON.
ARE YOU TIRED?
OF COURSE NOT. BUT IT'S QUITE CERTAIN I SHALL WEAR OUT MY WOODEN JOINTS IF I KEEP ON WALKING.
WHY DON'T YOU SIT DOWN?
WON'T IT STRAIN MY JOINTS?
OF COURSE NOT. IT'LL REST THEM.
CLATTER
IS YOUR HEAD CRACKED?

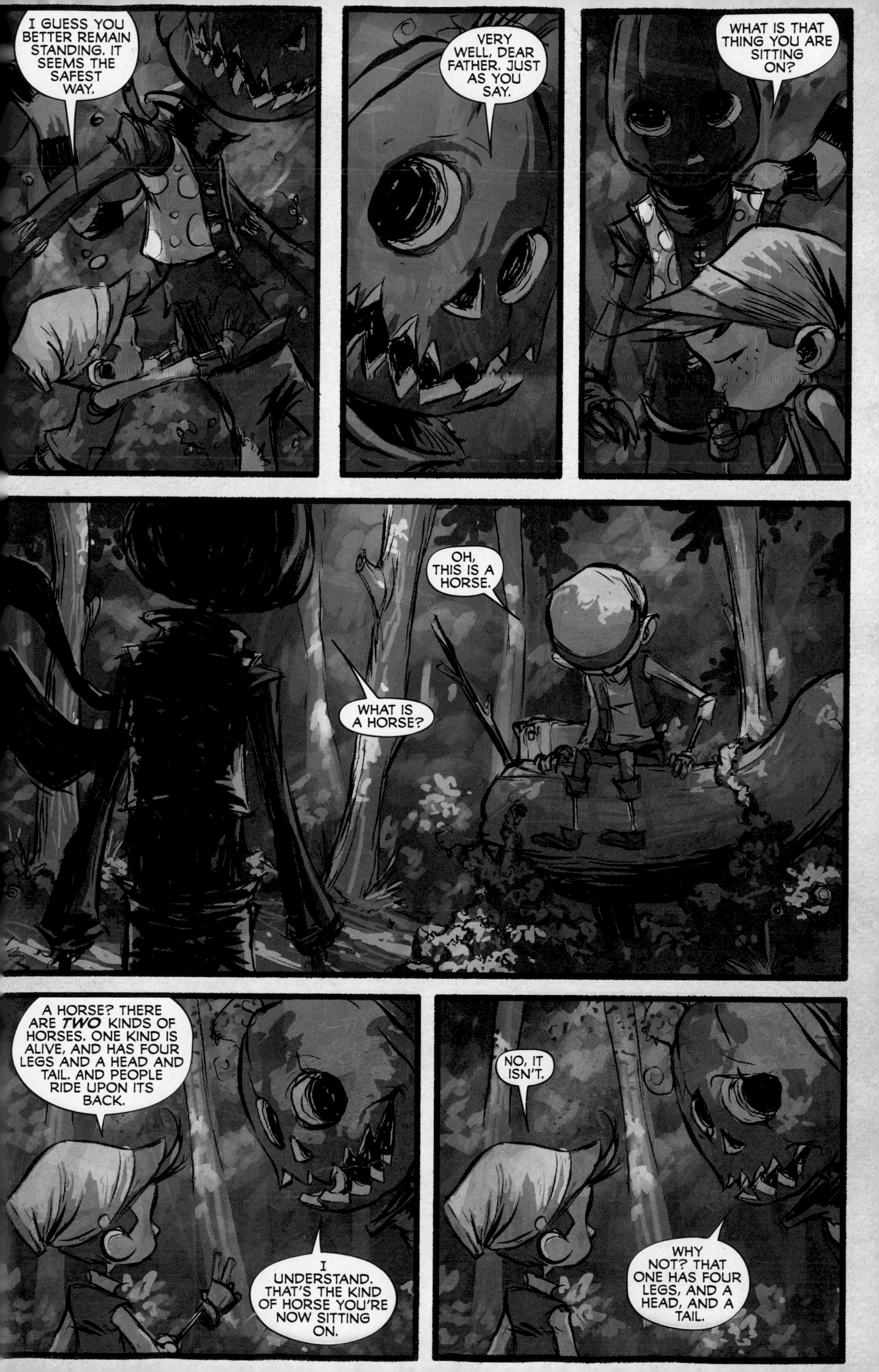
I GUESS YOU BETTER REMAIN STANDING. IT SEEMS THE SAFEST WAY.
VERY WELL, DEAR FATHER. JUST AS YOU SAY.
WHAT IS THAT THING YOU ARE SITTING ON?
OH, THIS IS A HORSE.
WHAT IS A HORSE?
A HORSE? THERE ARE *TWO* KINDS OF HORSES. ONE KIND IS ALIVE, AND HAS FOUR LEGS AND A HEAD AND TAIL. AND PEOPLE RIDE UPON ITS BACK.
I UNDERSTAND. THAT'S THE KIND OF HORSE YOU'RE NOW SITTING ON.
NO, IT ISN'T.
WHY NOT? THAT ONE HAS FOUR LEGS, AND A HEAD, AND A TAIL.

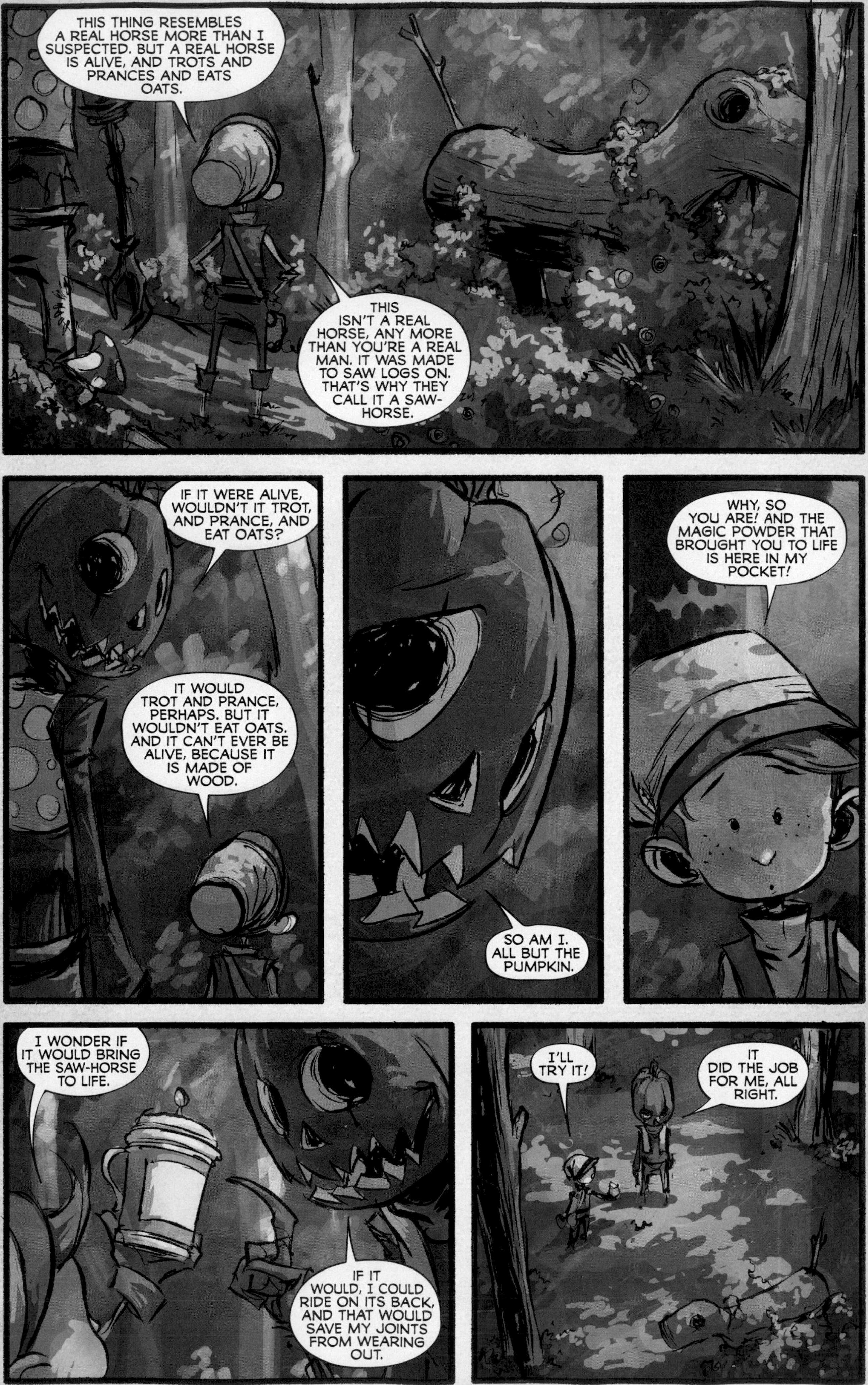
THIS THING RESEMBLES A REAL HORSE MORE THAN I SUSPECTED. BUT A REAL HORSE IS ALIVE, AND TROTS AND PRANCES AND EATS OATS.
THIS ISN'T A REAL HORSE, ANY MORE THAN YOU'RE A REAL MAN. IT WAS MADE TO SAW LOGS ON. THAT'S WHY THEY CALL IT A SAW-HORSE.
IF IT WERE ALIVE, WOULDN'T IT TROT, AND PRANCE, AND EAT OATS?
IT WOULD TROT AND PRANCE, PERHAPS. BUT IT WOULDN'T EAT OATS. AND IT CAN'T EVER BE ALIVE, BECAUSE IT IS MADE OF WOOD.
SO AM I. ALL BUT THE PUMPKIN.
WHY, SO YOU ARE! AND THE MAGIC POWDER THAT BROUGHT YOU TO LIFE IS HERE IN MY POCKET!
I WONDER IF IT WOULD BRING THE SAW-HORSE TO LIFE.
IF IT WOULD, I COULD RIDE ON ITS BACK, AND THAT WOULD SAVE MY JOINTS FROM WEARING OUT.
I'LL TRY IT!
IT DID THE JOB FOR ME, ALL RIGHT.

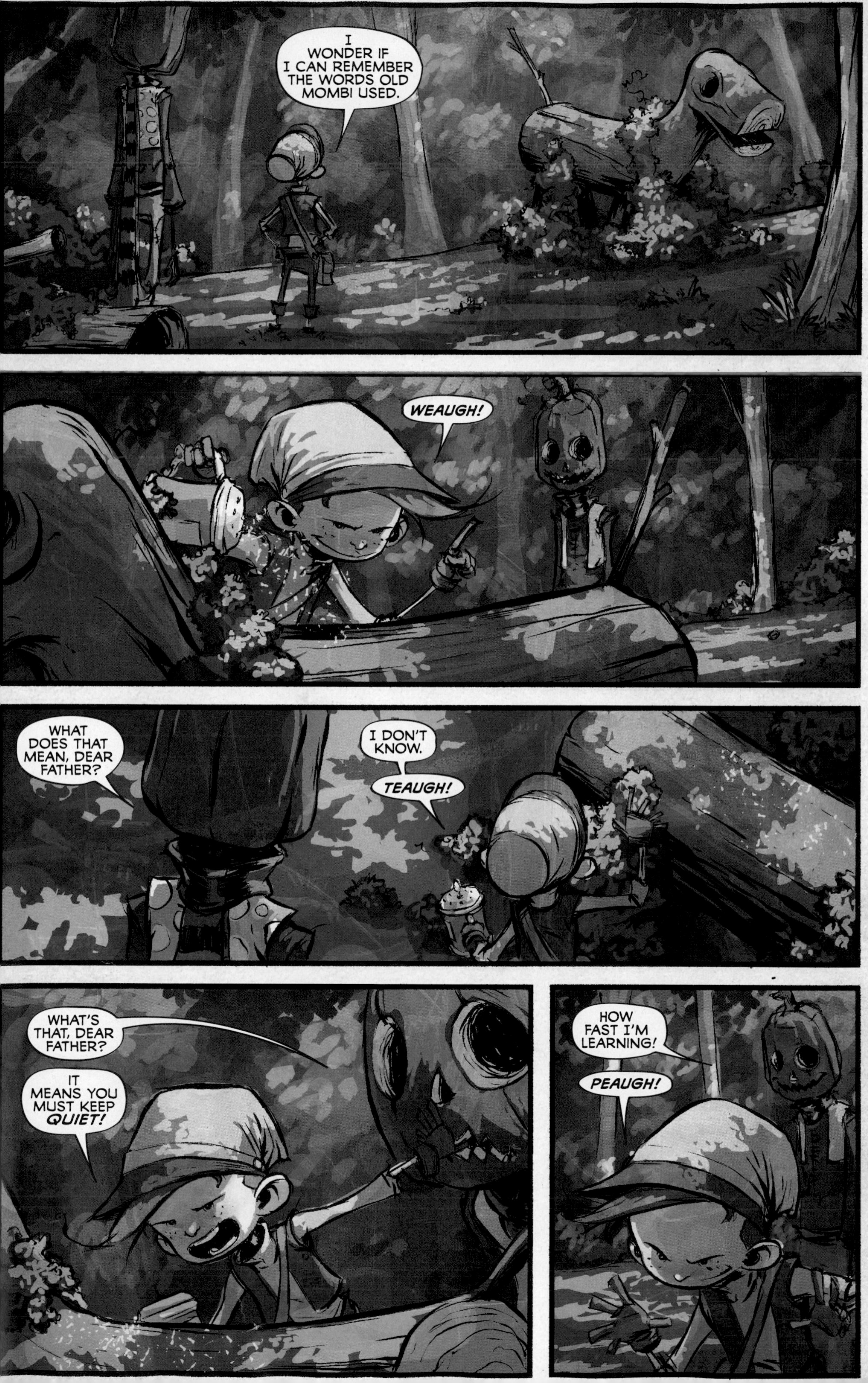
I WONDER IF I CAN REMEMBER THE WORDS OLD MOMBI USED.
WEAUGH!
WHAT DOES THAT MEAN, DEAR FATHER?
I DON'T KNOW.
TEAUGH!
WHAT'S THAT, DEAR FATHER?
IT MEANS YOU MUST KEEP QUIET!
HOW FAST I'M LEARNING!
PEAUGH!

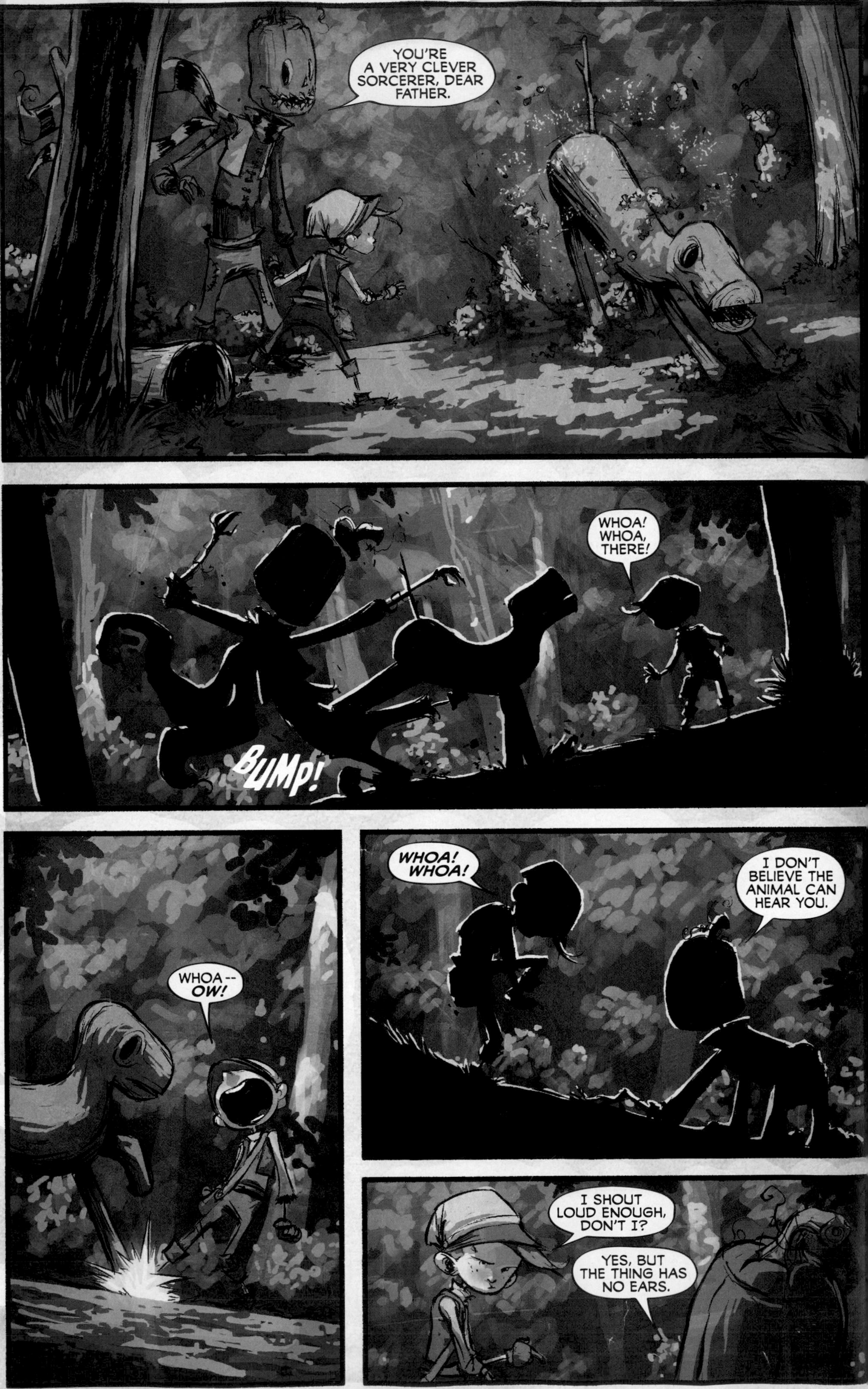
YOU'RE A VERY CLEVER SORCERER, DEAR FATHER.
WHOA! WHOA, THERE!
BUMP!
WHOA -- OW!
WHOA! WHOA!
I DON'T BELIEVE THE ANIMAL CAN HEAR YOU.
I SHOUT LOUD ENOUGH, DON'T I?
YES, BUT THE THING HAS NO EARS.

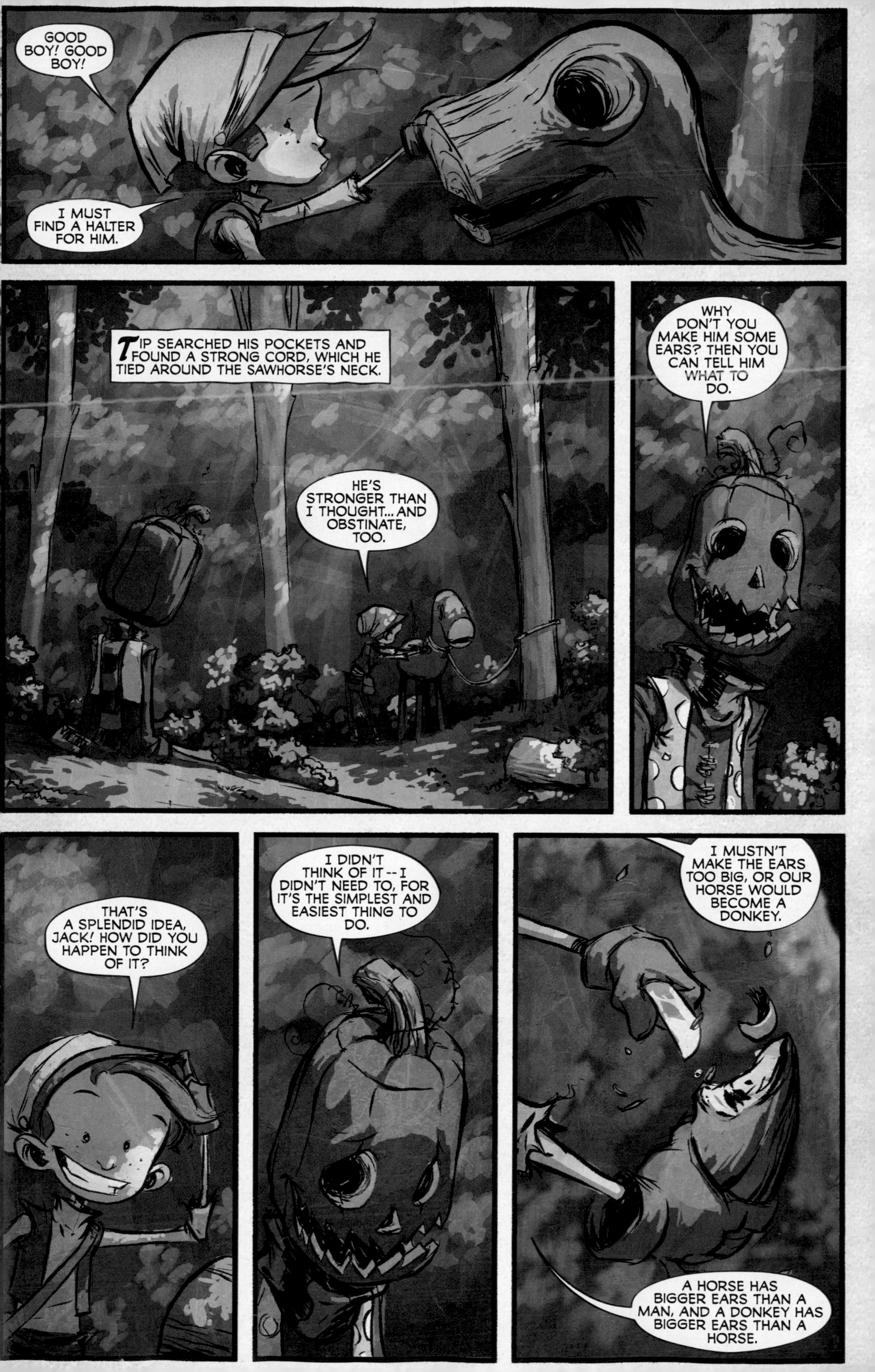
GOOD BOY! GOOD BOY!
I MUST FIND A HALTER FOR HIM.
TIP SEARCHED HIS POCKETS AND FOUND A STRONG CORD, WHICH HE TIED AROUND THE SAWHORSE'S NECK.
HE'S STRONGER THAN I THOUGHT... AND OBSTINATE, TOO.
WHY DON'T YOU MAKE HIM SOME EARS? THEN YOU CAN TELL HIM WHAT TO DO.
THAT'S A SPLENDID IDEA, JACK! HOW DID YOU HAPPEN TO THINK OF IT?
I DIDN'T THINK OF IT -- I DIDN'T NEED TO, FOR IT'S THE SIMPLEST AND EASIEST THING TO DO.
I MUSTN'T MAKE THE EARS TOO BIG, OR OUR HORSE WOULD BECOME A DONKEY.
A HORSE HAS BIGGER EARS THAN A MAN, AND A DONKEY HAS BIGGER EARS THAN A HORSE.

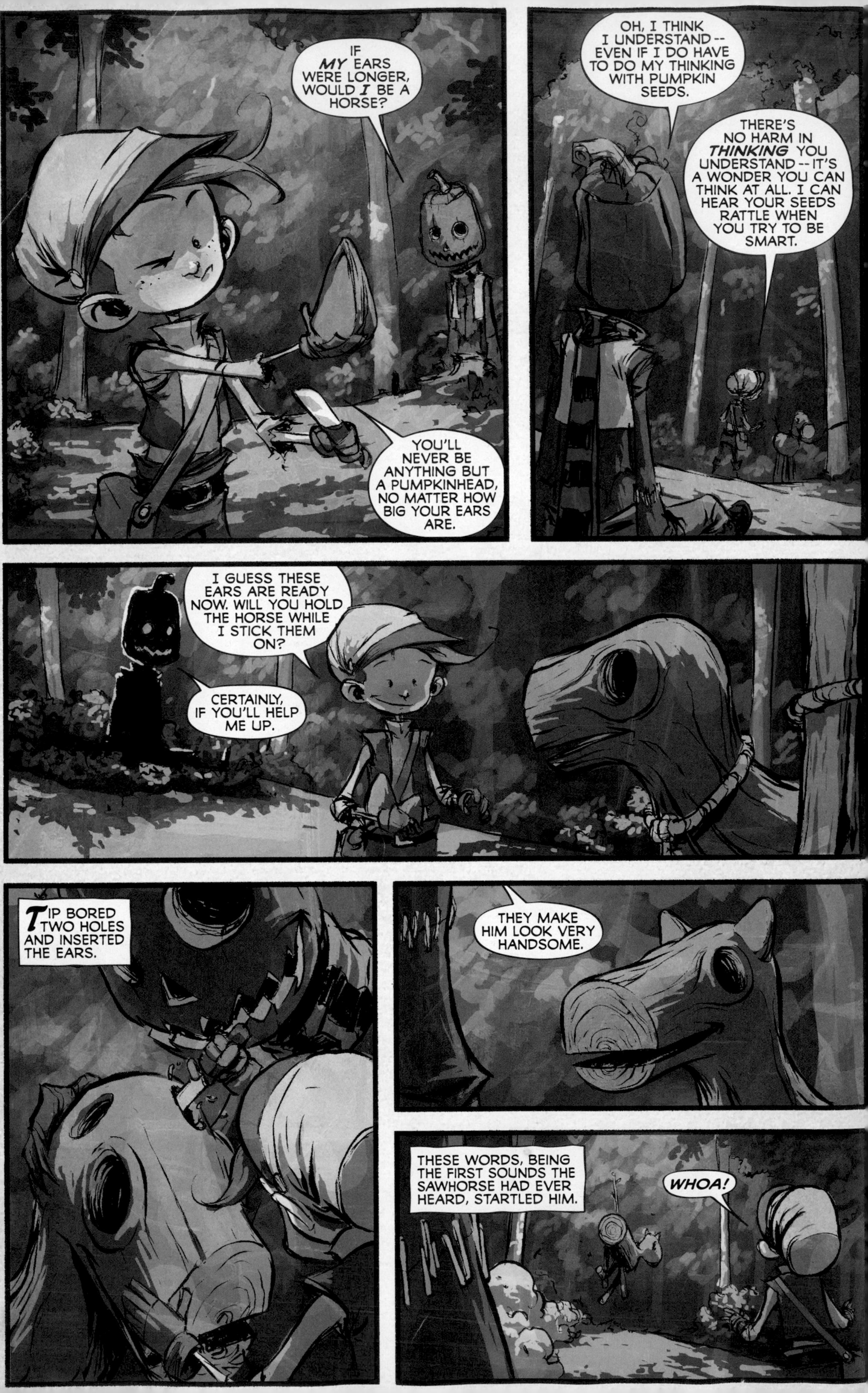

IF MY EARS WERE LONGER, WOULD I BE A HORSE?
YOU'LL NEVER BE ANYTHING BUT A PUMPKINHEAD, NO MATTER HOW BIG YOUR EARS ARE.
OH, I THINK I UNDERSTAND -- EVEN IF I DO HAVE TO DO MY THINKING WITH PUMPKIN SEEDS.
THERE'S NO HARM IN THINKING YOU UNDERSTAND -- IT'S A WONDER YOU CAN THINK AT ALL. I CAN HEAR YOUR SEEDS RATTLE WHEN YOU TRY TO BE SMART.
I GUESS THESE EARS ARE READY NOW. WILL YOU HOLD THE HORSE WHILE I STICK THEM ON?
CERTAINLY, IF YOU'LL HELP ME UP.
TIP BORED TWO HOLES AND INSERTED THE EARS.
THEY MAKE HIM LOOK VERY HANDSOME.
THESE WORDS, BEING THE FIRST SOUNDS THE SAWHORSE HAD EVER HEARD, STARTLED HIM.
WHOA!

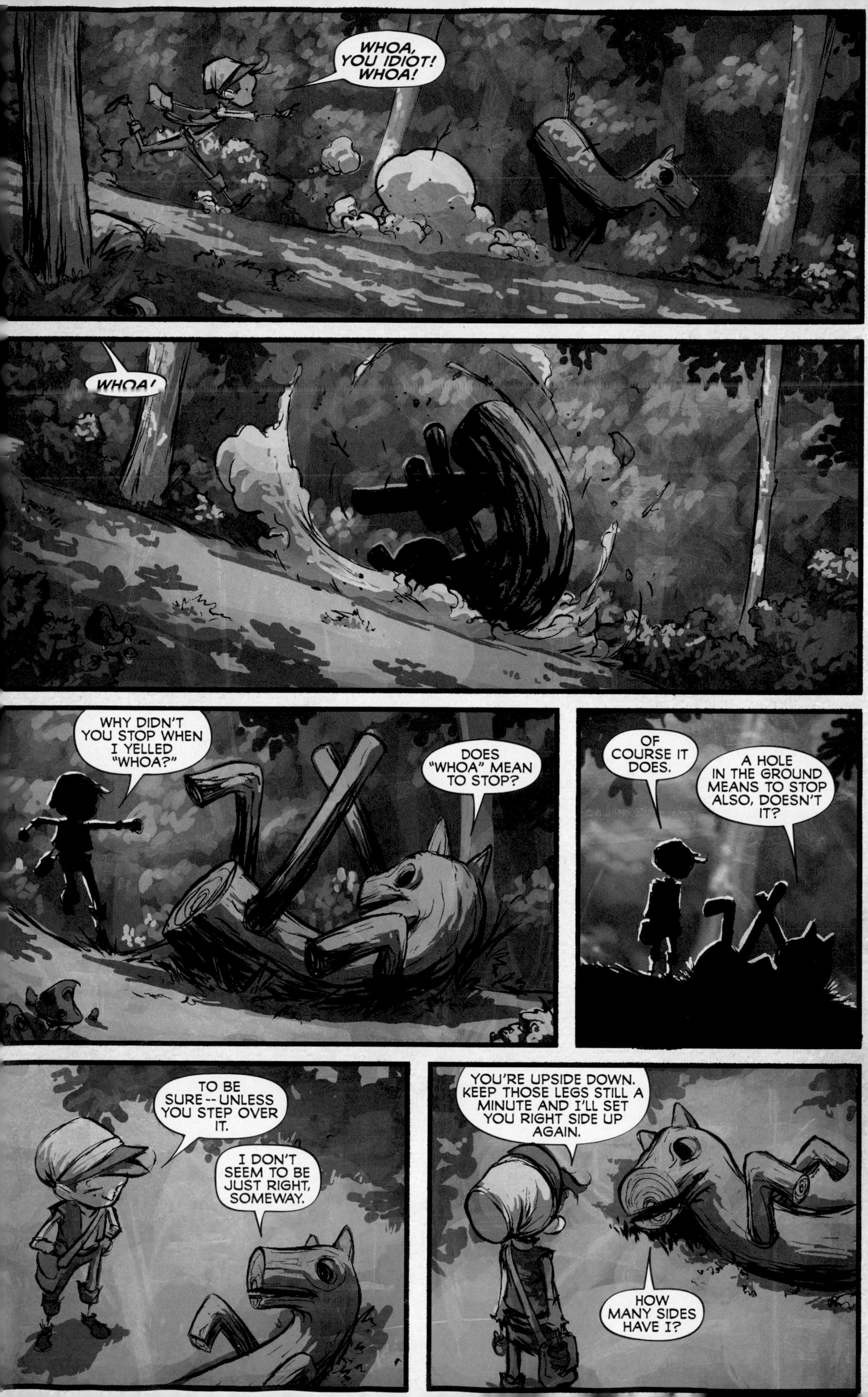
WHOA, YOU IDIOT! WHOA!
WHOA!
WHY DIDN'T YOU STOP WHEN I YELLED "WHOA?"
DOES "WHOA" MEAN TO STOP?
OF COURSE IT DOES.
A HOLE IN THE GROUND MEANS TO STOP ALSO, DOESN'T IT?
TO BE SURE--UNLESS YOU STEP OVER IT.
I DON'T SEEM TO BE JUST RIGHT, SOMEWAY.
YOU'RE UPSIDE DOWN. KEEP THOSE LEGS STILL A MINUTE AND I'LL SET YOU RIGHT SIDE UP AGAIN.
HOW MANY SIDES HAVE I?

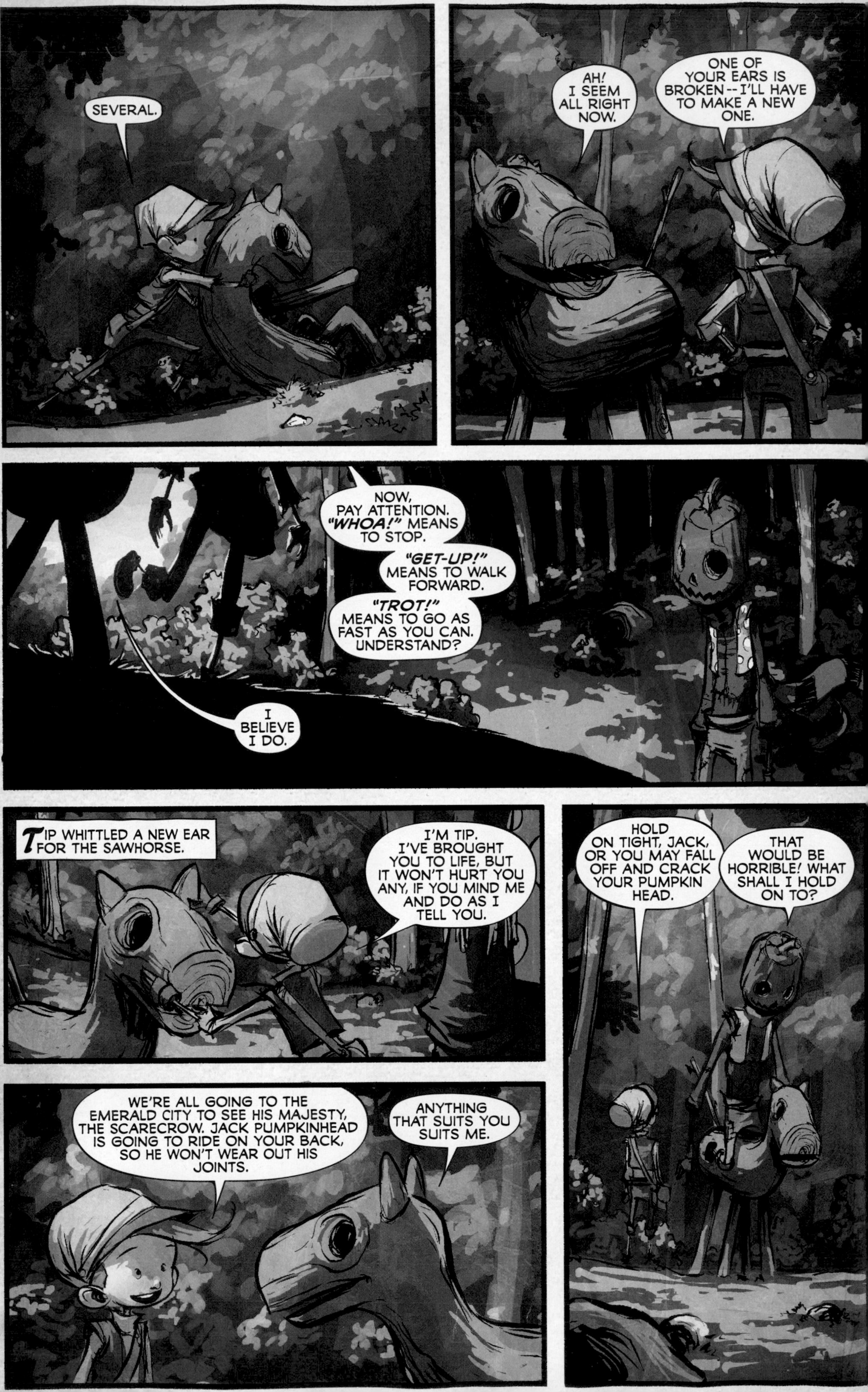
SEVERAL.
AH! I SEEM ALL RIGHT NOW.
ONE OF YOUR EARS IS BROKEN--I'LL HAVE TO MAKE A NEW ONE.
NOW, PAY ATTENTION. "WHOA!" MEANS TO STOP.
"GET-UP!" MEANS TO WALK FORWARD.
"TROT!" MEANS TO GO AS FAST AS YOU CAN. UNDERSTAND?
I BELIEVE I DO.
TIP WHITTLED A NEW EAR FOR THE SAWHORSE.
I'M TIP. I'VE BROUGHT YOU TO LIFE, BUT IT WON'T HURT YOU ANY, IF YOU MIND ME AND DO AS I TELL YOU.
WE'RE ALL GOING TO THE EMERALD CITY TO SEE HIS MAJESTY, THE SCARECROW. JACK PUMPKINHEAD IS GOING TO RIDE ON YOUR BACK, SO HE WON'T WEAR OUT HIS JOINTS.
ANYTHING THAT SUITS YOU SUITS ME.
HOLD ON TIGHT, JACK, OR YOU MAY FALL OFF AND CRACK YOUR PUMPKIN HEAD.
THAT WOULD BE HORRIBLE! WHAT SHALL I HOLD ON TO?

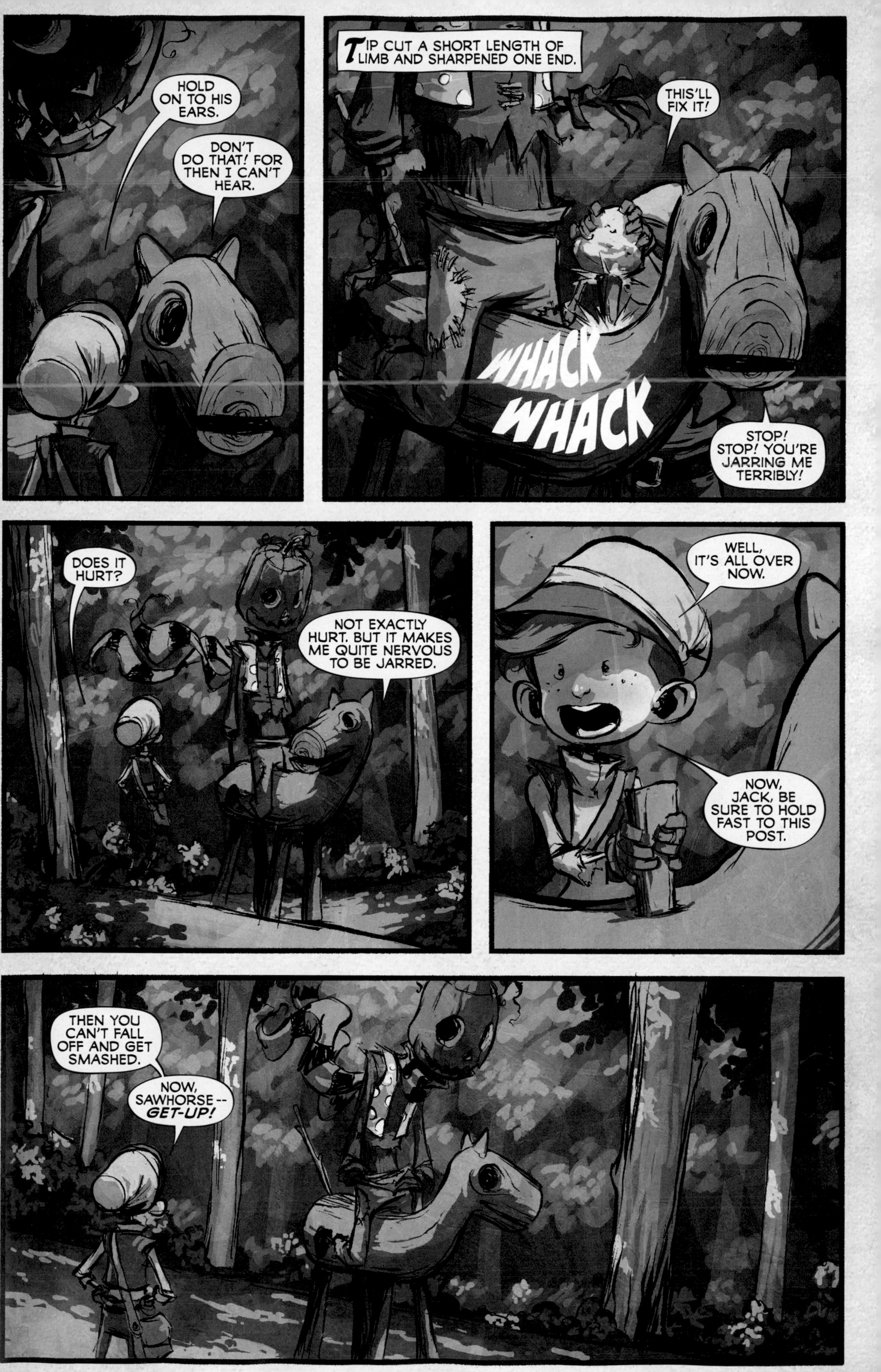
HOLD ON TO HIS EARS.
DON'T DO THAT! FOR THEN I CAN'T HEAR.
TIP CUT A SHORT LENGTH OF LIMB AND SHARPENED ONE END.
THIS'LL FIX IT!
WHACK
WHACK
STOP! STOP! YOU'RE JARRING ME TERRIBLY!
DOES IT HURT?
NOT EXACTLY HURT. BUT IT MAKES ME QUITE NERVOUS TO BE JARRED.
WELL, IT'S ALL OVER NOW.
NOW, JACK, BE SURE TO HOLD FAST TO THIS POST.
THEN YOU CAN'T FALL OFF AND GET SMASHED.
NOW, SAWHORSE -- GET-UP!

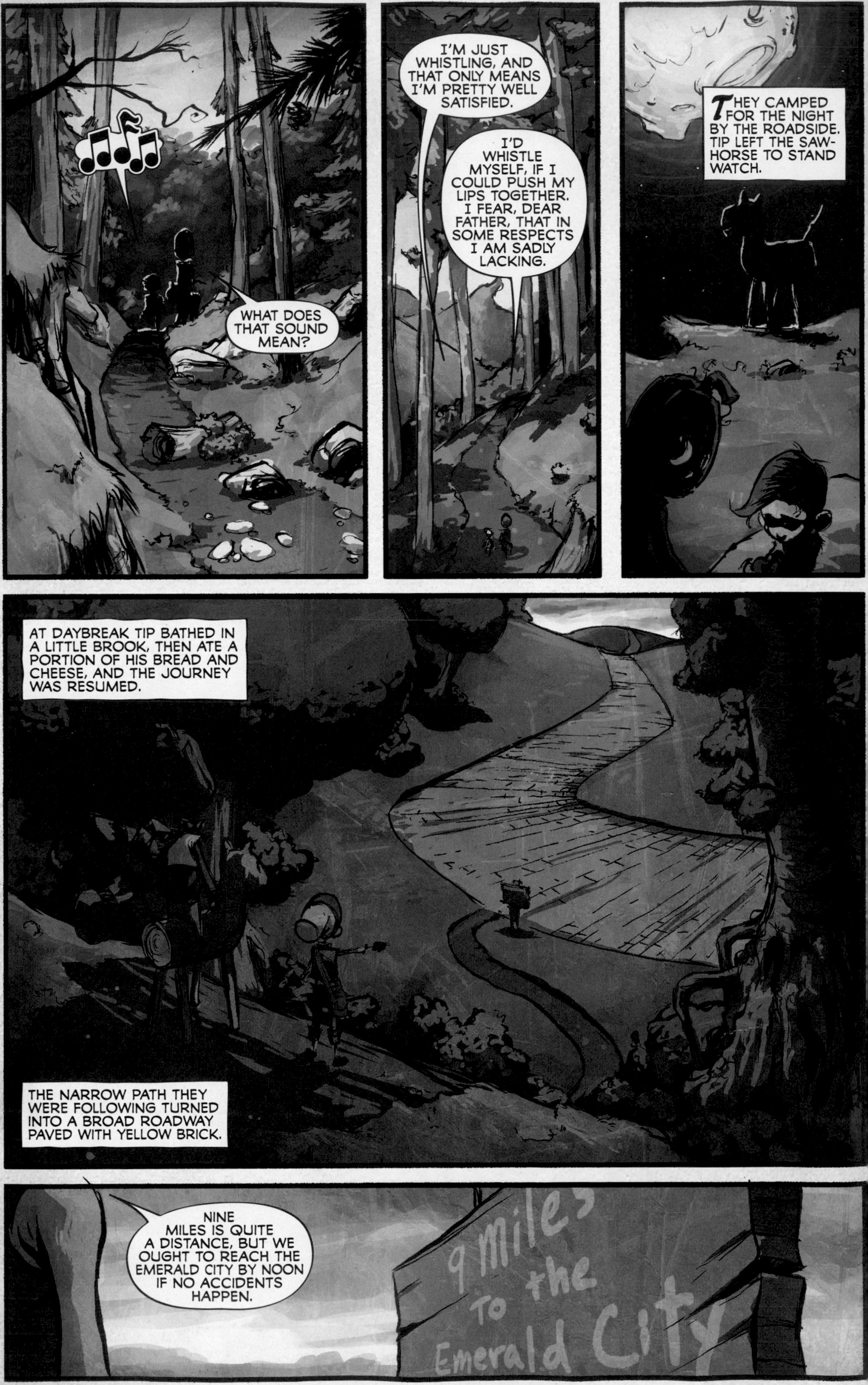
WHAT DOES THAT SOUND MEAN?
I'M JUST WHISTLING, AND THAT ONLY MEANS I'M PRETTY WELL SATISFIED.
I'D WHISTLE MYSELF, IF I COULD PUSH MY LIPS TOGETHER. I FEAR, DEAR FATHER, THAT IN SOME RESPECTS I AM SADLY LACKING.
THEY CAMPED FOR THE NIGHT BY THE ROADSIDE. TIP LEFT THE SAW-HORSE TO STAND WATCH.
AT DAYBREAK TIP BATHED IN A LITTLE BROOK, THEN ATE A PORTION OF HIS BREAD AND CHEESE, AND THE JOURNEY WAS RESUMED.
THE NARROW PATH THEY WERE FOLLOWING TURNED INTO A BROAD ROADWAY PAVED WITH YELLOW BRICK.
NINE MILES IS QUITE A DISTANCE, BUT WE OUGHT TO REACH THE EMERALD CITY BY NOON IF NO ACCIDENTS HAPPEN.
9 Miles To the Emerald City

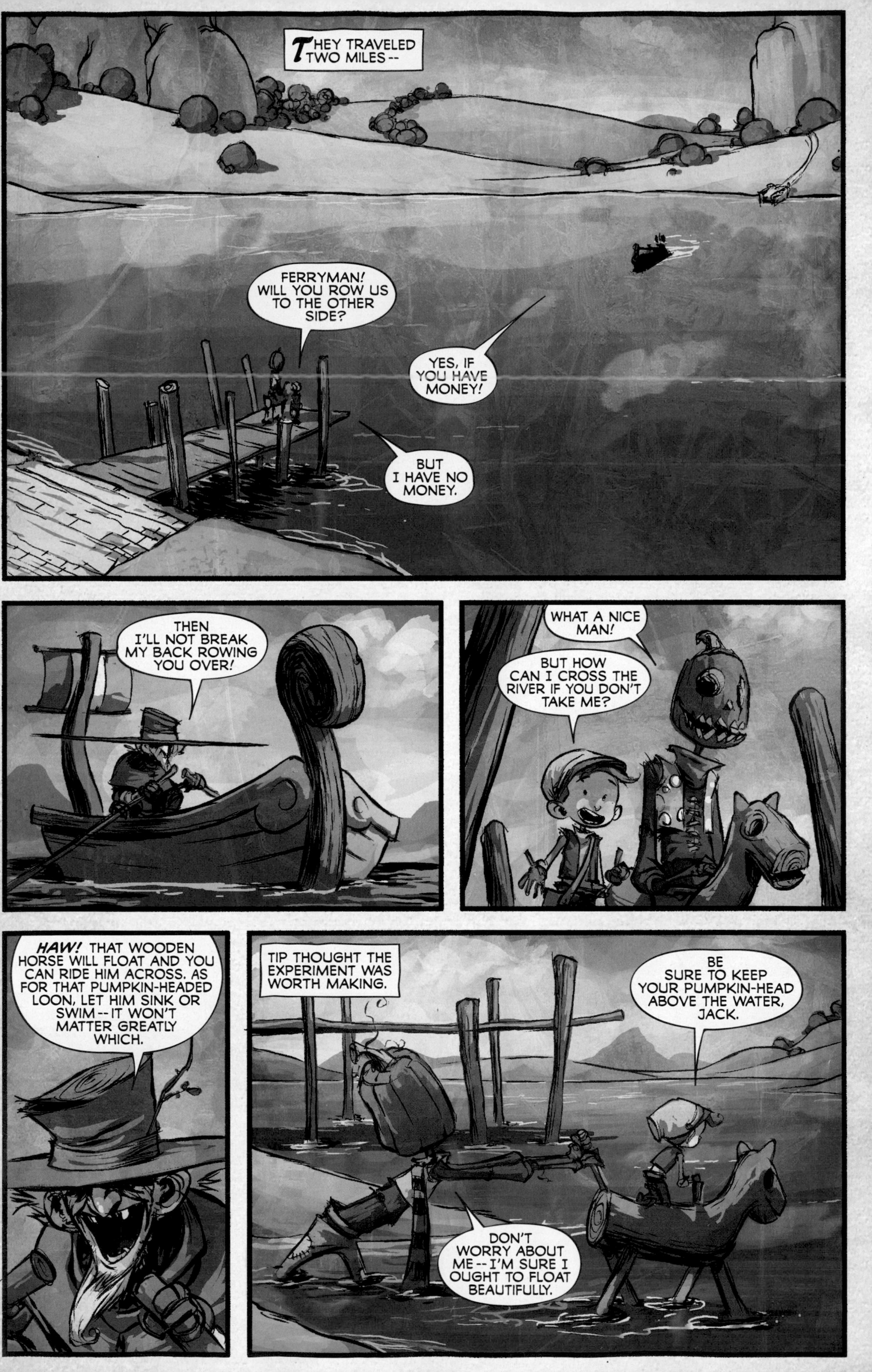

THEY TRAVELED TWO MILES --
FERRYMAN! WILL YOU ROW US TO THE OTHER SIDE?
YES, IF YOU HAVE MONEY!
BUT I HAVE NO MONEY.
THEN I'LL NOT BREAK MY BACK ROWING YOU OVER!
WHAT A NICE MAN!
BUT HOW CAN I CROSS THE RIVER IF YOU DON'T TAKE ME?
HAW! THAT WOODEN HORSE WILL FLOAT AND YOU CAN RIDE HIM ACROSS. AS FOR THAT PUMPKIN-HEADED LOON, LET HIM SINK OR SWIM -- IT WON'T MATTER GREATLY WHICH.
TIP THOUGHT THE EXPERIMENT WAS WORTH MAKING.
BE SURE TO KEEP YOUR PUMPKIN-HEAD ABOVE THE WATER, JACK.
DON'T WORRY ABOUT ME -- I'M SURE I OUGHT TO FLOAT BEAUTIFULLY.

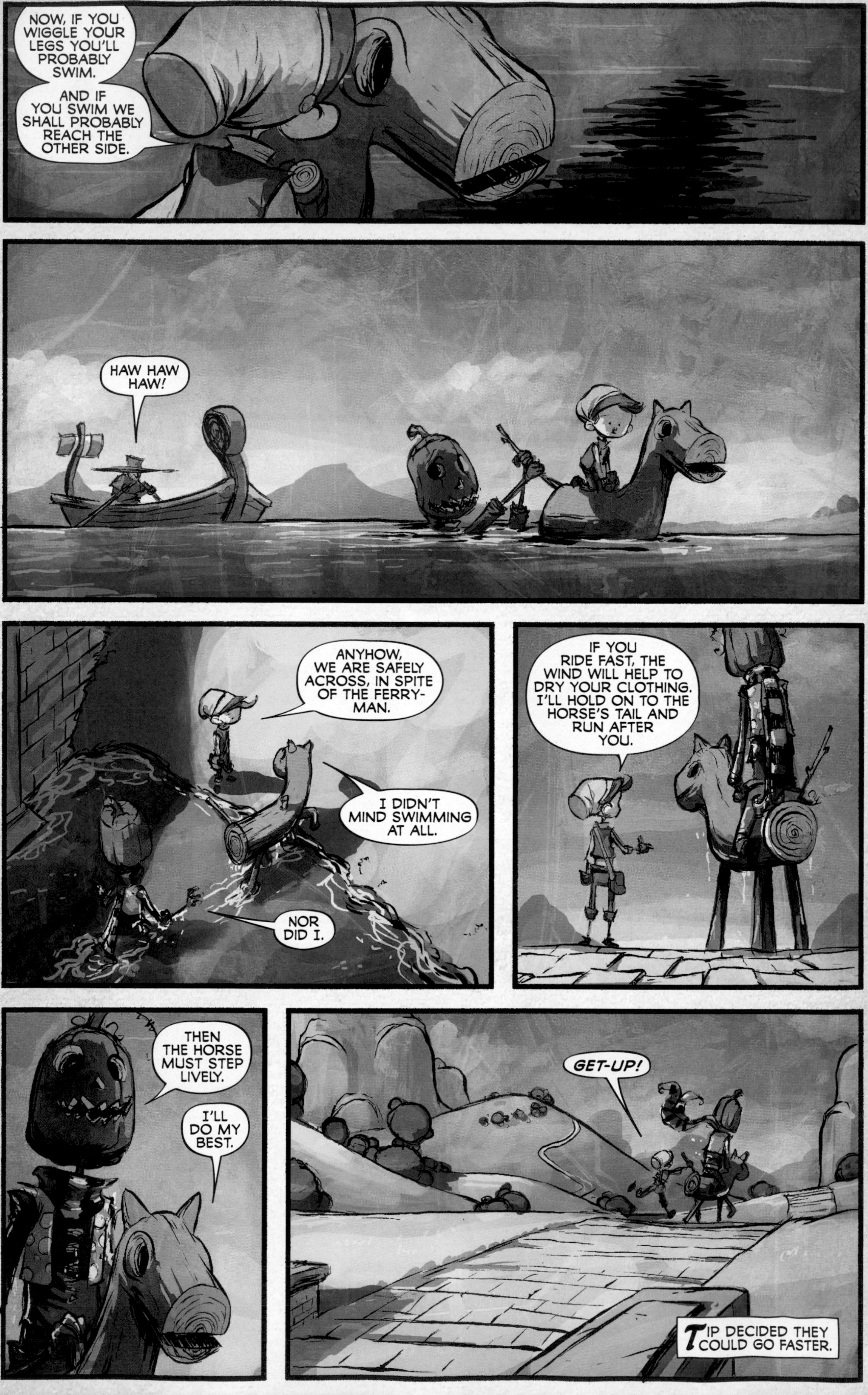
NOW, IF YOU WIGGLE YOUR LEGS YOU'LL PROBABLY SWIM.
AND IF YOU SWIM WE SHALL PROBABLY REACH THE OTHER SIDE.
HAW HAW HAW!
ANYHOW, WE ARE SAFELY ACROSS, IN SPITE OF THE FERRY-MAN.
I DIDN'T MIND SWIMMING AT ALL.
NOR DID I.
IF YOU RIDE FAST, THE WIND WILL HELP TO DRY YOUR CLOTHING. I'LL HOLD ON TO THE HORSE'S TAIL AND RUN AFTER YOU.
THEN THE HORSE MUST STEP LIVELY.
I'LL DO MY BEST.
GET-UP!
TIP DECIDED THEY COULD GO FASTER.

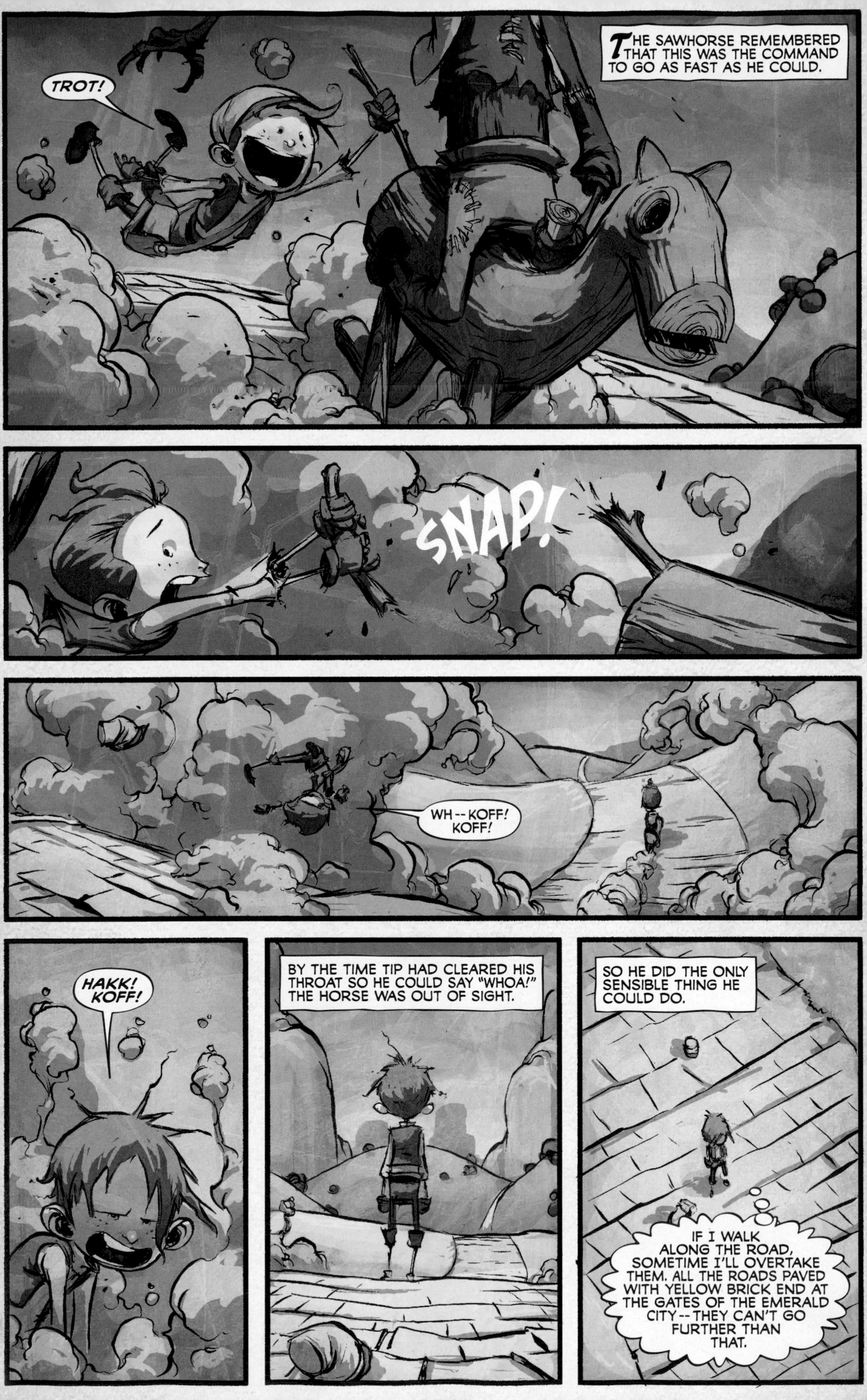
THE SAWHORSE REMEMBERED THAT THIS WAS THE COMMAND TO GO AS FAST AS HE COULD.
TROT!
SNAP!
WH--KOFF! KOFF!
HAKK! KOFF!
BY THE TIME TIP HAD CLEARED HIS THROAT SO HE COULD SAY "WHOA!" THE HORSE WAS OUT OF SIGHT.
SO HE DID THE ONLY SENSIBLE THING HE COULD DO.
IF I WALK ALONG THE ROAD, SOMETIME I'LL OVERTAKE THEM. ALL THE ROADS PAVED WITH YELLOW BRICK END AT THE GATES OF THE EMERALD CITY--THEY CAN'T GO FURTHER THAN THAT.

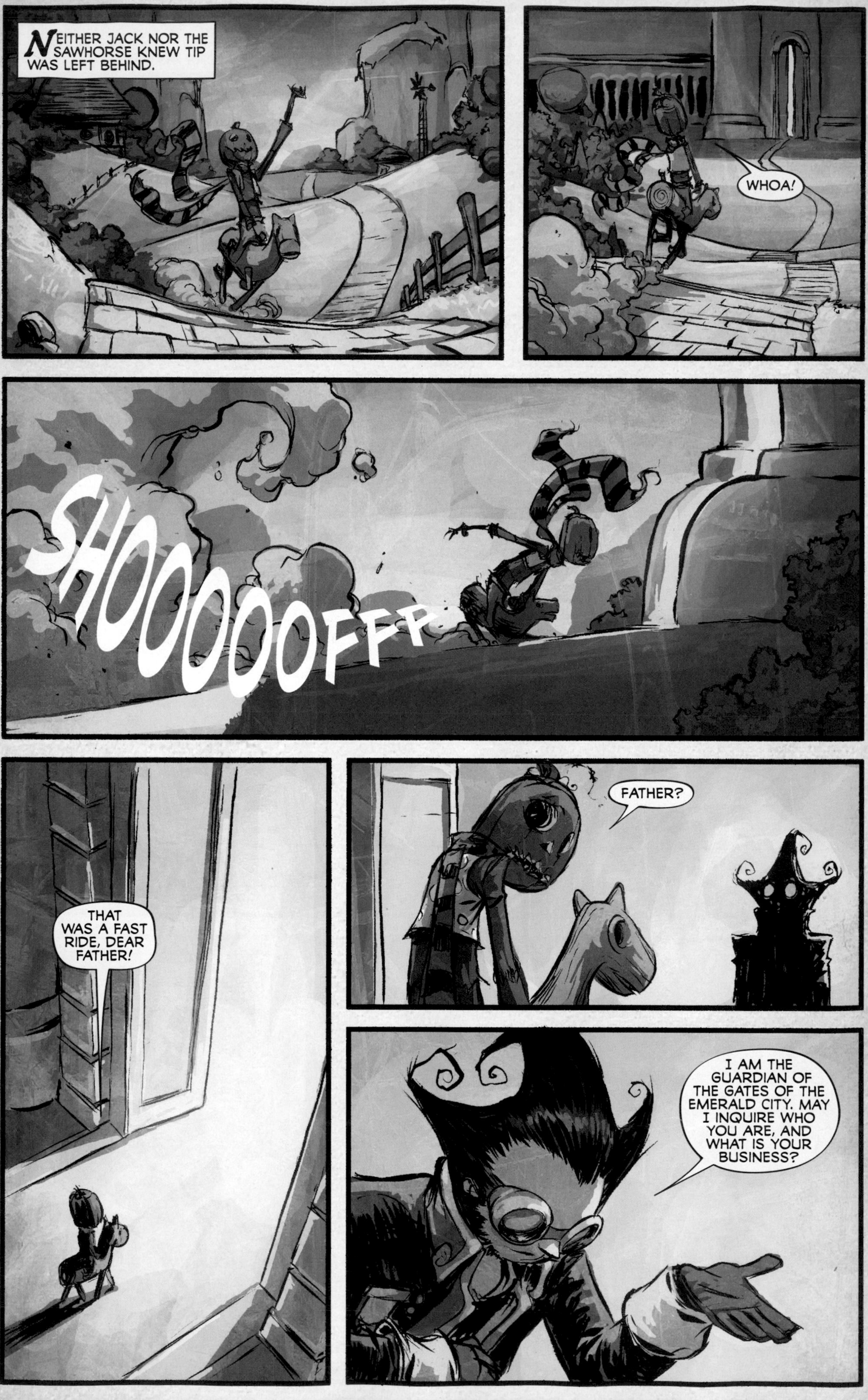
NEITHER JACK NOR THE SAWHORSE KNEW TIP WAS LEFT BEHIND.
WHOA!
SHOOOOOOFFF
THAT WAS A FAST RIDE, DEAR FATHER!
FATHER?
I AM THE GUARDIAN OF THE GATES OF THE EMERALD CITY. MAY I INQUIRE WHO YOU ARE, AND WHAT IS YOUR BUSINESS?

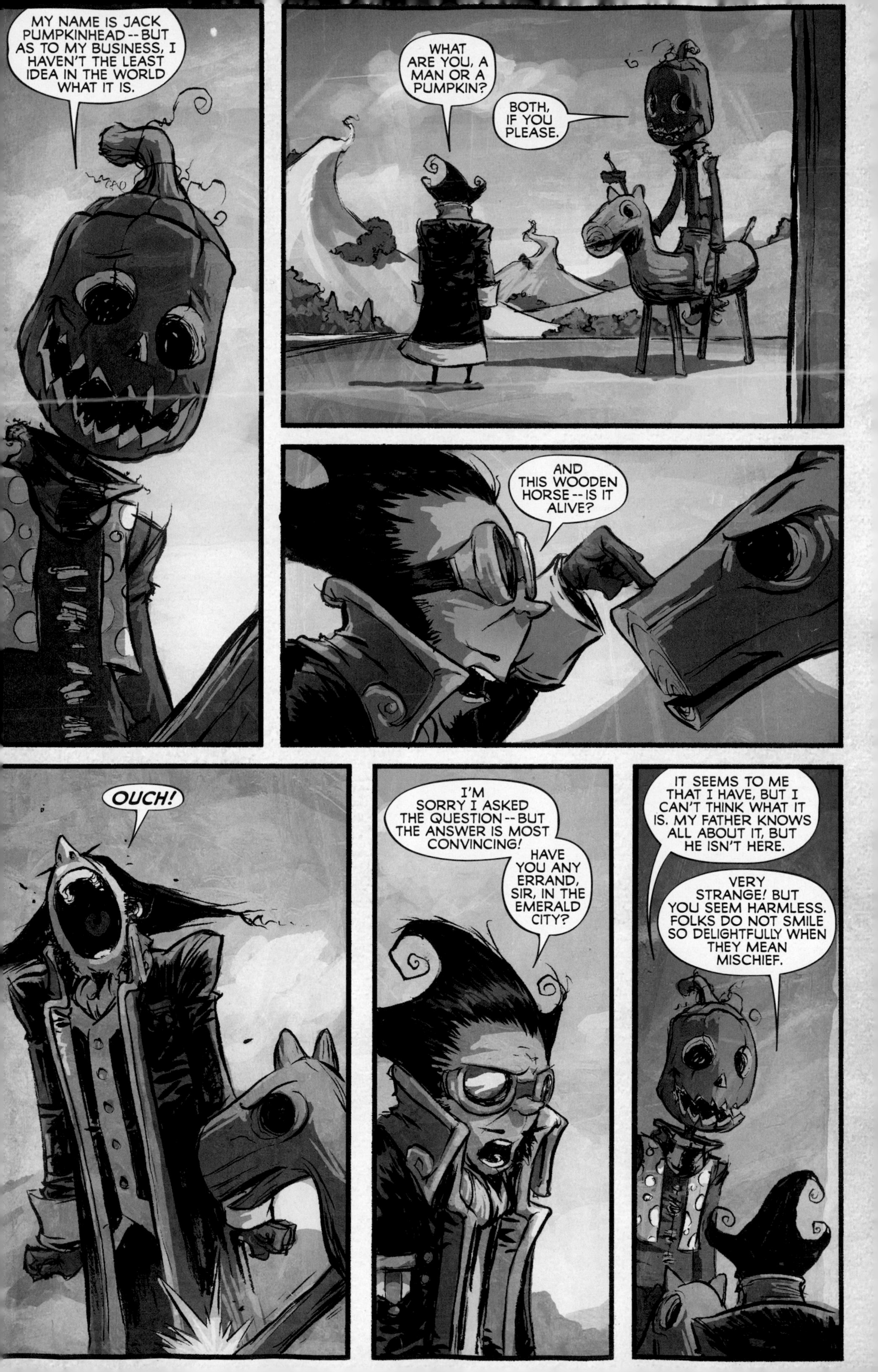
MY NAME IS JACK PUMPKINHEAD -- BUT AS TO MY BUSINESS, I HAVEN'T THE LEAST IDEA IN THE WORLD WHAT IT IS.
WHAT ARE YOU, A MAN OR A PUMPKIN?
BOTH, IF YOU PLEASE.
AND THIS WOODEN HORSE -- IS IT ALIVE?
OUCH!
I'M SORRY I ASKED THE QUESTION -- BUT THE ANSWER IS MOST CONVINCING!
HAVE YOU ANY ERRAND, SIR, IN THE EMERALD CITY?
IT SEEMS TO ME THAT I HAVE, BUT I CAN'T THINK WHAT IT IS. MY FATHER KNOWS ALL ABOUT IT, BUT HE ISN'T HERE.
VERY STRANGE! BUT YOU SEEM HARMLESS. FOLKS DO NOT SMILE SO DELIGHTFULLY WHEN THEY MEAN MISCHIEF.

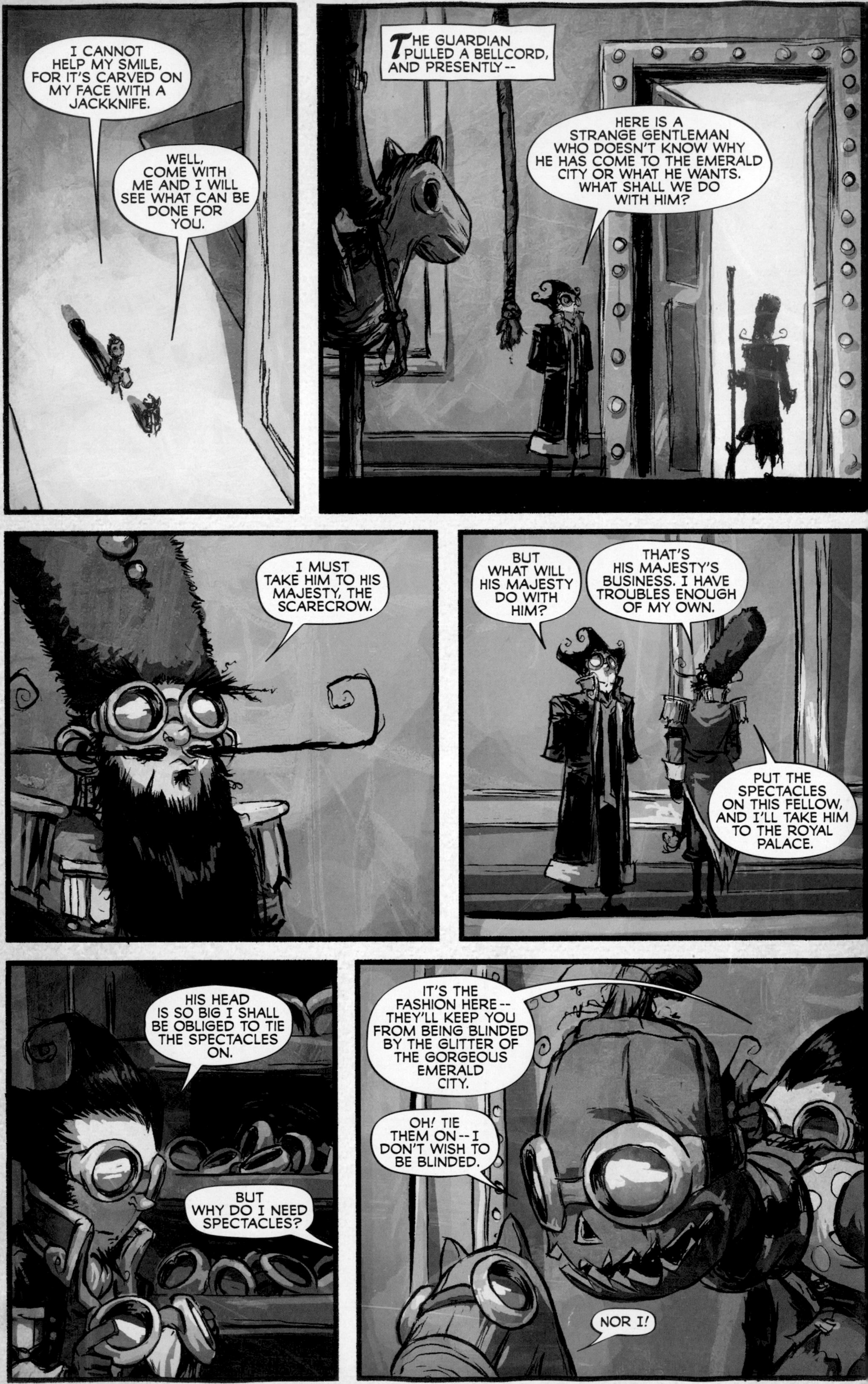
I CANNOT HELP MY SMILE, FOR IT'S CARVED ON MY FACE WITH A JACKKNIFE.
WELL, COME WITH ME AND I WILL SEE WHAT CAN BE DONE FOR YOU.
THE GUARDIAN PULLED A BELLCORD, AND PRESENTLY--
HERE IS A STRANGE GENTLEMAN WHO DOESN'T KNOW WHY HE HAS COME TO THE EMERALD CITY OR WHAT HE WANTS. WHAT SHALL WE DO WITH HIM?
I MUST TAKE HIM TO HIS MAJESTY, THE SCARECROW.
BUT WHAT WILL HIS MAJESTY DO WITH HIM?
THAT'S HIS MAJESTY'S BUSINESS. I HAVE TROUBLES ENOUGH OF MY OWN.
PUT THE SPECTACLES ON THIS FELLOW, AND I'LL TAKE HIM TO THE ROYAL PALACE.
HIS HEAD IS SO BIG I SHALL BE OBLIGED TO TIE THE SPECTACLES ON.
BUT WHY DO I NEED SPECTACLES?
IT'S THE FASHION HERE-- THEY'LL KEEP YOU FROM BEING BLINDED BY THE GLITTER OF THE GORGEOUS EMERALD CITY.
OH! TIE THEM ON--I DON'T WISH TO BE BLINDED.
NOR I!

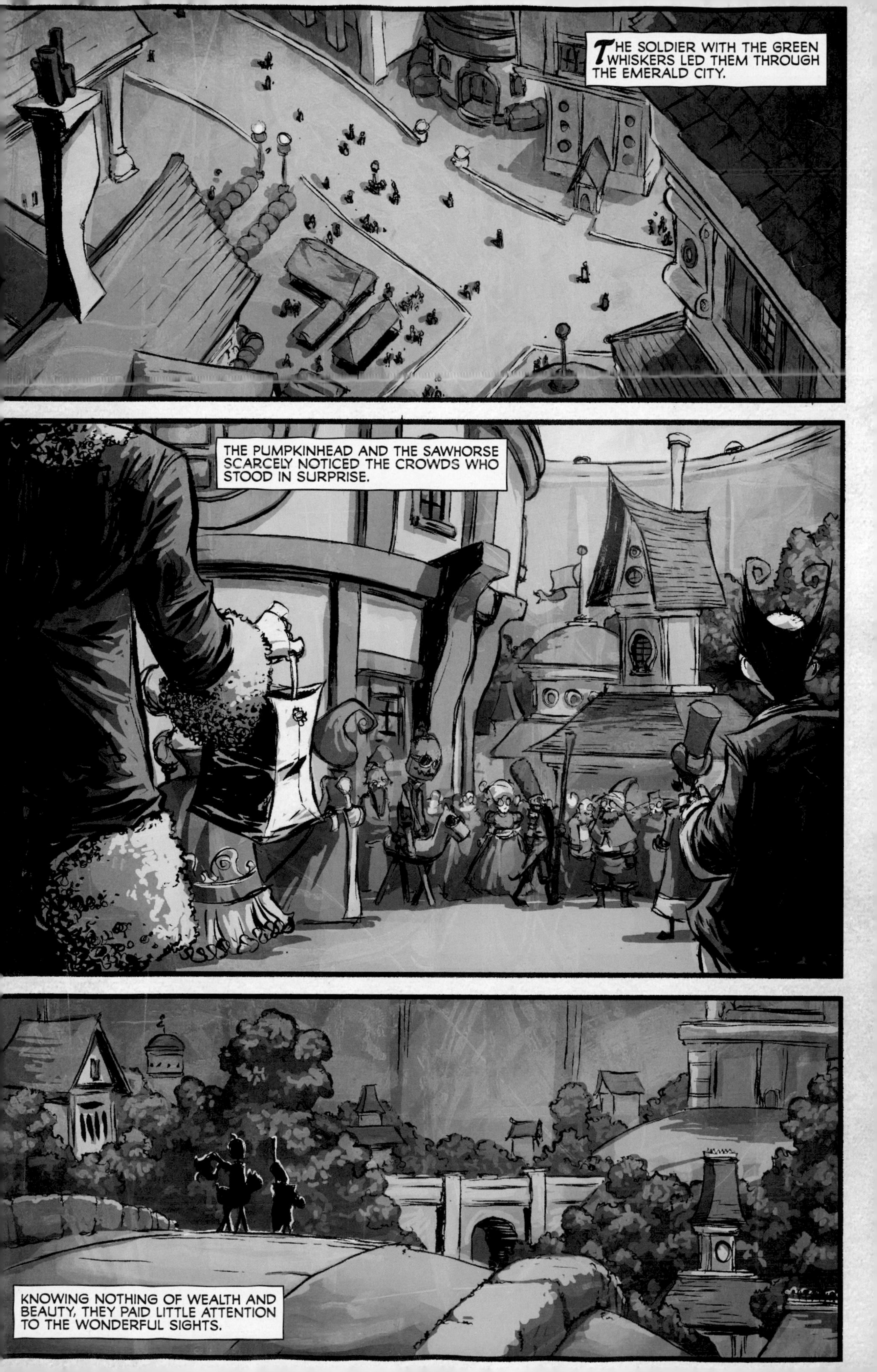
THE SOLDIER WITH THE GREEN WHISKERS LED THEM THROUGH THE EMERALD CITY.
THE PUMPKINHEAD AND THE SAWHORSE SCARCELY NOTICED THE CROWDS WHO STOOD IN SURPRISE.
KNOWING NOTHING OF WEALTH AND BEAUTY, THEY PAID LITTLE ATTENTION TO THE WONDERFUL SIGHTS.

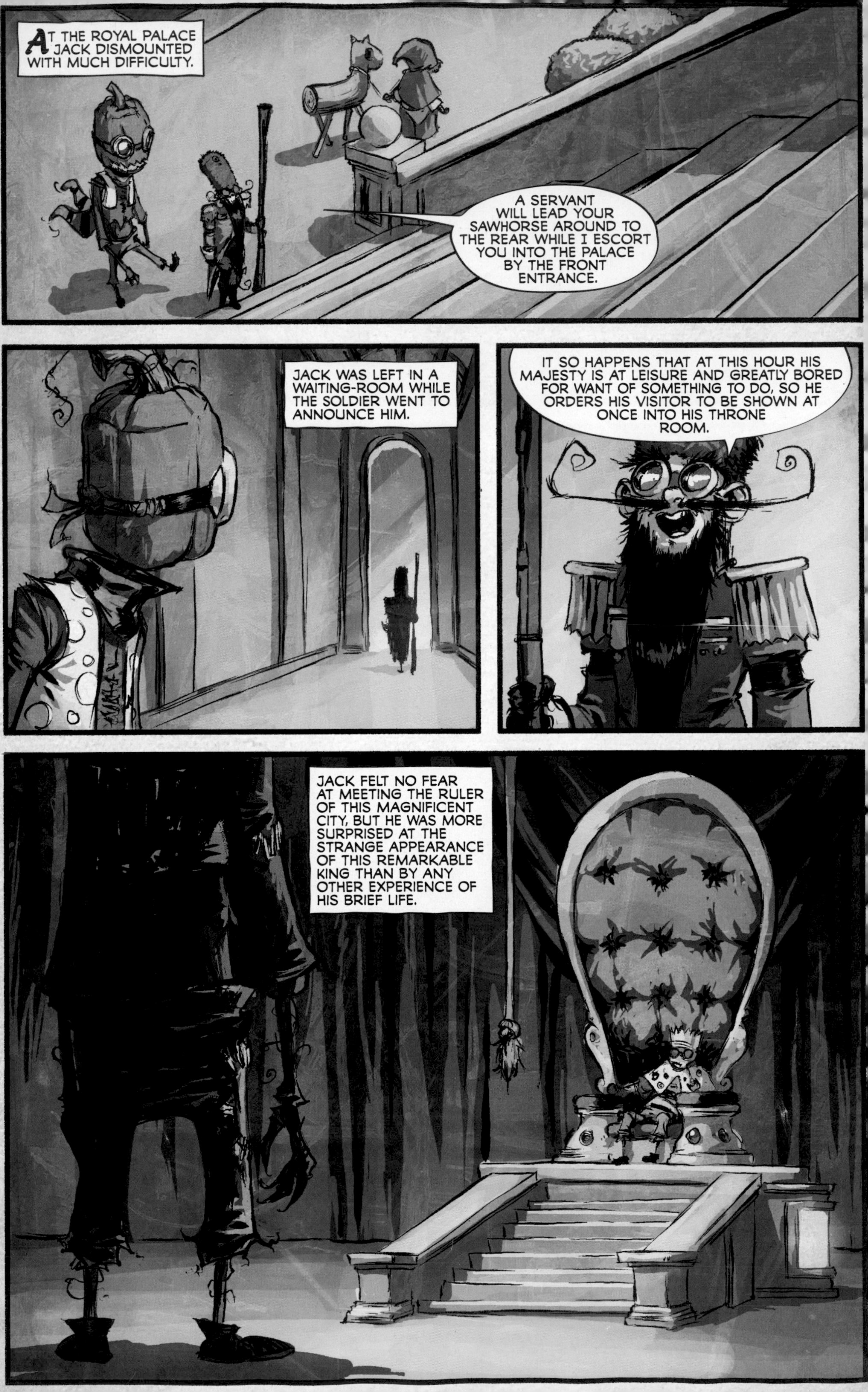
AT THE ROYAL PALACE JACK DISMOUNTED WITH MUCH DIFFICULTY.
A SERVANT WILL LEAD YOUR SAWHORSE AROUND TO THE REAR WHILE I ESCORT YOU INTO THE PALACE BY THE FRONT ENTRANCE.
JACK WAS LEFT IN A WAITING-ROOM WHILE THE SOLDIER WENT TO ANNOUNCE HIM.
IT SO HAPPENS THAT AT THIS HOUR HIS MAJESTY IS AT LEISURE AND GREATLY BORED FOR WANT OF SOMETHING TO DO, SO HE ORDERS HIS VISITOR TO BE SHOWN AT ONCE INTO HIS THRONE ROOM.
JACK FELT NO FEAR AT MEETING THE RULER OF THIS MAGNIFICENT CITY, BUT HE WAS MORE SURPRISED AT THE STRANGE APPEARANCE OF THIS REMARKABLE KING THAN BY ANY OTHER EXPERIENCE OF HIS BRIEF LIFE.

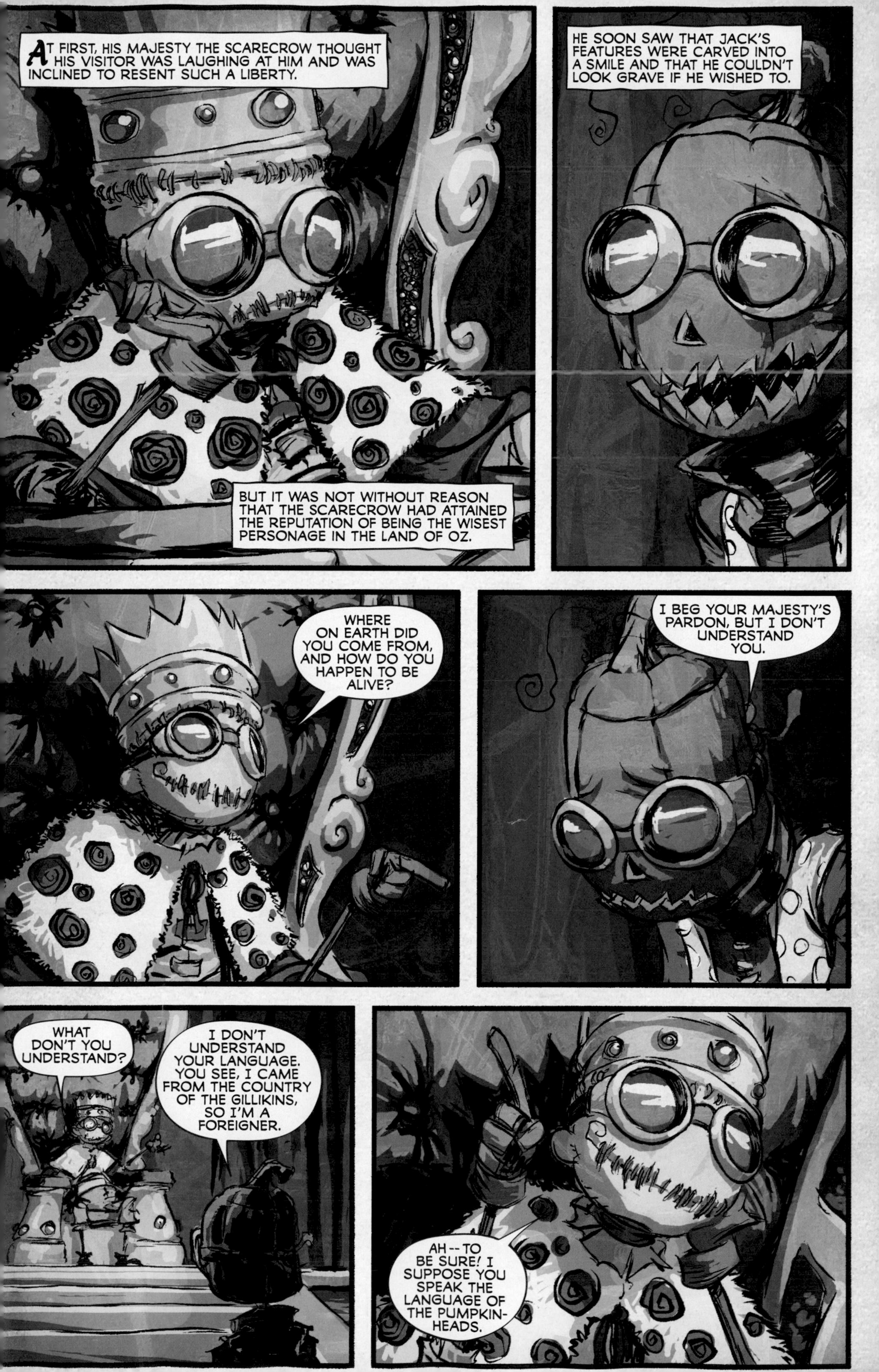

AT FIRST, HIS MAJESTY THE SCARECROW THOUGHT HIS VISITOR WAS LAUGHING AT HIM AND WAS INCLINED TO RESENT SUCH A LIBERTY.
BUT IT WAS NOT WITHOUT REASON THAT THE SCARECROW HAD ATTAINED THE REPUTATION OF BEING THE WISEST PERSONAGE IN THE LAND OF OZ.
HE SOON SAW THAT JACK'S FEATURES WERE CARVED INTO A SMILE AND THAT HE COULDN'T LOOK GRAVE IF HE WISHED TO.
WHERE ON EARTH DID YOU COME FROM, AND HOW DO YOU HAPPEN TO BE ALIVE?
I BEG YOUR MAJESTY'S PARDON, BUT I DON'T UNDERSTAND YOU.
WHAT DON'T YOU UNDERSTAND?
I DON'T UNDERSTAND YOUR LANGUAGE. YOU SEE, I CAME FROM THE COUNTRY OF THE GILLIKINS, SO I'M A FOREIGNER.
AH--TO BE SURE! I SUPPOSE YOU SPEAK THE LANGUAGE OF THE PUMPKIN-HEADS.

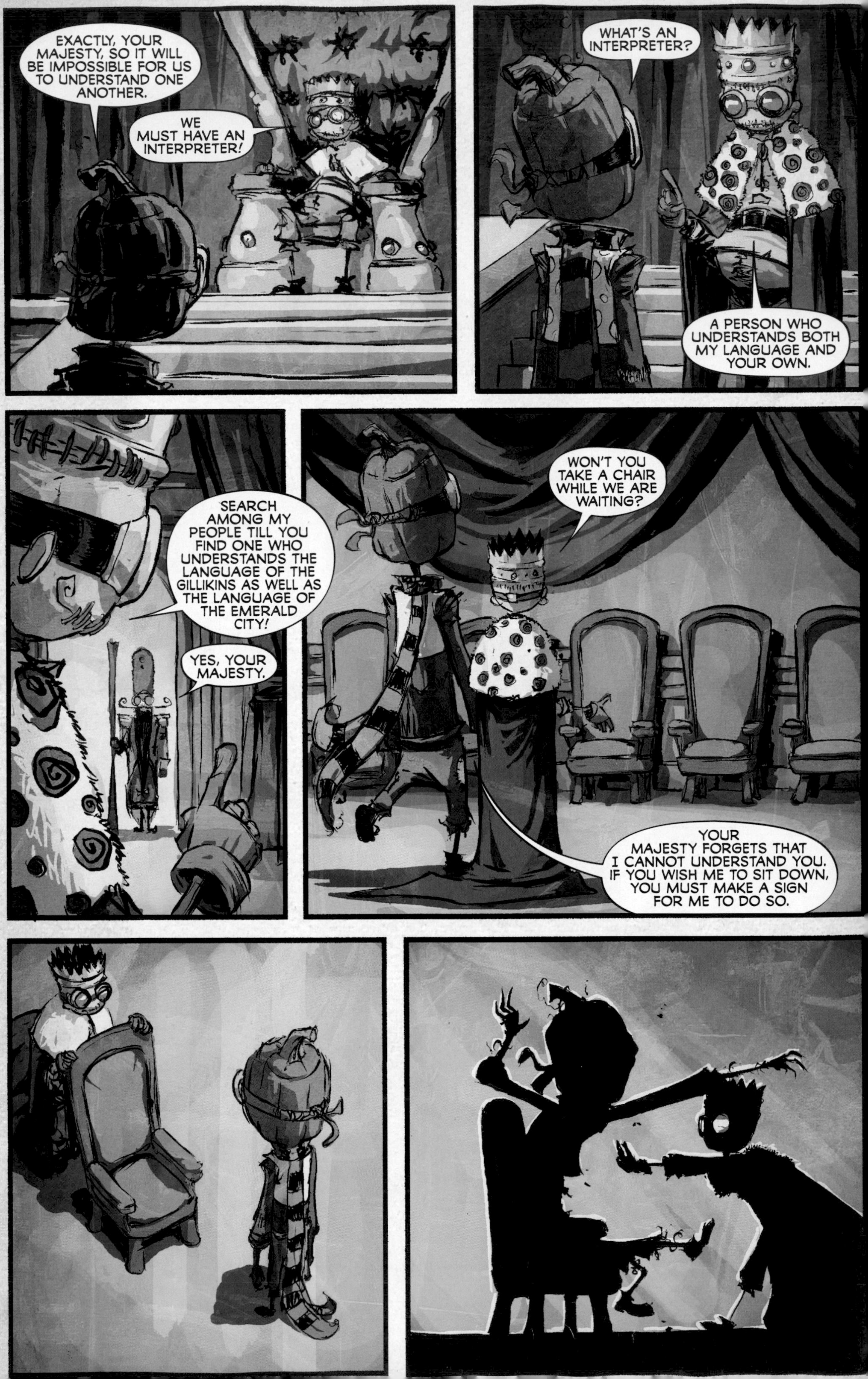
EXACTLY, YOUR MAJESTY, SO IT WILL BE IMPOSSIBLE FOR US TO UNDERSTAND ONE ANOTHER.
WE MUST HAVE AN INTERPRETER!
WHAT'S AN INTERPRETER?
A PERSON WHO UNDERSTANDS BOTH MY LANGUAGE AND YOUR OWN.
SEARCH AMONG MY PEOPLE TILL YOU FIND ONE WHO UNDERSTANDS THE LANGUAGE OF THE GILLIKINS AS WELL AS THE LANGUAGE OF THE EMERALD CITY!
YES, YOUR MAJESTY.
WON'T YOU TAKE A CHAIR WHILE WE ARE WAITING?
YOUR MAJESTY FORGETS THAT I CANNOT UNDERSTAND YOU. IF YOU WISH ME TO SIT DOWN, YOU MUST MAKE A SIGN FOR ME TO DO SO.

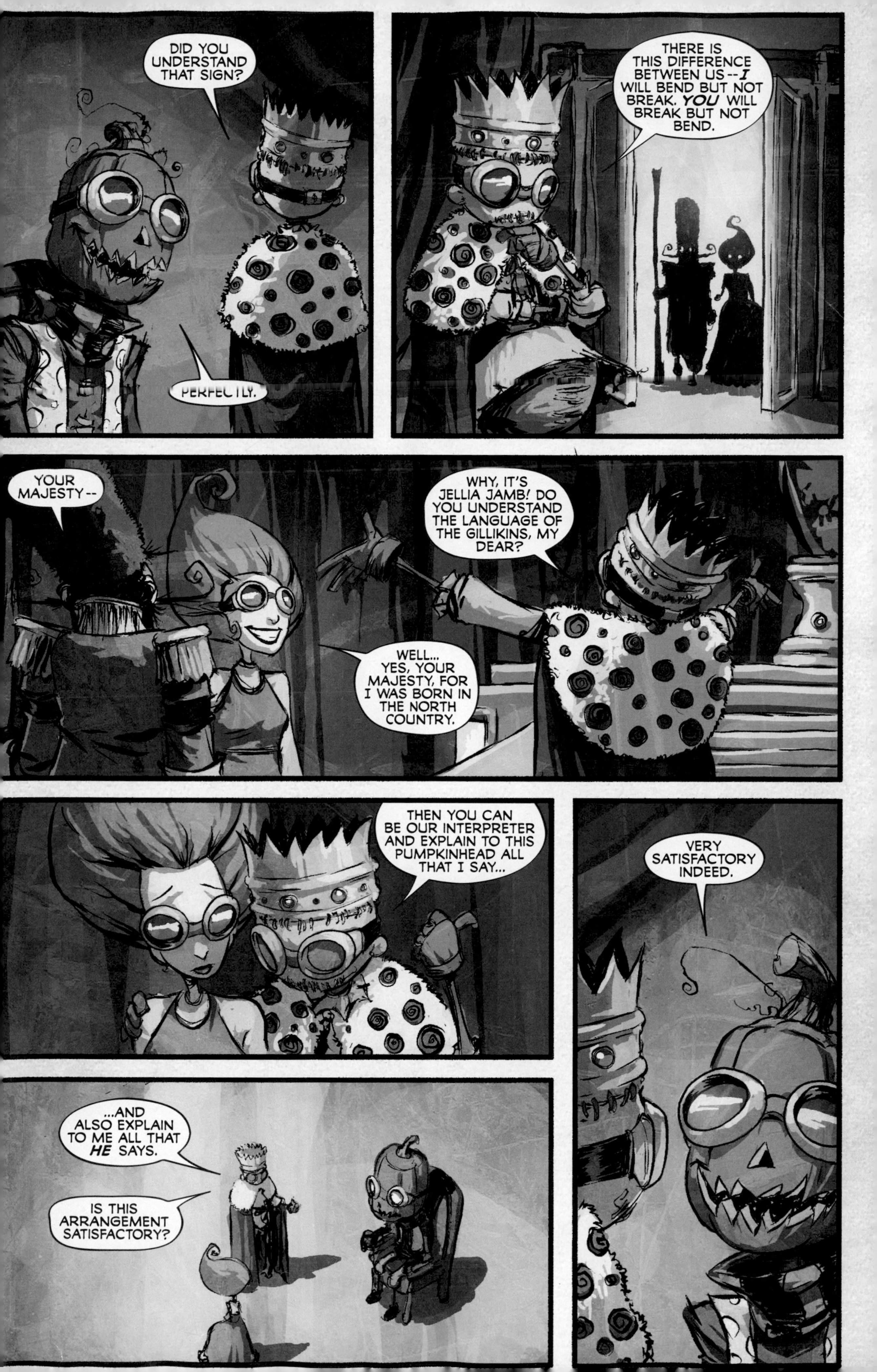
DID YOU UNDERSTAND THAT SIGN?
PERFECTLY.
THERE IS THIS DIFFERENCE BETWEEN US--*I* WILL BEND BUT NOT BREAK. *YOU* WILL BREAK BUT NOT BEND.
YOUR MAJESTY--
WHY, IT'S JELLIA JAMB! DO YOU UNDERSTAND THE LANGUAGE OF THE GILLIKINS, MY DEAR?
WELL... YES, YOUR MAJESTY, FOR I WAS BORN IN THE NORTH COUNTRY.
THEN YOU CAN BE OUR INTERPRETER AND EXPLAIN TO THIS PUMPKINHEAD ALL THAT I SAY...
...AND ALSO EXPLAIN TO ME ALL THAT *HE* SAYS.
IS THIS ARRANGEMENT SATISFACTORY?
VERY SATISFACTORY INDEED.

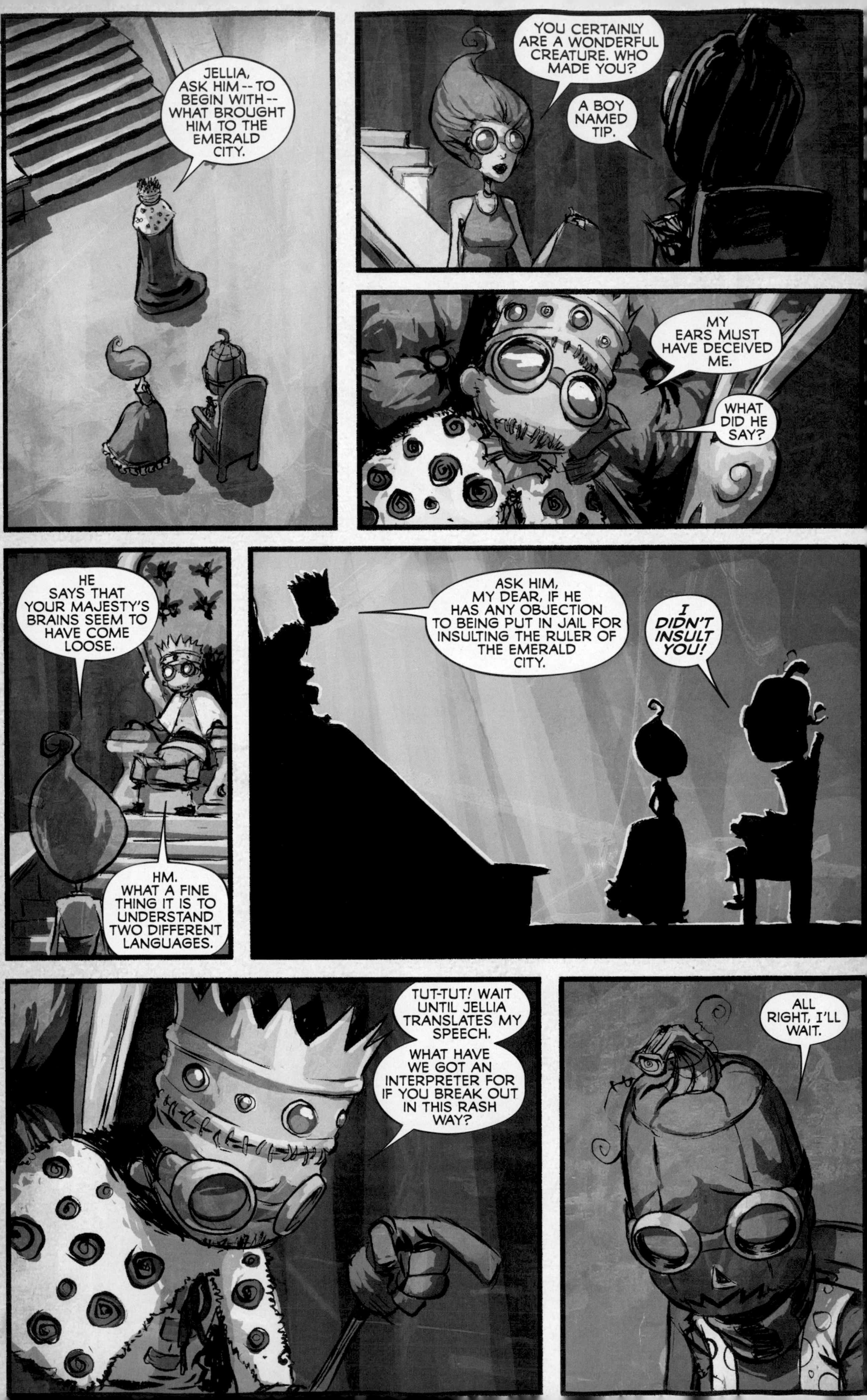
JELLIA, ASK HIM -- TO BEGIN WITH -- WHAT BROUGHT HIM TO THE EMERALD CITY.
YOU CERTAINLY ARE A WONDERFUL CREATURE. WHO MADE YOU?
A BOY NAMED TIP.
MY EARS MUST HAVE DECEIVED ME.
WHAT DID HE SAY?
HE SAYS THAT YOUR MAJESTY'S BRAINS SEEM TO HAVE COME LOOSE.
HM. WHAT A FINE THING IT IS TO UNDERSTAND TWO DIFFERENT LANGUAGES.
ASK HIM, MY DEAR, IF HE HAS ANY OBJECTION TO BEING PUT IN JAIL FOR INSULTING THE RULER OF THE EMERALD CITY.
I DIDN'T INSULT YOU!
TUT-TUT! WAIT UNTIL JELLIA TRANSLATES MY SPEECH.
WHAT HAVE WE GOT AN INTERPRETER FOR IF YOU BREAK OUT IN THIS RASH WAY?
ALL RIGHT, I'LL WAIT.

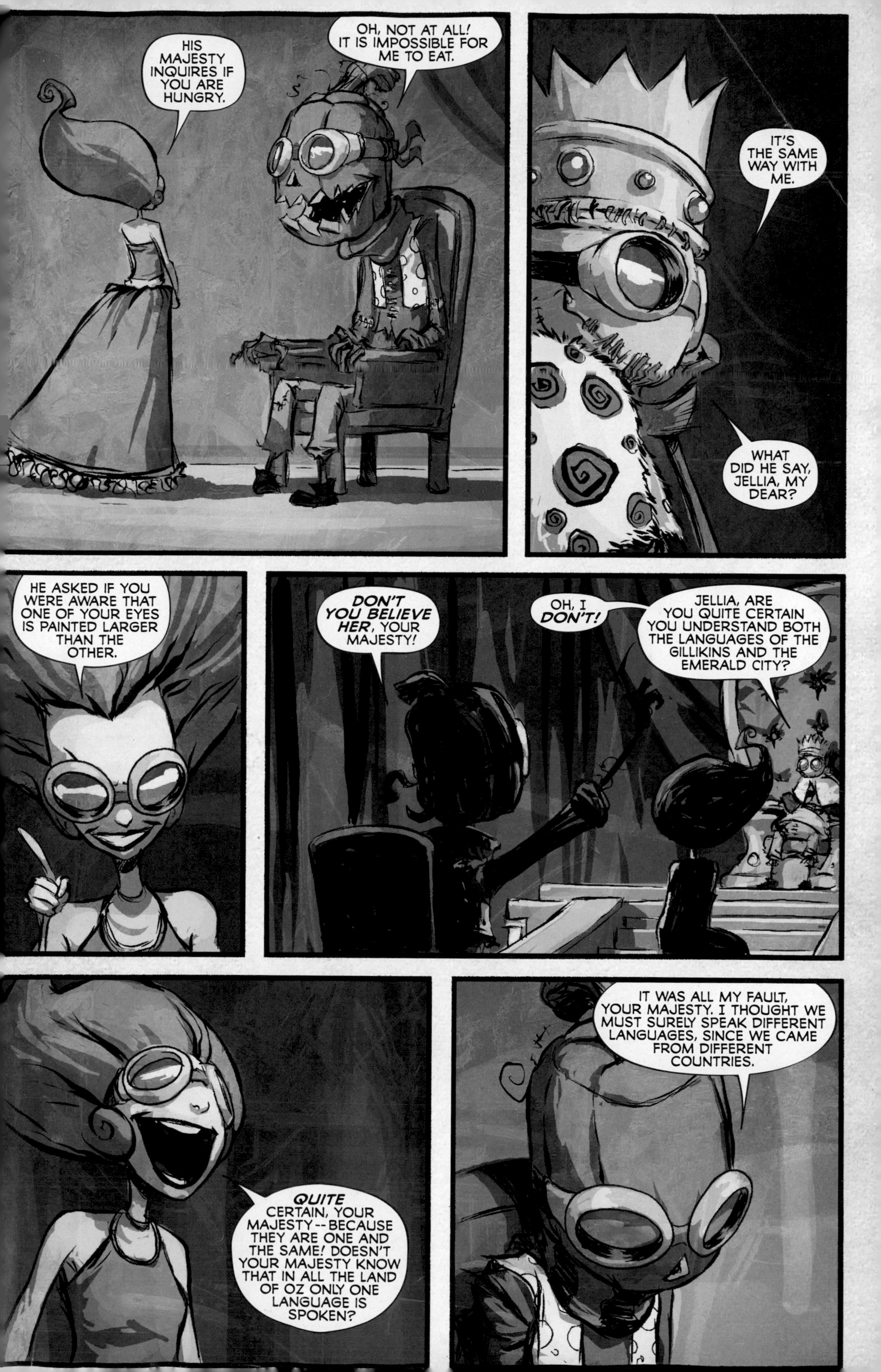
HIS MAJESTY INQUIRES IF YOU ARE HUNGRY.
OH, NOT AT ALL! IT IS IMPOSSIBLE FOR ME TO EAT.
IT'S THE SAME WAY WITH ME.
WHAT DID HE SAY, JELLIA, MY DEAR?
HE ASKED IF YOU WERE AWARE THAT ONE OF YOUR EYES IS PAINTED LARGER THAN THE OTHER.
DON'T YOU BELIEVE HER, YOUR MAJESTY!
OH, I *DON'T!*
JELLIA, ARE YOU QUITE CERTAIN YOU UNDERSTAND BOTH THE LANGUAGES OF THE GILLIKINS AND THE EMERALD CITY?
QUITE CERTAIN, YOUR MAJESTY--BECAUSE THEY ARE ONE AND THE SAME! DOESN'T YOUR MAJESTY KNOW THAT IN ALL THE LAND OF OZ ONLY ONE LANGUAGE IS SPOKEN?
IT WAS ALL MY FAULT, YOUR MAJESTY. I THOUGHT WE MUST SURELY SPEAK DIFFERENT LANGUAGES, SINCE WE CAME FROM DIFFERENT COUNTRIES.

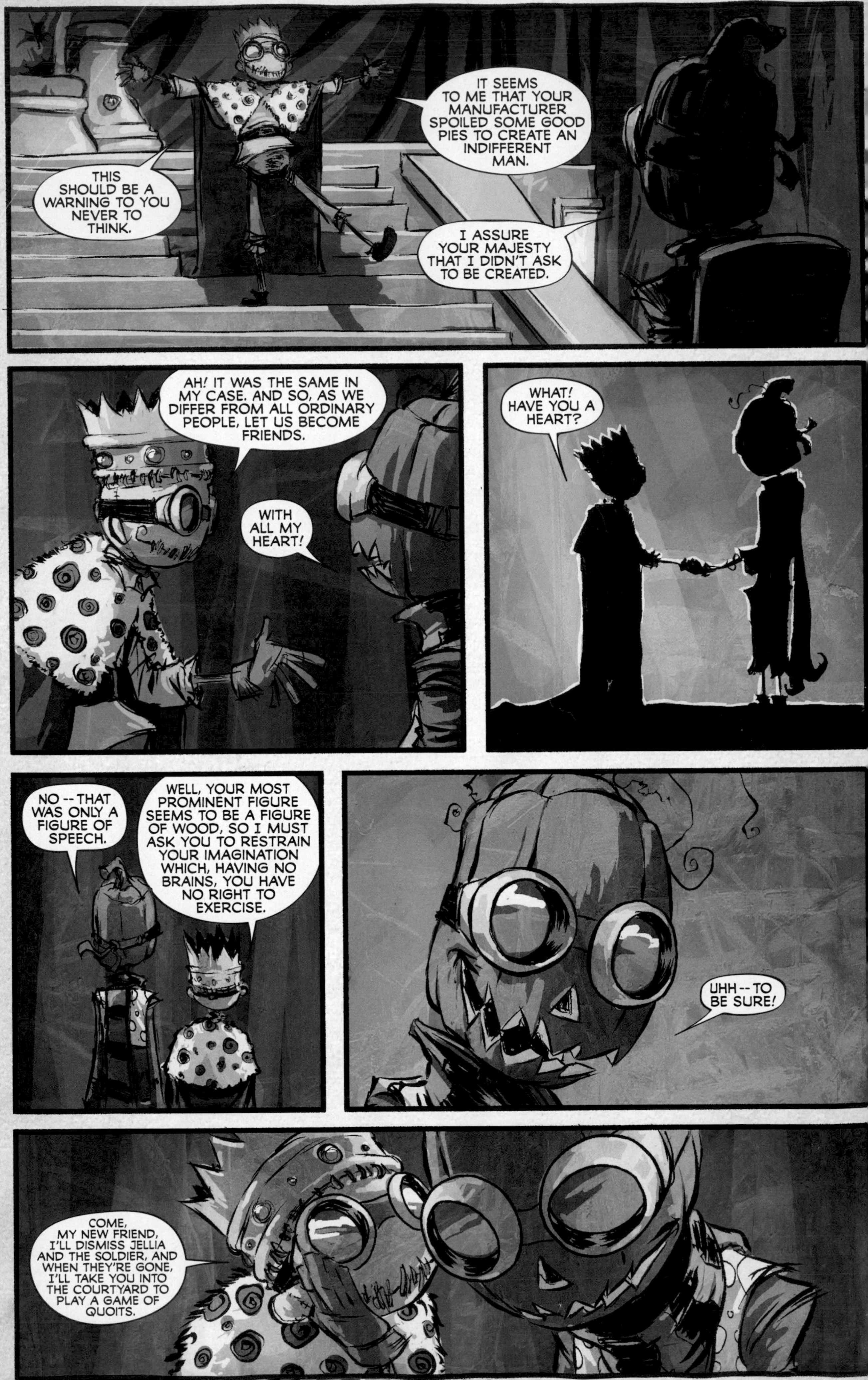
IT SEEMS TO ME THAT YOUR MANUFACTURER SPOILED SOME GOOD PIES TO CREATE AN INDIFFERENT MAN.
THIS SHOULD BE A WARNING TO YOU NEVER TO THINK.
I ASSURE YOUR MAJESTY THAT I DIDN'T ASK TO BE CREATED.
AH! IT WAS THE SAME IN MY CASE. AND SO, AS WE DIFFER FROM ALL ORDINARY PEOPLE, LET US BECOME FRIENDS.
WITH ALL MY HEART!
WHAT! HAVE YOU A HEART?
NO -- THAT WAS ONLY A FIGURE OF SPEECH.
WELL, YOUR MOST PROMINENT FIGURE SEEMS TO BE A FIGURE OF WOOD, SO I MUST ASK YOU TO RESTRAIN YOUR IMAGINATION WHICH, HAVING NO BRAINS, YOU HAVE NO RIGHT TO EXERCISE.
UHH -- TO BE SURE!
COME, MY NEW FRIEND, I'LL DISMISS JELLIA AND THE SOLDIER, AND WHEN THEY'RE GONE, I'LL TAKE YOU INTO THE COURTYARD TO PLAY A GAME OF QUOITS.

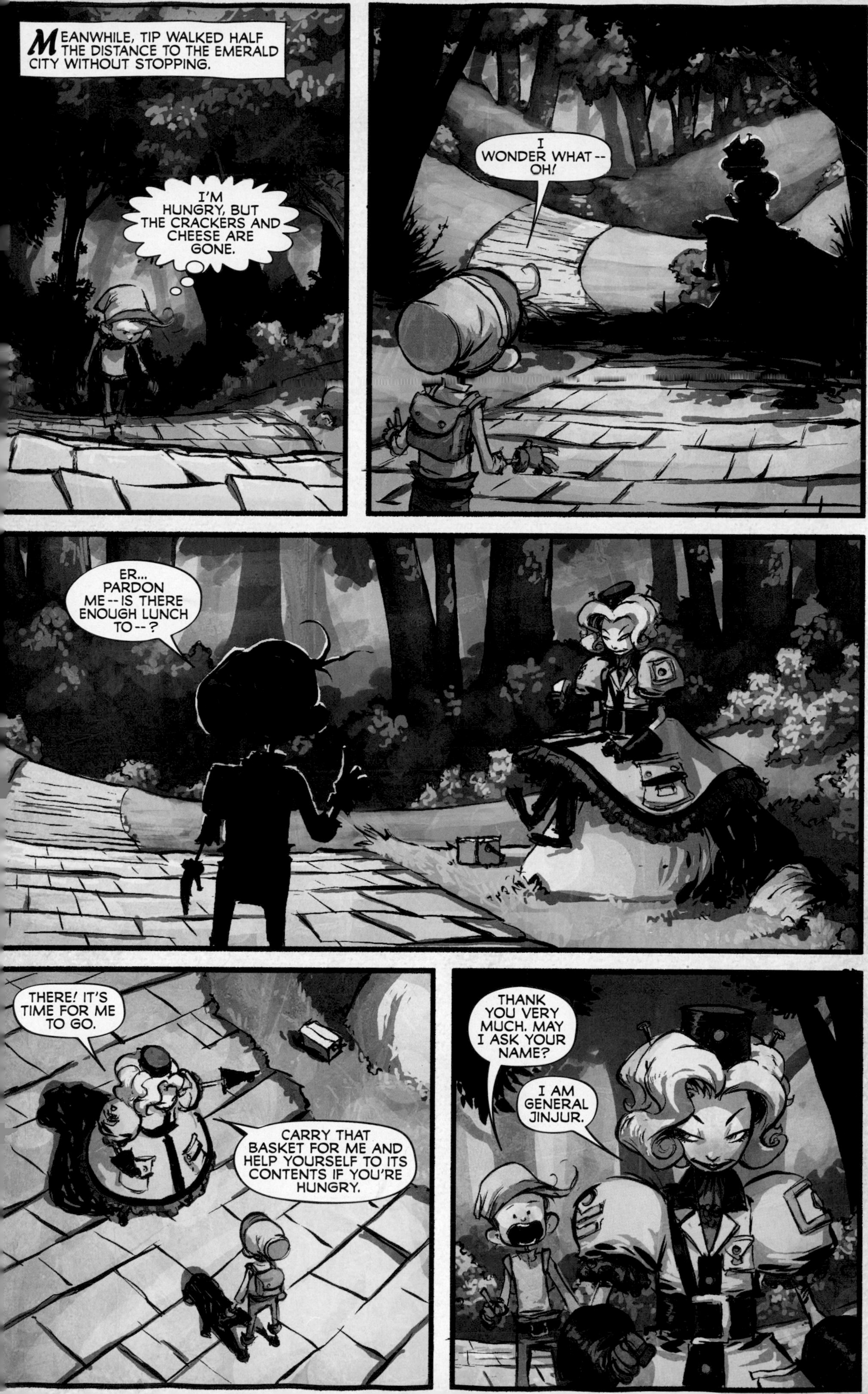
MEANWHILE, TIP WALKED HALF THE DISTANCE TO THE EMERALD CITY WITHOUT STOPPING.
I'M HUNGRY, BUT THE CRACKERS AND CHEESE ARE GONE.
I WONDER WHAT -- OH!
ER... PARDON ME -- IS THERE ENOUGH LUNCH TO -- ?
THERE! IT'S TIME FOR ME TO GO.
CARRY THAT BASKET FOR ME AND HELP YOURSELF TO ITS CONTENTS IF YOU'RE HUNGRY.
THANK YOU VERY MUCH. MAY I ASK YOUR NAME?
I AM GENERAL JINJUR.

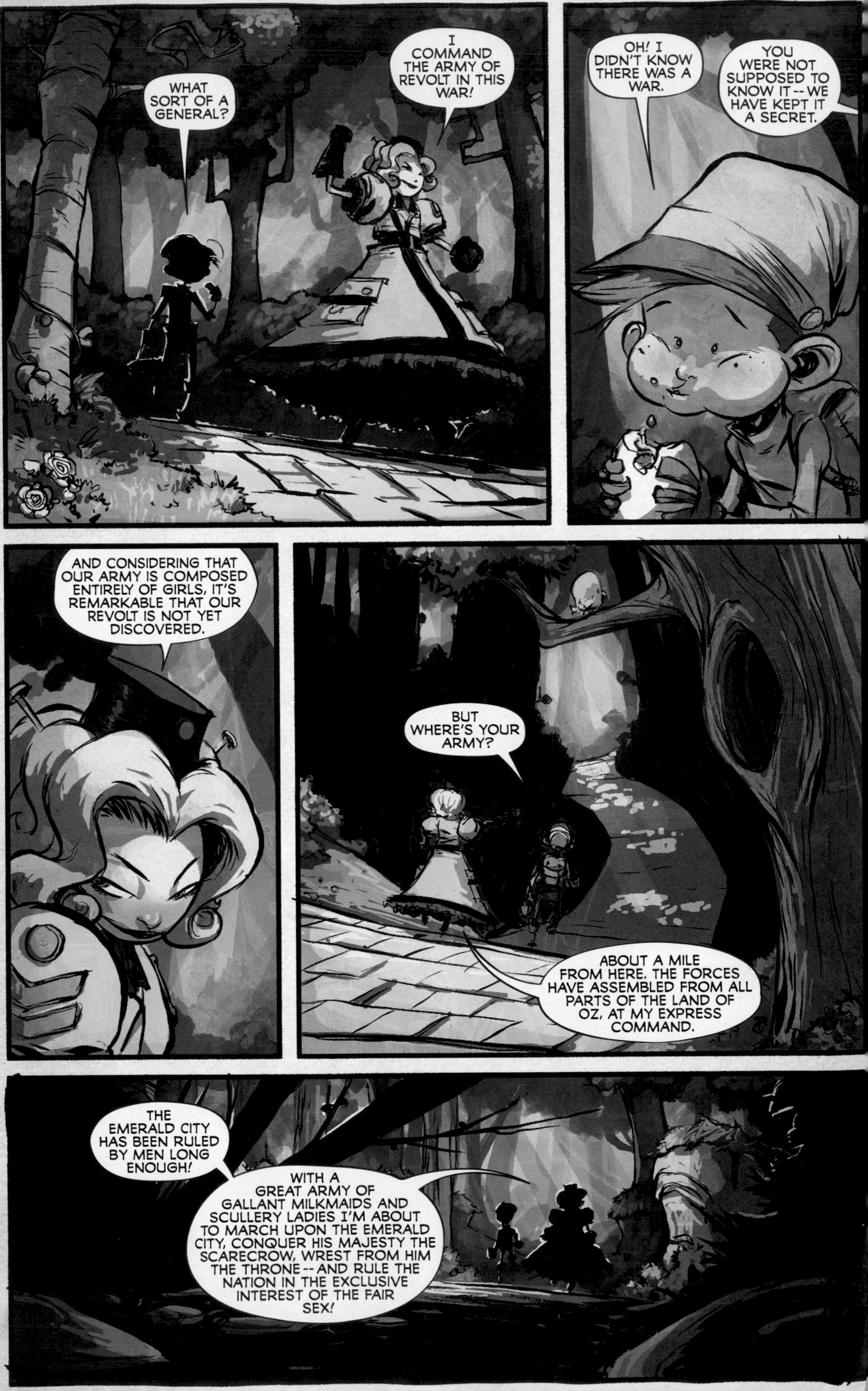
WHAT SORT OF A GENERAL?
I COMMAND THE ARMY OF REVOLT IN THIS WAR!
OH! I DIDN'T KNOW THERE WAS A WAR.
YOU WERE NOT SUPPOSED TO KNOW IT -- WE HAVE KEPT IT A SECRET.
AND CONSIDERING THAT OUR ARMY IS COMPOSED ENTIRELY OF GIRLS, IT'S REMARKABLE THAT OUR REVOLT IS NOT YET DISCOVERED.
BUT WHERE'S YOUR ARMY?
ABOUT A MILE FROM HERE. THE FORCES HAVE ASSEMBLED FROM ALL PARTS OF THE LAND OF OZ, AT MY EXPRESS COMMAND.
THE EMERALD CITY HAS BEEN RULED BY MEN LONG ENOUGH!
WITH A GREAT ARMY OF GALLANT MILKMAIDS AND SCULLERY LADIES I'M ABOUT TO MARCH UPON THE EMERALD CITY, CONQUER HIS MAJESTY THE SCARECROW, WREST FROM HIM THE THRONE -- AND RULE THE NATION IN THE EXCLUSIVE INTEREST OF THE FAIR SEX!

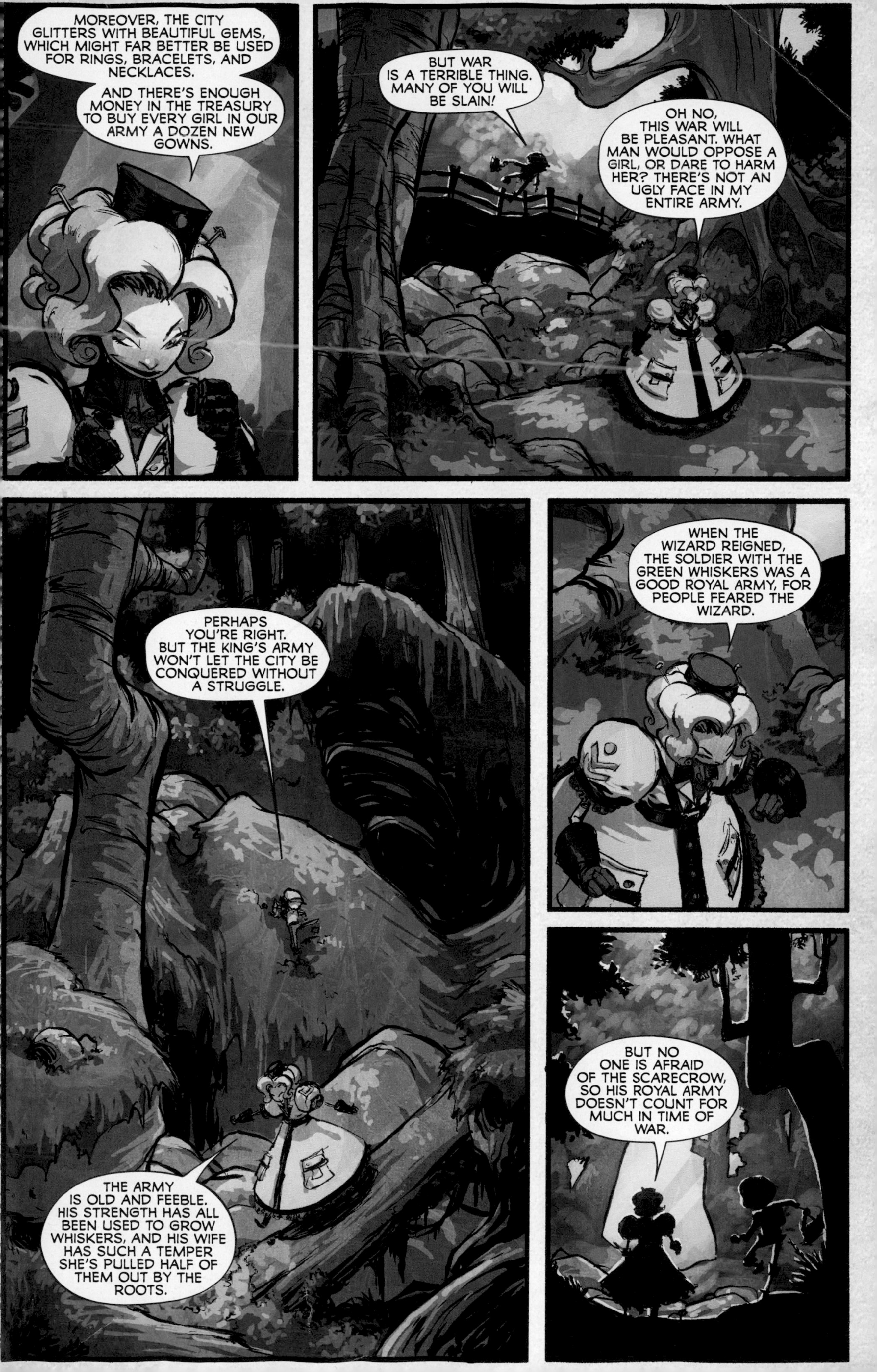
MOREOVER, THE CITY GLITTERS WITH BEAUTIFUL GEMS, WHICH MIGHT FAR BETTER BE USED FOR RINGS, BRACELETS, AND NECKLACES.
AND THERE'S ENOUGH MONEY IN THE TREASURY TO BUY EVERY GIRL IN OUR ARMY A DOZEN NEW GOWNS.
BUT WAR IS A TERRIBLE THING. MANY OF YOU WILL BE SLAIN!
OH NO, THIS WAR WILL BE PLEASANT. WHAT MAN WOULD OPPOSE A GIRL, OR DARE TO HARM HER? THERE'S NOT AN UGLY FACE IN MY ENTIRE ARMY.
PERHAPS YOU'RE RIGHT. BUT THE KING'S ARMY WON'T LET THE CITY BE CONQUERED WITHOUT A STRUGGLE.
THE ARMY IS OLD AND FEEBLE. HIS STRENGTH HAS ALL BEEN USED TO GROW WHISKERS, AND HIS WIFE HAS SUCH A TEMPER SHE'S PULLED HALF OF THEM OUT BY THE ROOTS.
WHEN THE WIZARD REIGNED, THE SOLDIER WITH THE GREEN WHISKERS WAS A GOOD ROYAL ARMY, FOR PEOPLE FEARED THE WIZARD.
BUT NO ONE IS AFRAID OF THE SCARECROW, SO HIS ROYAL ARMY DOESN'T COUNT FOR MUCH IN TIME OF WAR.

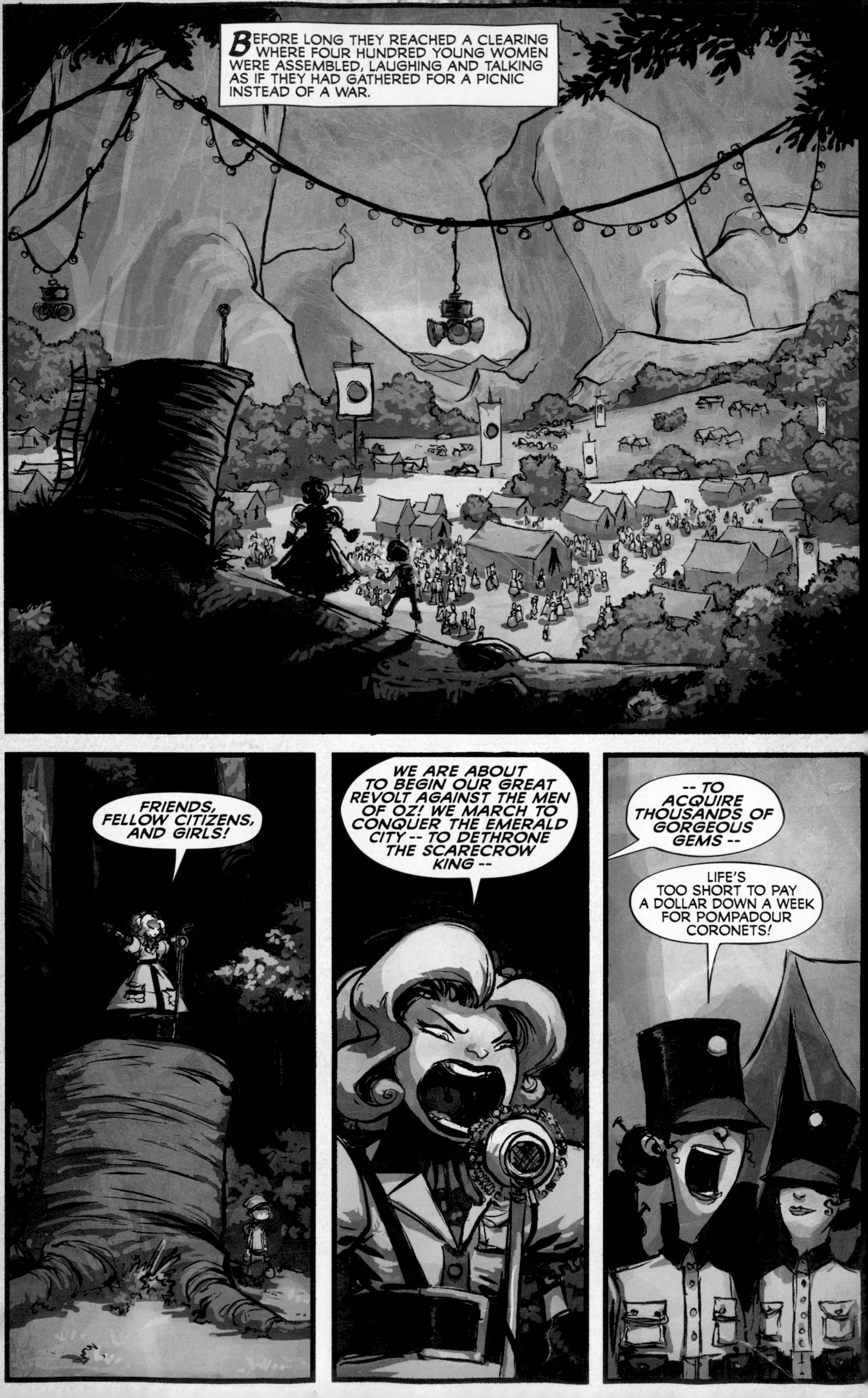
BEFORE LONG THEY REACHED A CLEARING WHERE FOUR HUNDRED YOUNG WOMEN WERE ASSEMBLED, LAUGHING AND TALKING AS IF THEY HAD GATHERED FOR A PICNIC INSTEAD OF A WAR.
FRIENDS, FELLOW CITIZENS, AND GIRLS!
WE ARE ABOUT TO BEGIN OUR GREAT REVOLT AGAINST THE MEN OF OZ! WE MARCH TO CONQUER THE EMERALD CITY -- TO DETHRONE THE SCARECROW KING --
-- TO ACQUIRE THOUSANDS OF GORGEOUS GEMS --
LIFE'S TOO SHORT TO PAY A DOLLAR DOWN A WEEK FOR POMPADOUR CORONETS!

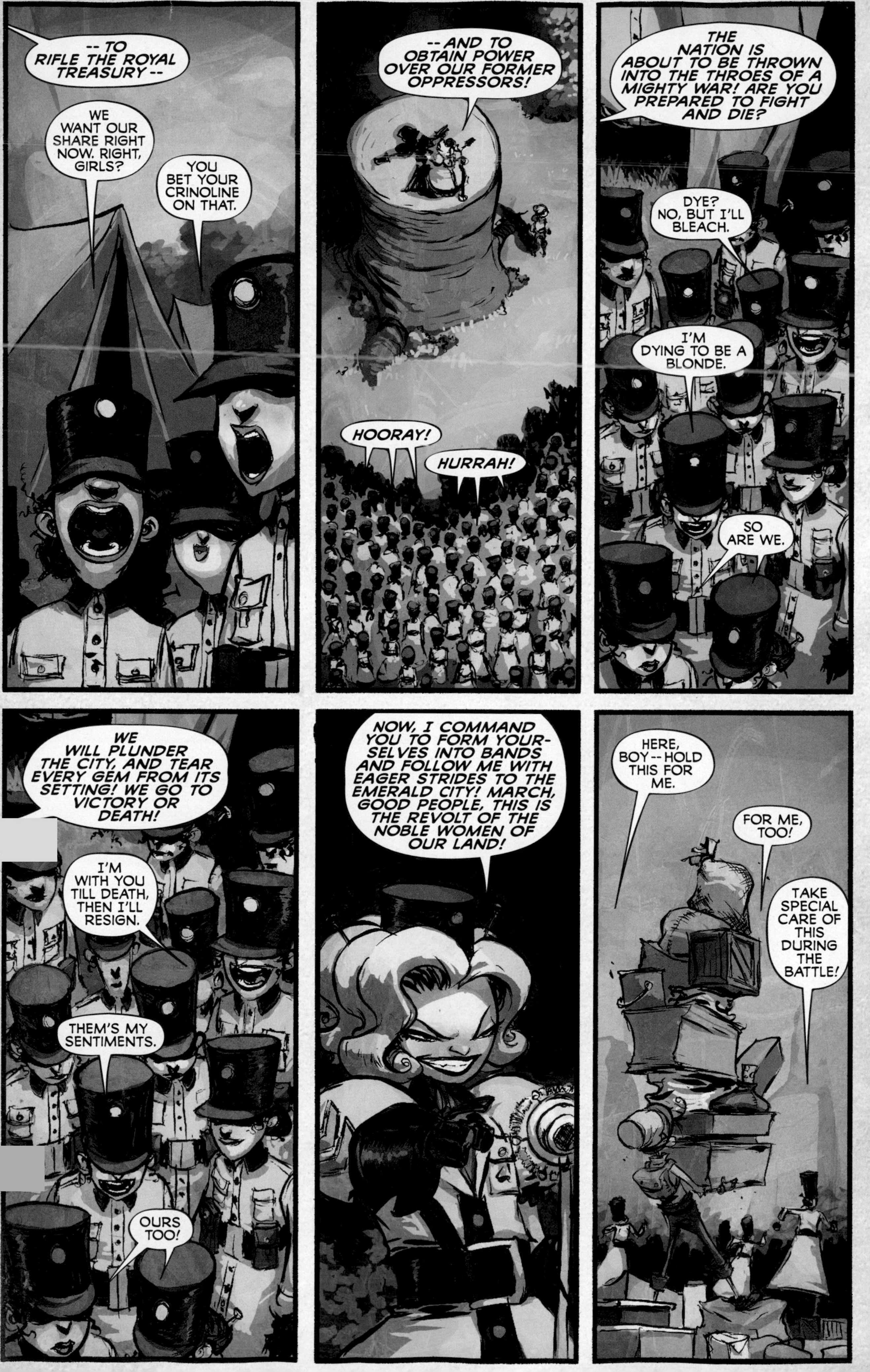
-- TO RIFLE THE ROYAL TREASURY --
WE WANT OUR SHARE RIGHT NOW. RIGHT, GIRLS?
YOU BET YOUR CRINOLINE ON THAT.
-- AND TO OBTAIN POWER OVER OUR FORMER OPPRESSORS!
HOORAY!
HURRAH!
THE NATION IS ABOUT TO BE THROWN INTO THE THROES OF A MIGHTY WAR! ARE YOU PREPARED TO FIGHT AND DIE?
DYE? NO, BUT I'LL BLEACH.
I'M DYING TO BE A BLONDE.
SO ARE WE.
WE WILL PLUNDER THE CITY, AND TEAR EVERY GEM FROM ITS SETTING! WE GO TO VICTORY OR DEATH!
I'M WITH YOU TILL DEATH, THEN I'LL RESIGN.
THEM'S MY SENTIMENTS.
OURS TOO!
NOW, I COMMAND YOU TO FORM YOUR-SELVES INTO BANDS AND FOLLOW ME WITH EAGER STRIDES TO THE EMERALD CITY! MARCH, GOOD PEOPLE, THIS IS THE REVOLT OF THE NOBLE WOMEN OF OUR LAND!
HERE, BOY -- HOLD THIS FOR ME.
FOR ME, TOO!
TAKE SPECIAL CARE OF THIS DURING THE BATTLE!

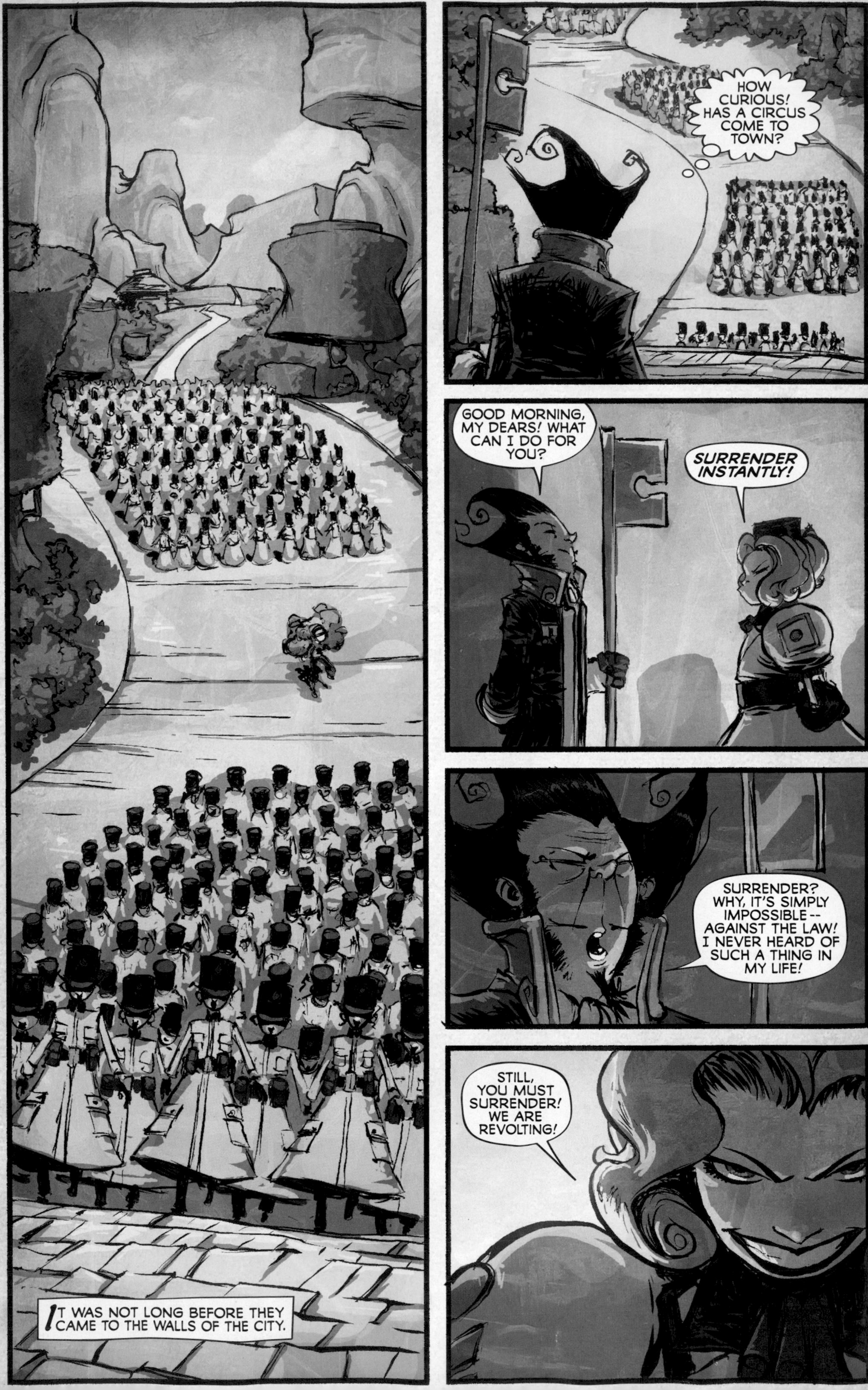
IT WAS NOT LONG BEFORE THEY CAME TO THE WALLS OF THE CITY.
HOW CURIOUS! HAS A CIRCUS COME TO TOWN?
GOOD MORNING, MY DEARS! WHAT CAN I DO FOR YOU?
SURRENDER INSTANTLY!
SURRENDER? WHY, IT'S SIMPLY IMPOSSIBLE -- AGAINST THE LAW! I NEVER HEARD OF SUCH A THING IN MY LIFE!
STILL, YOU MUST SURRENDER! WE ARE REVOLTING!

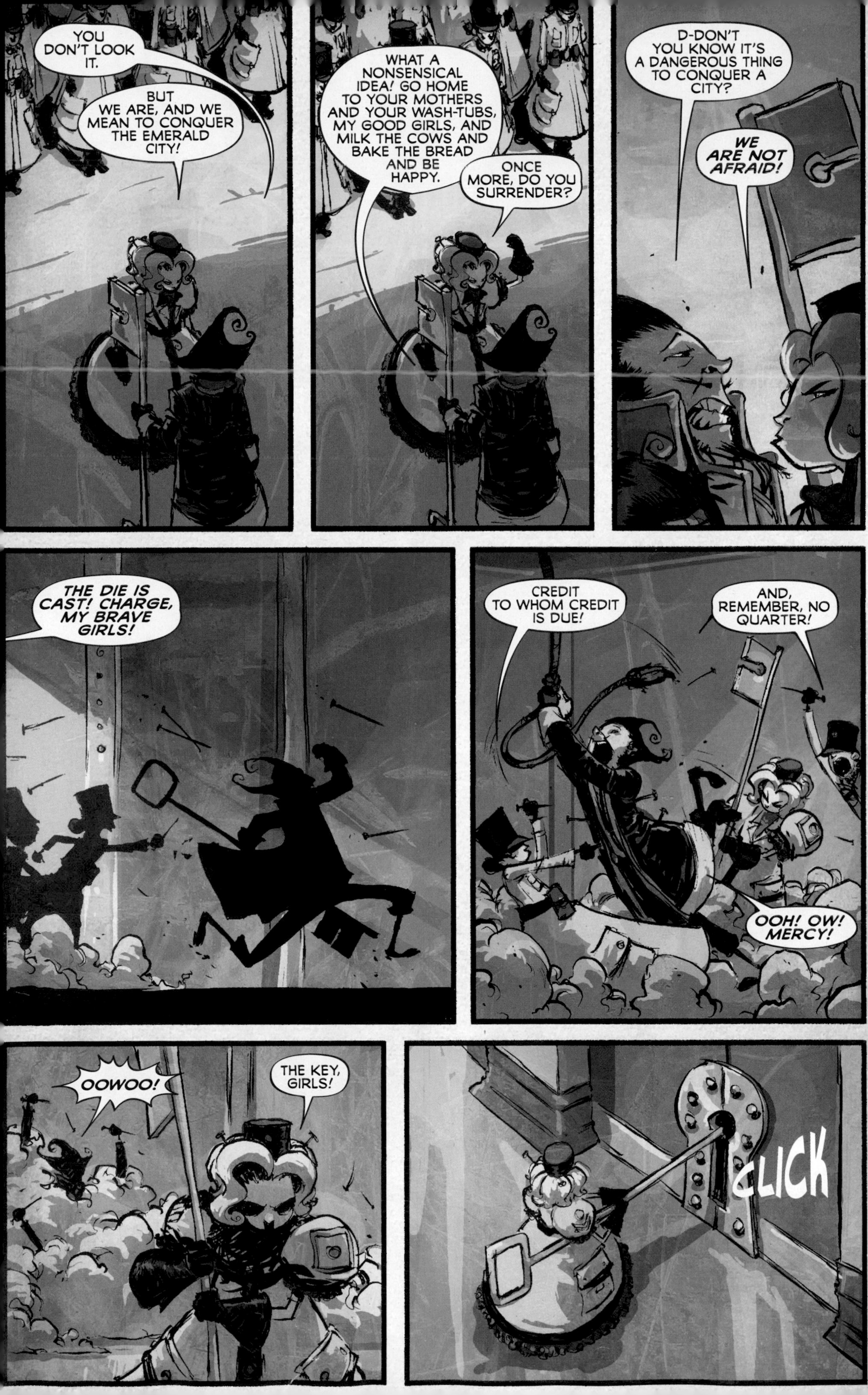
YOU DON'T LOOK IT.
BUT WE ARE, AND WE MEAN TO CONQUER THE EMERALD CITY!
WHAT A NONSENSICAL IDEA! GO HOME TO YOUR MOTHERS AND YOUR WASH-TUBS, MY GOOD GIRLS, AND MILK THE COWS AND BAKE THE BREAD AND BE HAPPY.
ONCE MORE, DO YOU SURRENDER?
D-DON'T YOU KNOW IT'S A DANGEROUS THING TO CONQUER A CITY?
WE ARE NOT AFRAID!
THE DIE IS CAST! CHARGE, MY BRAVE GIRLS!
CREDIT TO WHOM CREDIT IS DUE!
AND, REMEMBER, NO QUARTER!
OOH! OW! MERCY!
OOWOO!
THE KEY, GIRLS!
CLICK

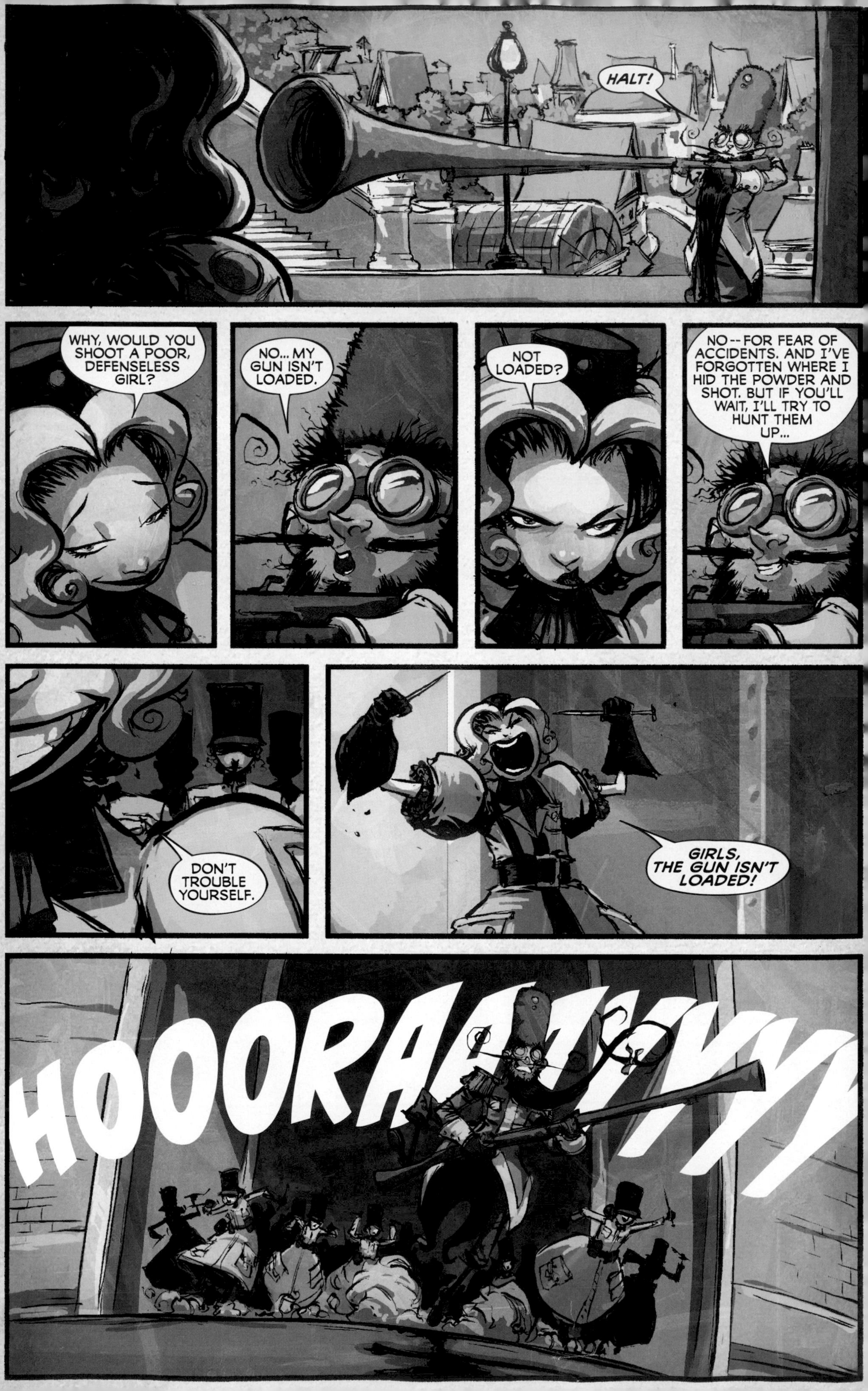

HALT!
WHY, WOULD YOU SHOOT A POOR, DEFENSELESS GIRL?
NO... MY GUN ISN'T LOADED.
NOT LOADED?
NO--FOR FEAR OF ACCIDENTS. AND I'VE FORGOTTEN WHERE I HID THE POWDER AND SHOT. BUT IF YOU'LL WAIT, I'LL TRY TO HUNT THEM UP...
DON'T TROUBLE YOURSELF.
GIRLS, THE GUN ISN'T LOADED!
HOOORAAYYY

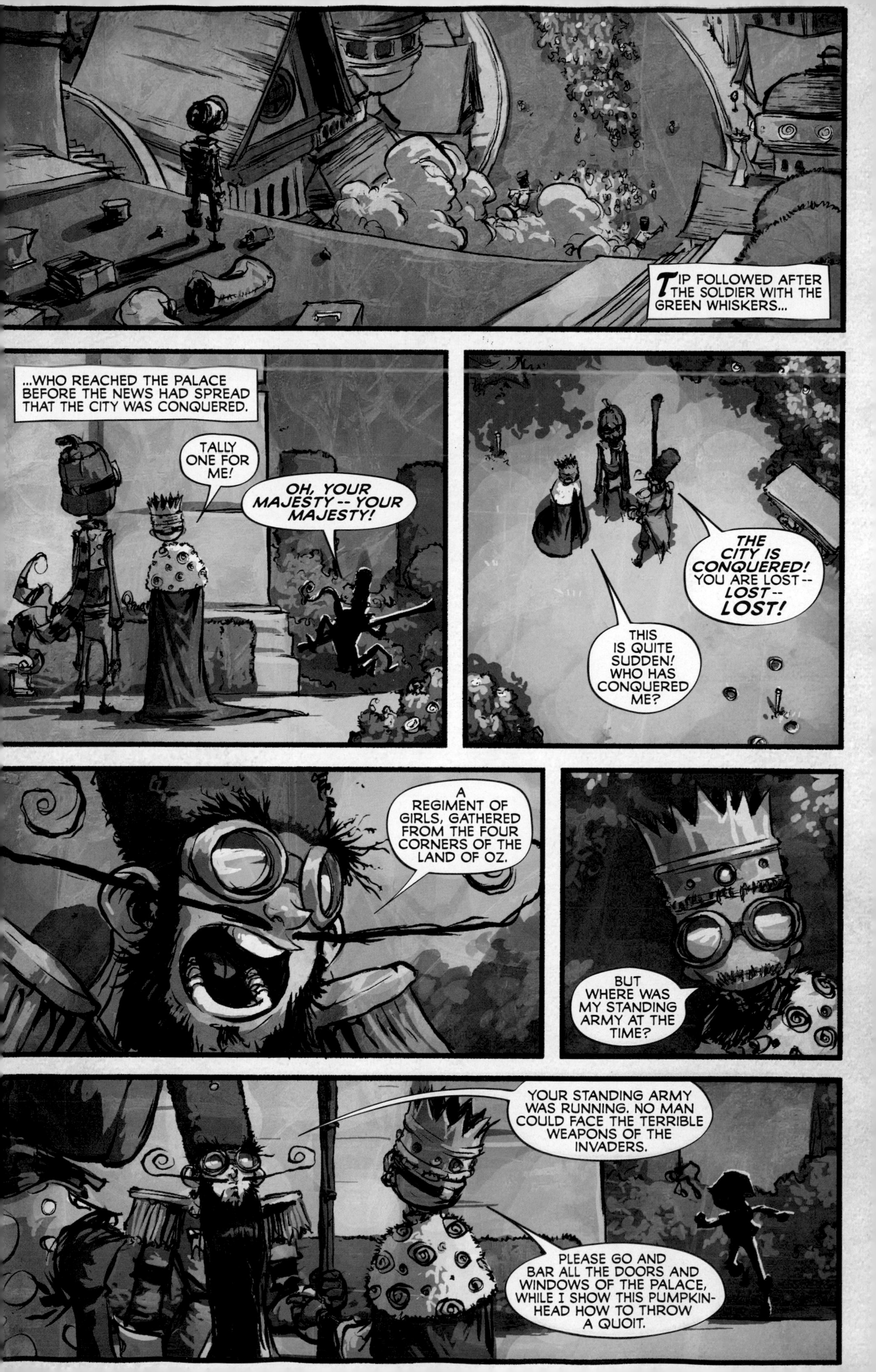
TIP FOLLOWED AFTER THE SOLDIER WITH THE GREEN WHISKERS...
...WHO REACHED THE PALACE BEFORE THE NEWS HAD SPREAD THAT THE CITY WAS CONQUERED.
TALLY ONE FOR ME!
OH, YOUR MAJESTY -- YOUR MAJESTY!
THE CITY IS CONQUERED! YOU ARE LOST -- LOST -- LOST!
THIS IS QUITE SUDDEN! WHO HAS CONQUERED ME?
A REGIMENT OF GIRLS, GATHERED FROM THE FOUR CORNERS OF THE LAND OF OZ.
BUT WHERE WAS MY STANDING ARMY AT THE TIME?
YOUR STANDING ARMY WAS RUNNING. NO MAN COULD FACE THE TERRIBLE WEAPONS OF THE INVADERS.
PLEASE GO AND BAR ALL THE DOORS AND WINDOWS OF THE PALACE, WHILE I SHOW THIS PUMPKIN-HEAD HOW TO THROW A QUOIT.

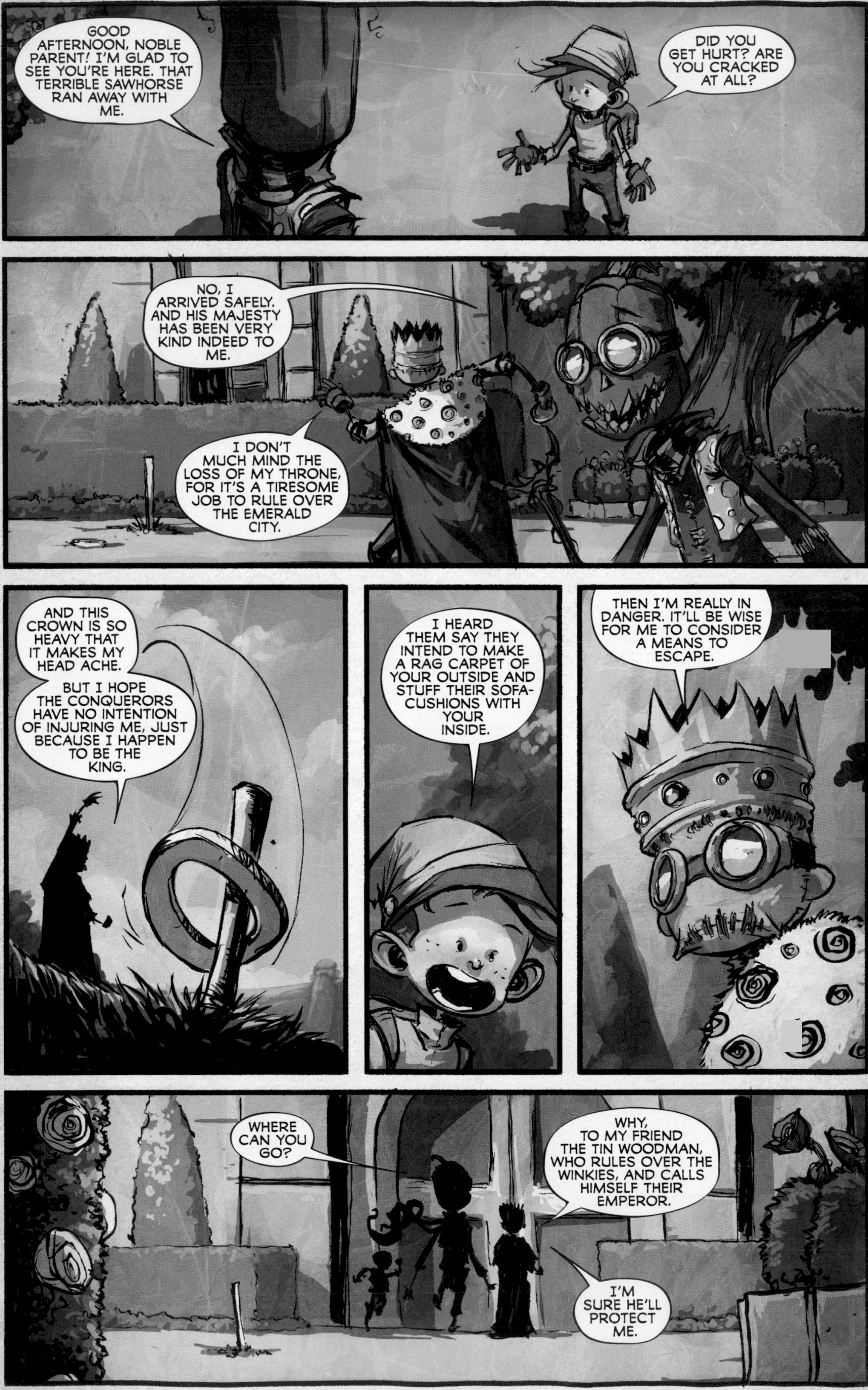

GOOD AFTERNOON, NOBLE PARENT! I'M GLAD TO SEE YOU'RE HERE. THAT TERRIBLE SAWHORSE RAN AWAY WITH ME.
DID YOU GET HURT? ARE YOU CRACKED AT ALL?
NO, I ARRIVED SAFELY. AND HIS MAJESTY HAS BEEN VERY KIND INDEED TO ME.
I DON'T MUCH MIND THE LOSS OF MY THRONE, FOR IT'S A TIRESOME JOB TO RULE OVER THE EMERALD CITY.
AND THIS CROWN IS SO HEAVY THAT IT MAKES MY HEAD ACHE.
BUT I HOPE THE CONQUERORS HAVE NO INTENTION OF INJURING ME, JUST BECAUSE I HAPPEN TO BE THE KING.
I HEARD THEM SAY THEY INTEND TO MAKE A RAG CARPET OF YOUR OUTSIDE AND STUFF THEIR SOFA-CUSHIONS WITH YOUR INSIDE.
THEN I'M REALLY IN DANGER. IT'LL BE WISE FOR ME TO CONSIDER A MEANS TO ESCAPE.
WHERE CAN YOU GO?
WHY, TO MY FRIEND THE TIN WOODMAN, WHO RULES OVER THE WINKIES, AND CALLS HIMSELF THEIR EMPEROR.
I'M SURE HE'LL PROTECT ME.

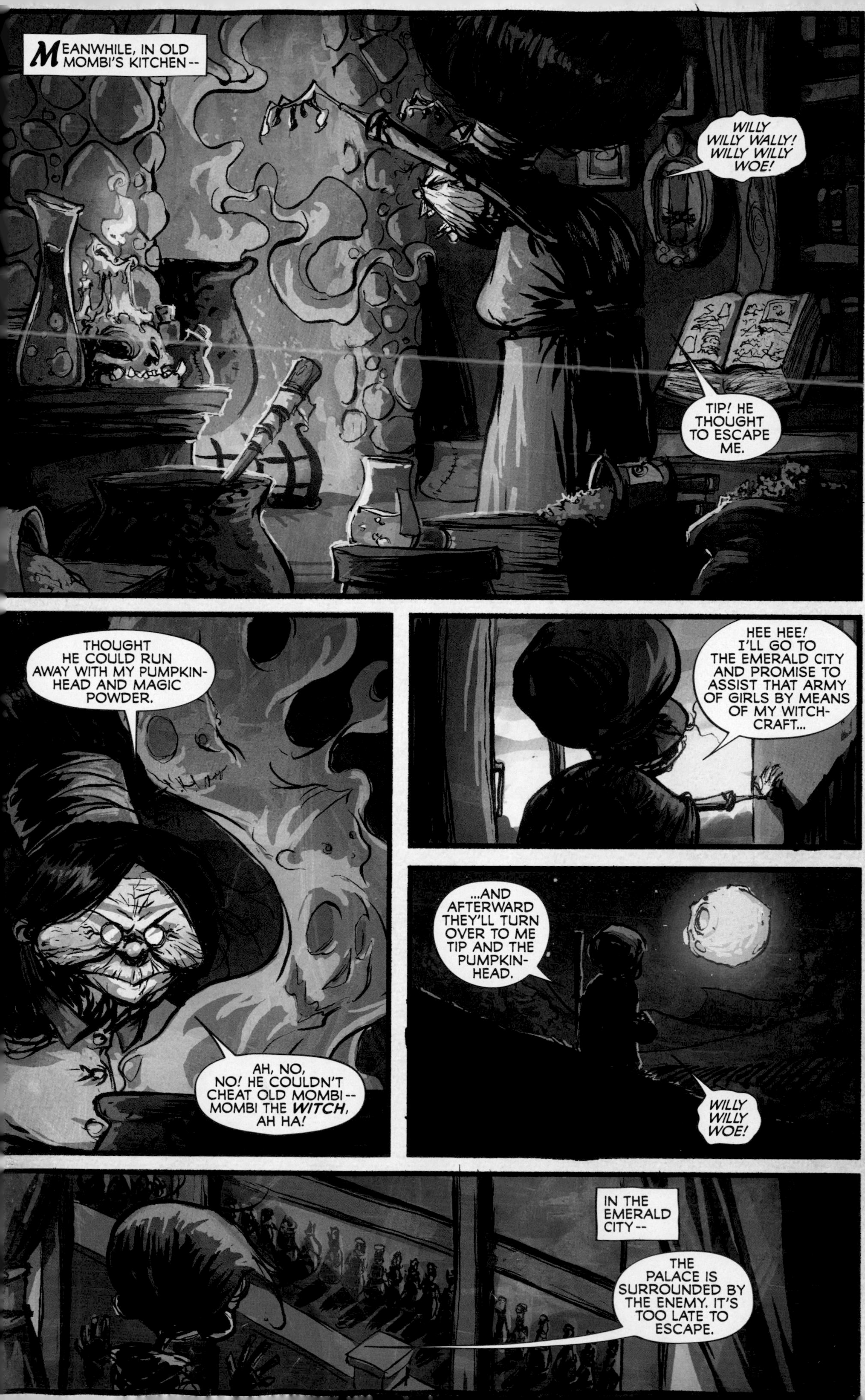

MEANWHILE, IN OLD MOMBI'S KITCHEN--
WILLY WILLY WALLY! WILLY WILLY WOE!
TIP! HE THOUGHT TO ESCAPE ME.
THOUGHT HE COULD RUN AWAY WITH MY PUMPKIN-HEAD AND MAGIC POWDER.
AH, NO, NO! HE COULDN'T CHEAT OLD MOMBI--MOMBI THE WITCH, AH HA!
HEE HEE! I'LL GO TO THE EMERALD CITY AND PROMISE TO ASSIST THAT ARMY OF GIRLS BY MEANS OF MY WITCH-CRAFT...
...AND AFTERWARD THEY'LL TURN OVER TO ME TIP AND THE PUMPKIN-HEAD.
WILLY WILLY WOE!
IN THE EMERALD CITY--
THE PALACE IS SURROUNDED BY THE ENEMY. IT'S TOO LATE TO ESCAPE.

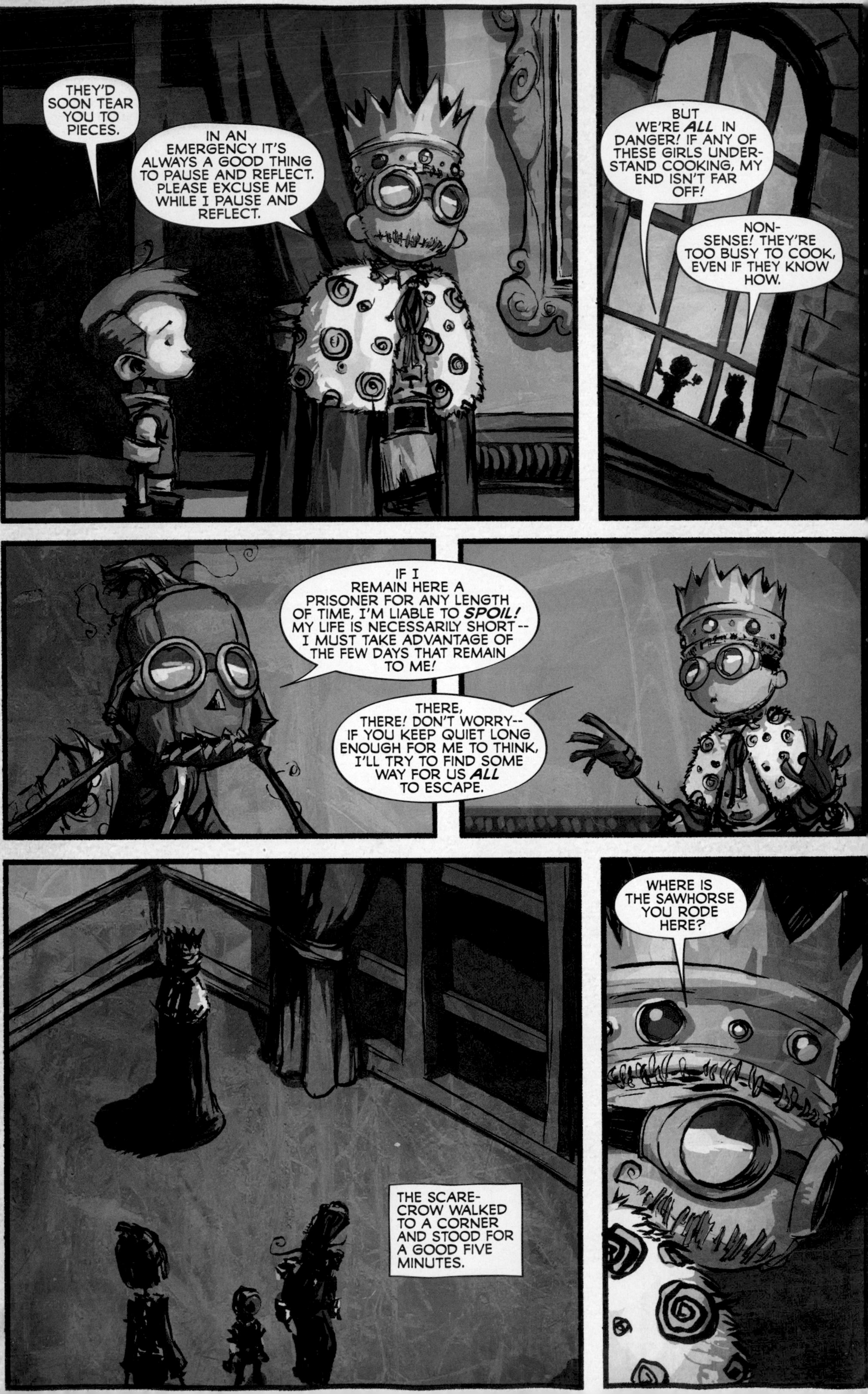
THEY'D SOON TEAR YOU TO PIECES.
IN AN EMERGENCY IT'S ALWAYS A GOOD THING TO PAUSE AND REFLECT. PLEASE EXCUSE ME WHILE I PAUSE AND REFLECT.
BUT WE'RE *ALL* IN DANGER! IF ANY OF THESE GIRLS UNDERSTAND COOKING, MY END ISN'T FAR OFF!
NON-SENSE! THEY'RE TOO BUSY TO COOK, EVEN IF THEY KNOW HOW.
IF I REMAIN HERE A PRISONER FOR ANY LENGTH OF TIME, I'M LIABLE TO *SPOIL!* MY LIFE IS NECESSARILY SHORT-- I MUST TAKE ADVANTAGE OF THE FEW DAYS THAT REMAIN TO ME!
THERE, THERE! DON'T WORRY-- IF YOU KEEP QUIET LONG ENOUGH FOR ME TO THINK, I'LL TRY TO FIND SOME WAY FOR US *ALL* TO ESCAPE.
THE SCARE-CROW WALKED TO A CORNER AND STOOD FOR A GOOD FIVE MINUTES.
WHERE IS THE SAWHORSE YOU RODE HERE?

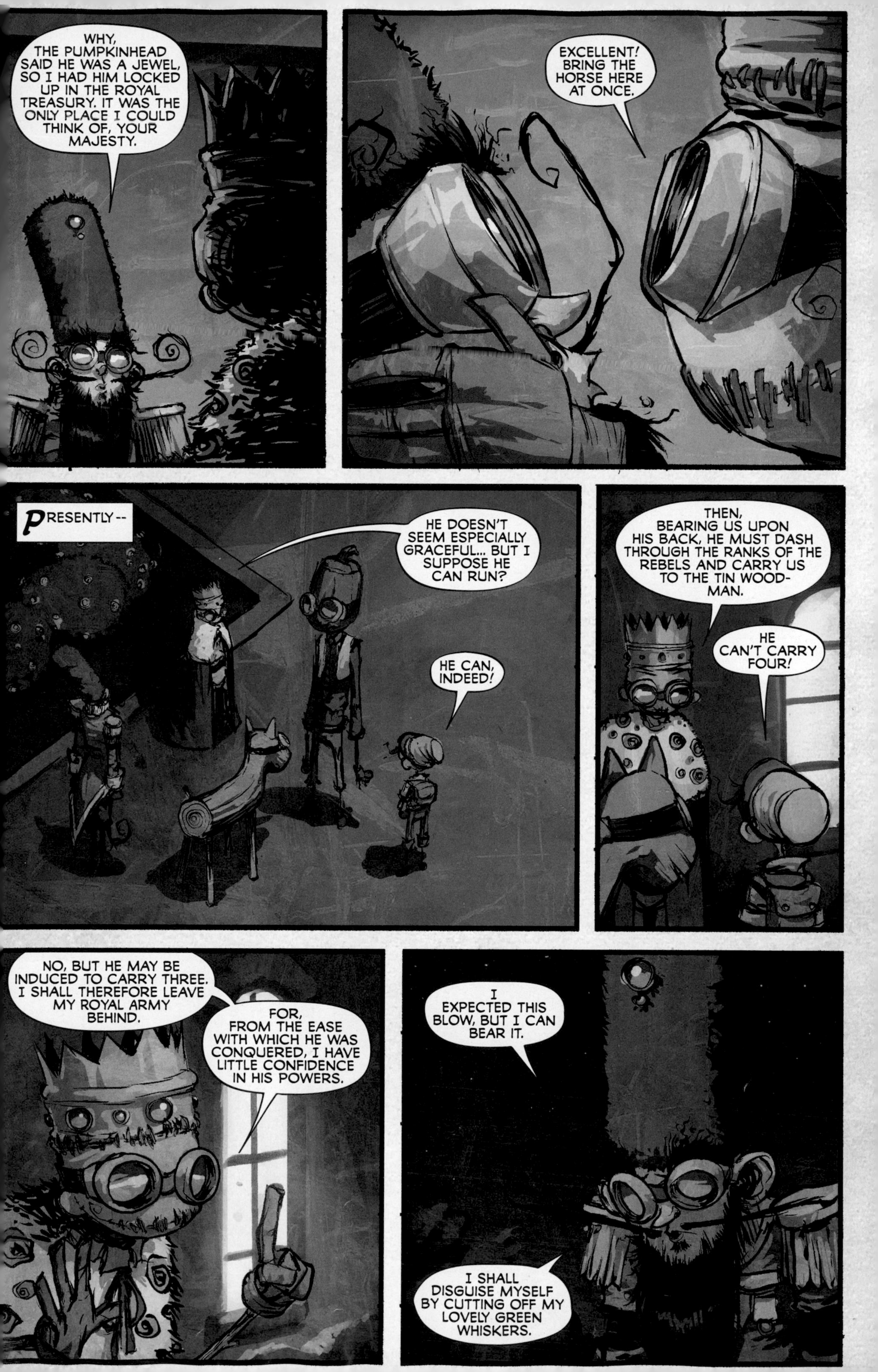
WHY, THE PUMPKINHEAD SAID HE WAS A JEWEL, SO I HAD HIM LOCKED UP IN THE ROYAL TREASURY. IT WAS THE ONLY PLACE I COULD THINK OF, YOUR MAJESTY.
EXCELLENT! BRING THE HORSE HERE AT ONCE.
PRESENTLY --
HE DOESN'T SEEM ESPECIALLY GRACEFUL... BUT I SUPPOSE HE CAN RUN?
HE CAN, INDEED!
THEN, BEARING US UPON HIS BACK, HE MUST DASH THROUGH THE RANKS OF THE REBELS AND CARRY US TO THE TIN WOOD-MAN.
HE CAN'T CARRY FOUR!
NO, BUT HE MAY BE INDUCED TO CARRY THREE. I SHALL THEREFORE LEAVE MY ROYAL ARMY BEHIND.
FOR, FROM THE EASE WITH WHICH HE WAS CONQUERED, I HAVE LITTLE CONFIDENCE IN HIS POWERS.
I EXPECTED THIS BLOW, BUT I CAN BEAR IT.
I SHALL DISGUISE MYSELF BY CUTTING OFF MY LOVELY GREEN WHISKERS.

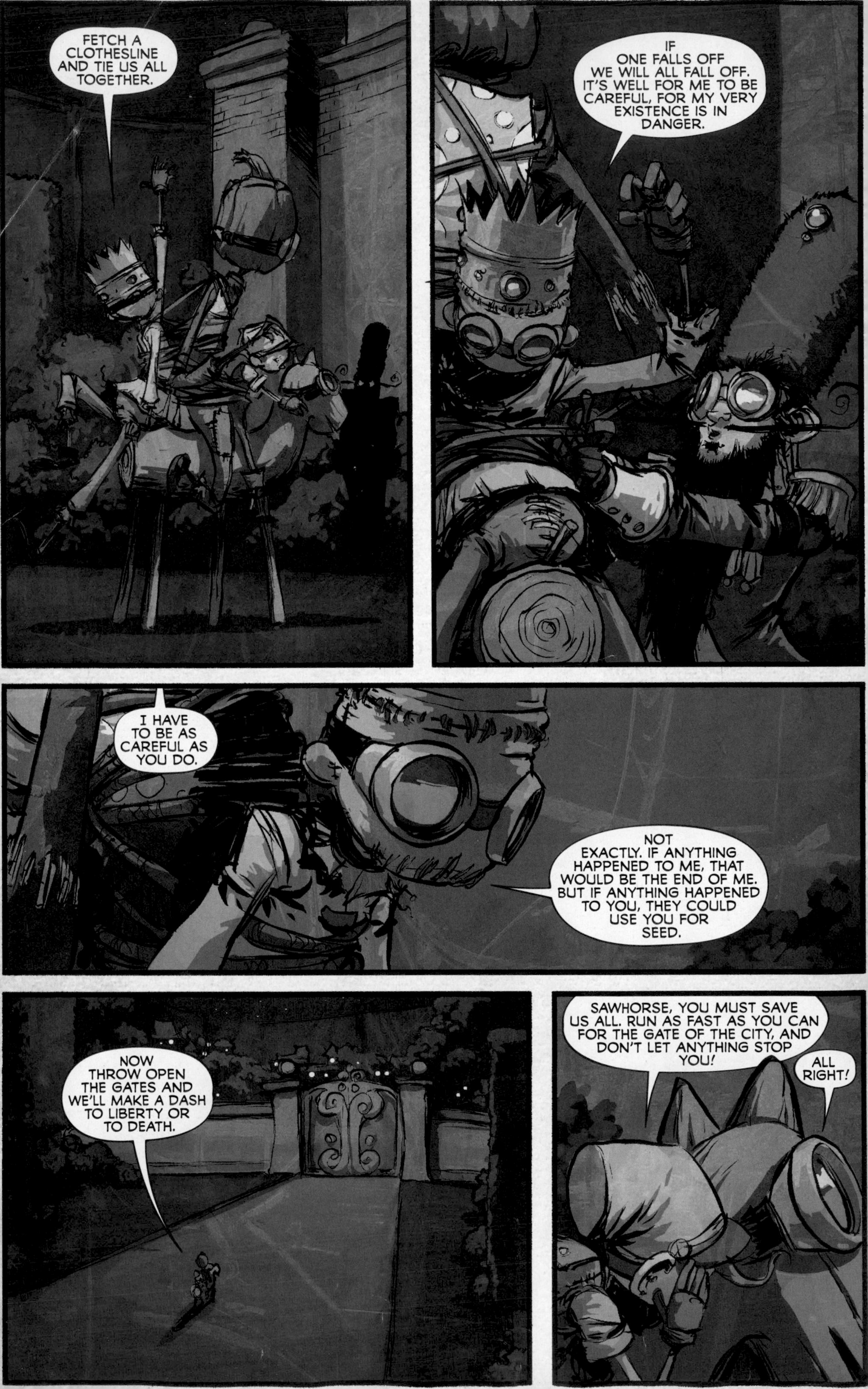
FETCH A CLOTHESLINE AND TIE US ALL TOGETHER.
IF ONE FALLS OFF WE WILL ALL FALL OFF. IT'S WELL FOR ME TO BE CAREFUL, FOR MY VERY EXISTENCE IS IN DANGER.
I HAVE TO BE AS CAREFUL AS YOU DO.
NOT EXACTLY. IF ANYTHING HAPPENED TO ME, THAT WOULD BE THE END OF ME. BUT IF ANYTHING HAPPENED TO YOU, THEY COULD USE YOU FOR SEED.
NOW THROW OPEN THE GATES AND WE'LL MAKE A DASH TO LIBERTY OR TO DEATH.
SAWHORSE, YOU MUST SAVE US ALL. RUN AS FAST AS YOU CAN FOR THE GATE OF THE CITY, AND DON'T LET ANYTHING STOP YOU!
ALL RIGHT!

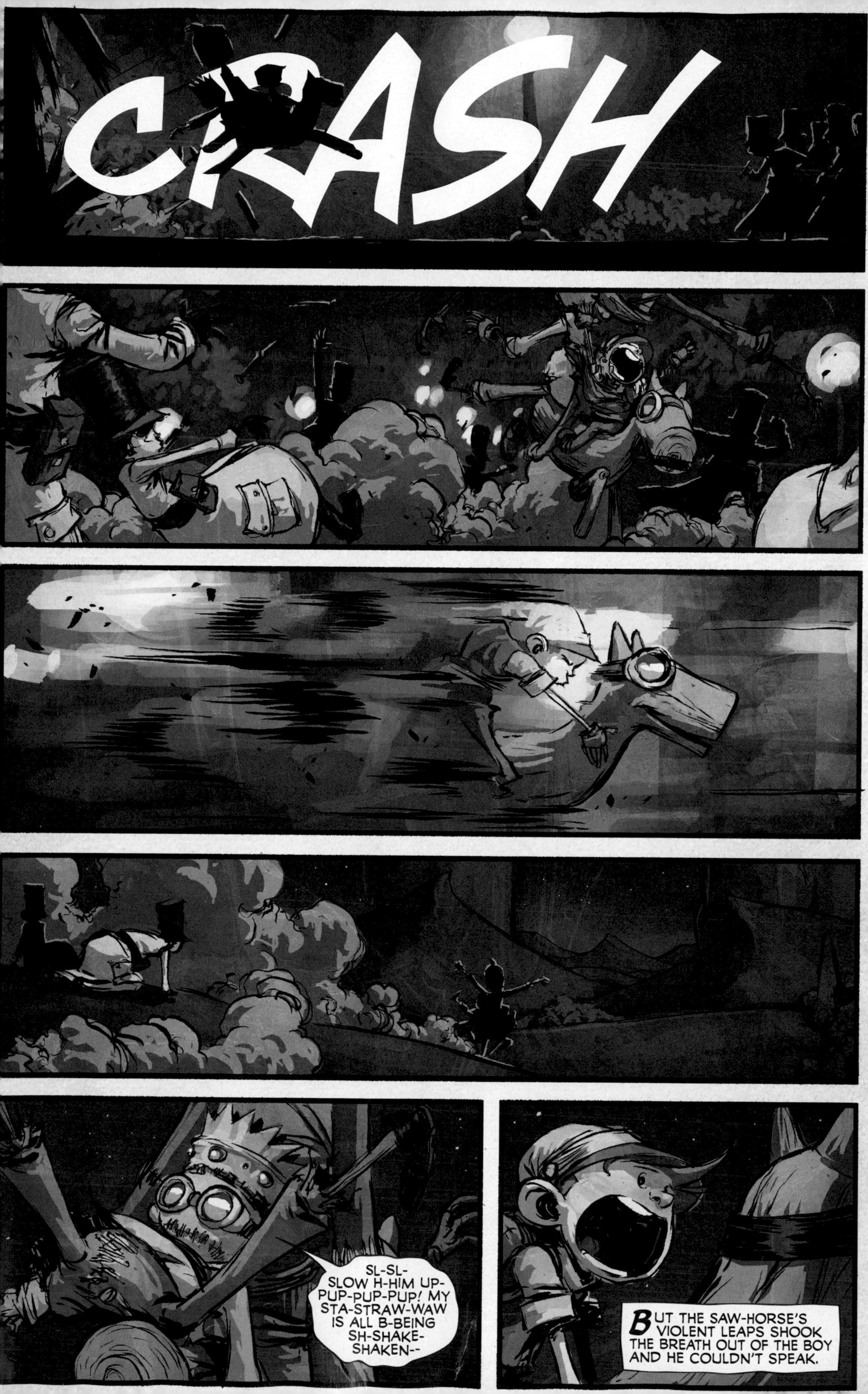
CRASH
SL-SL-
SLOW H-HIM UP-
PUP-PUP-PUP! MY
STA-STRAW-WAW
IS ALL B-BEING
SH-SHAKE-
SHAKEN--
BUT THE SAW-HORSE'S VIOLENT LEAPS SHOOK THE BREATH OUT OF THE BOY AND HE COULDN'T SPEAK.

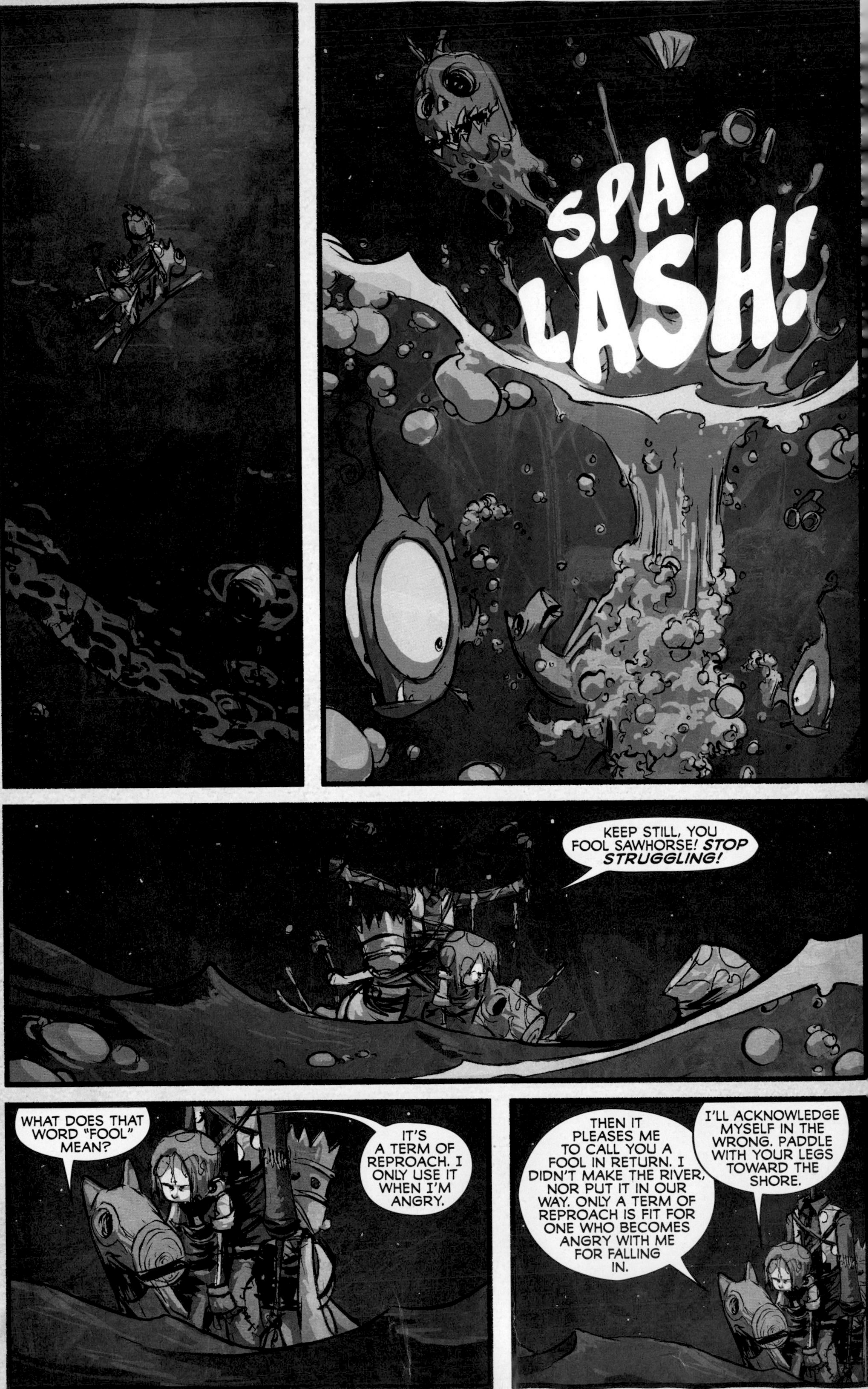
SPA-
LASH!
KEEP STILL, YOU FOOL SAWHORSE! *STOP STRUGGLING!*
WHAT DOES THAT WORD "FOOL" MEAN?
IT'S A TERM OF REPROACH. I ONLY USE IT WHEN I'M ANGRY.
THEN IT PLEASES ME TO CALL YOU A FOOL IN RETURN. I DIDN'T MAKE THE RIVER, NOR PUT IT IN OUR WAY. ONLY A TERM OF REPROACH IS FIT FOR ONE WHO BECOMES ANGRY WITH ME FOR FALLING IN.
I'LL ACKNOWLEDGE MYSELF IN THE WRONG. PADDLE WITH YOUR LEGS TOWARD THE SHORE.

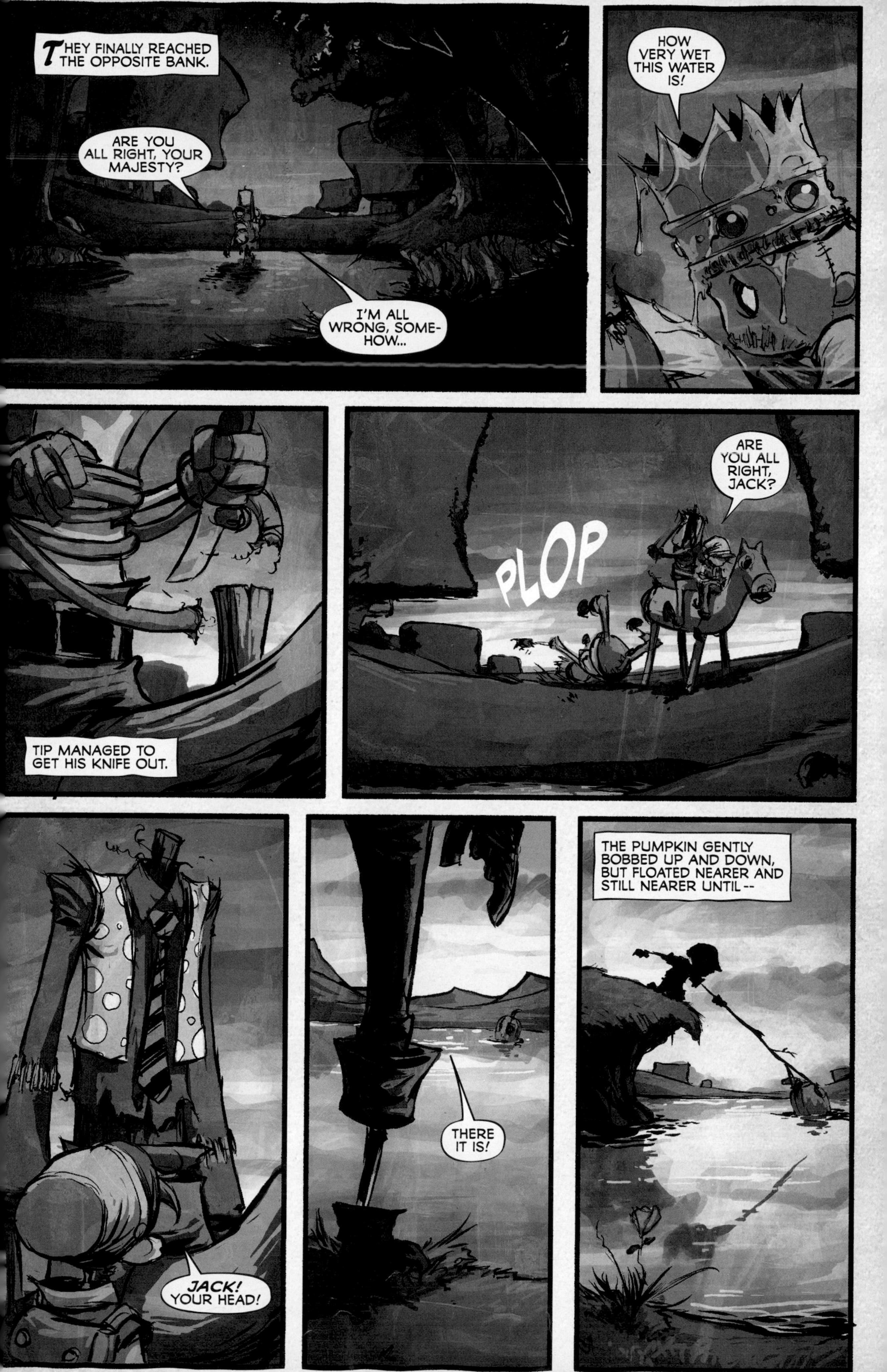
THEY FINALLY REACHED THE OPPOSITE BANK.
ARE YOU ALL RIGHT, YOUR MAJESTY?
I'M ALL WRONG, SOME-HOW...
HOW VERY WET THIS WATER IS!
TIP MANAGED TO GET HIS KNIFE OUT.
PLOP
ARE YOU ALL RIGHT, JACK?
JACK! YOUR HEAD!
THERE IT IS!
THE PUMPKIN GENTLY BOBBED UP AND DOWN, BUT FLOATED NEARER AND STILL NEARER UNTIL--

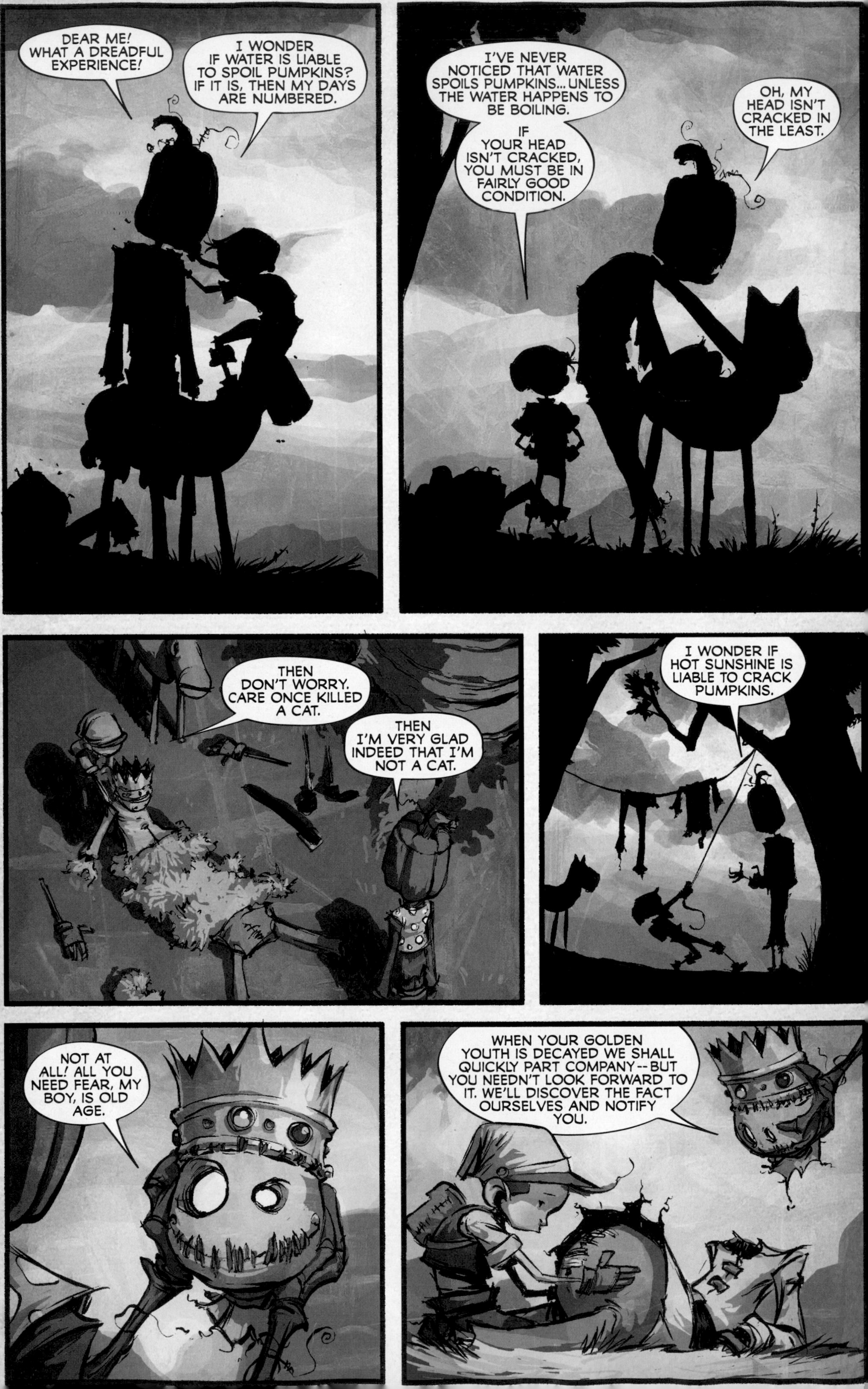
DEAR ME! WHAT A DREADFUL EXPERIENCE!
I WONDER IF WATER IS LIABLE TO SPOIL PUMPKINS? IF IT IS, THEN MY DAYS ARE NUMBERED.
I'VE NEVER NOTICED THAT WATER SPOILS PUMPKINS... UNLESS THE WATER HAPPENS TO BE BOILING.
IF YOUR HEAD ISN'T CRACKED, YOU MUST BE IN FAIRLY GOOD CONDITION.
OH, MY HEAD ISN'T CRACKED IN THE LEAST.
THEN DON'T WORRY. CARE ONCE KILLED A CAT.
THEN I'M VERY GLAD INDEED THAT I'M NOT A CAT.
I WONDER IF HOT SUNSHINE IS LIABLE TO CRACK PUMPKINS.
NOT AT ALL! ALL YOU NEED FEAR, MY BOY, IS OLD AGE.
WHEN YOUR GOLDEN YOUTH IS DECAYED WE SHALL QUICKLY PART COMPANY--BUT YOU NEEDN'T LOOK FORWARD TO IT. WE'LL DISCOVER THE FACT OURSELVES AND NOTIFY YOU.

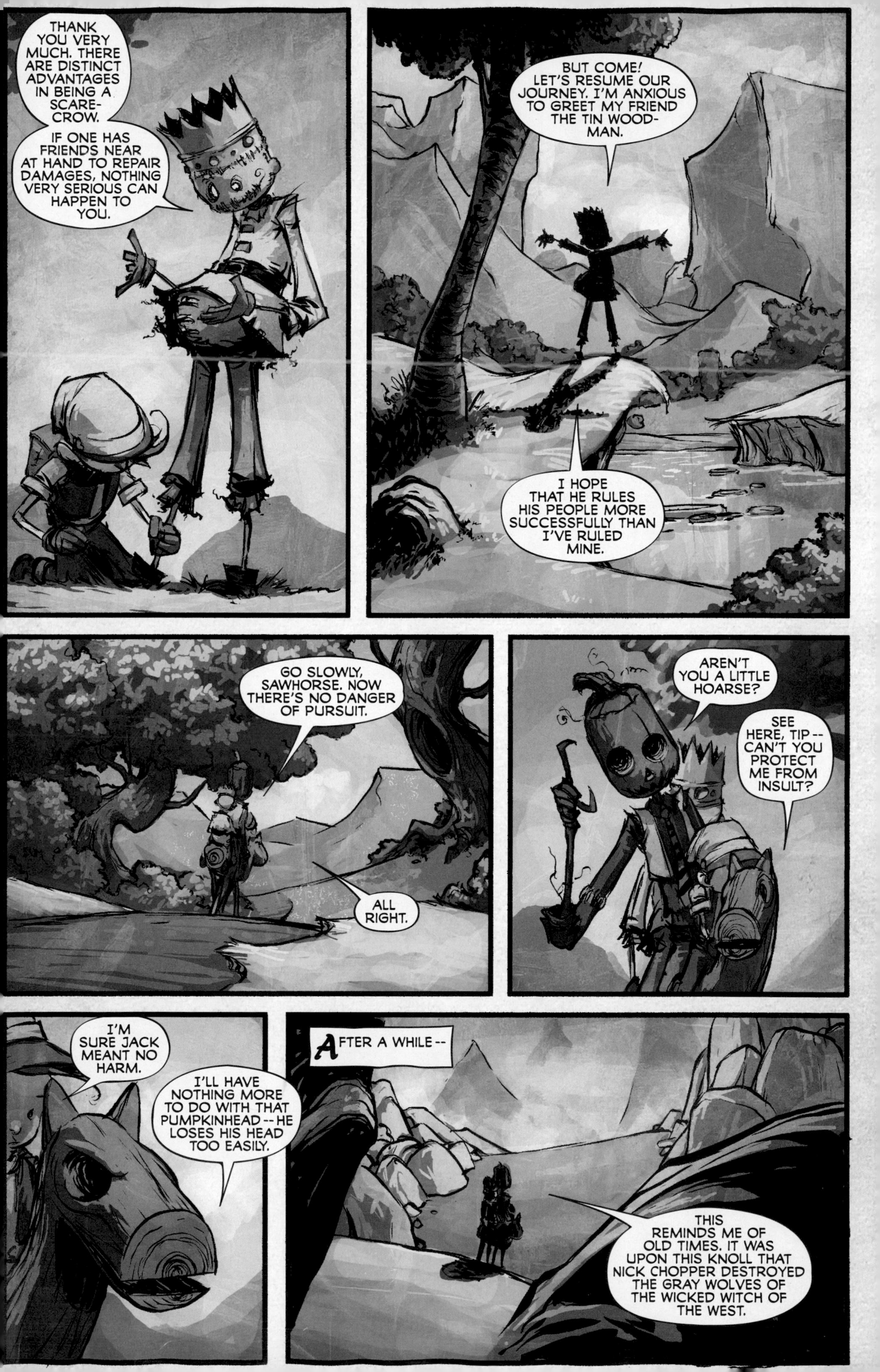
THANK YOU VERY MUCH. THERE ARE DISTINCT ADVANTAGES IN BEING A SCARE-CROW.
IF ONE HAS FRIENDS NEAR AT HAND TO REPAIR DAMAGES, NOTHING VERY SERIOUS CAN HAPPEN TO YOU.
BUT COME! LET'S RESUME OUR JOURNEY. I'M ANXIOUS TO GREET MY FRIEND THE TIN WOOD-MAN.
I HOPE THAT HE RULES HIS PEOPLE MORE SUCCESSFULLY THAN I'VE RULED MINE.
GO SLOWLY, SAWHORSE. NOW THERE'S NO DANGER OF PURSUIT.
ALL RIGHT.
AREN'T YOU A LITTLE HOARSE?
SEE HERE, TIP -- CAN'T YOU PROTECT ME FROM INSULT?
I'M SURE JACK MEANT NO HARM.
I'LL HAVE NOTHING MORE TO DO WITH THAT PUMPKINHEAD -- HE LOSES HIS HEAD TOO EASILY.
AFTER A WHILE --
THIS REMINDS ME OF OLD TIMES. IT WAS UPON THIS KNOLL THAT NICK CHOPPER DESTROYED THE GRAY WOLVES OF THE WICKED WITCH OF THE WEST.

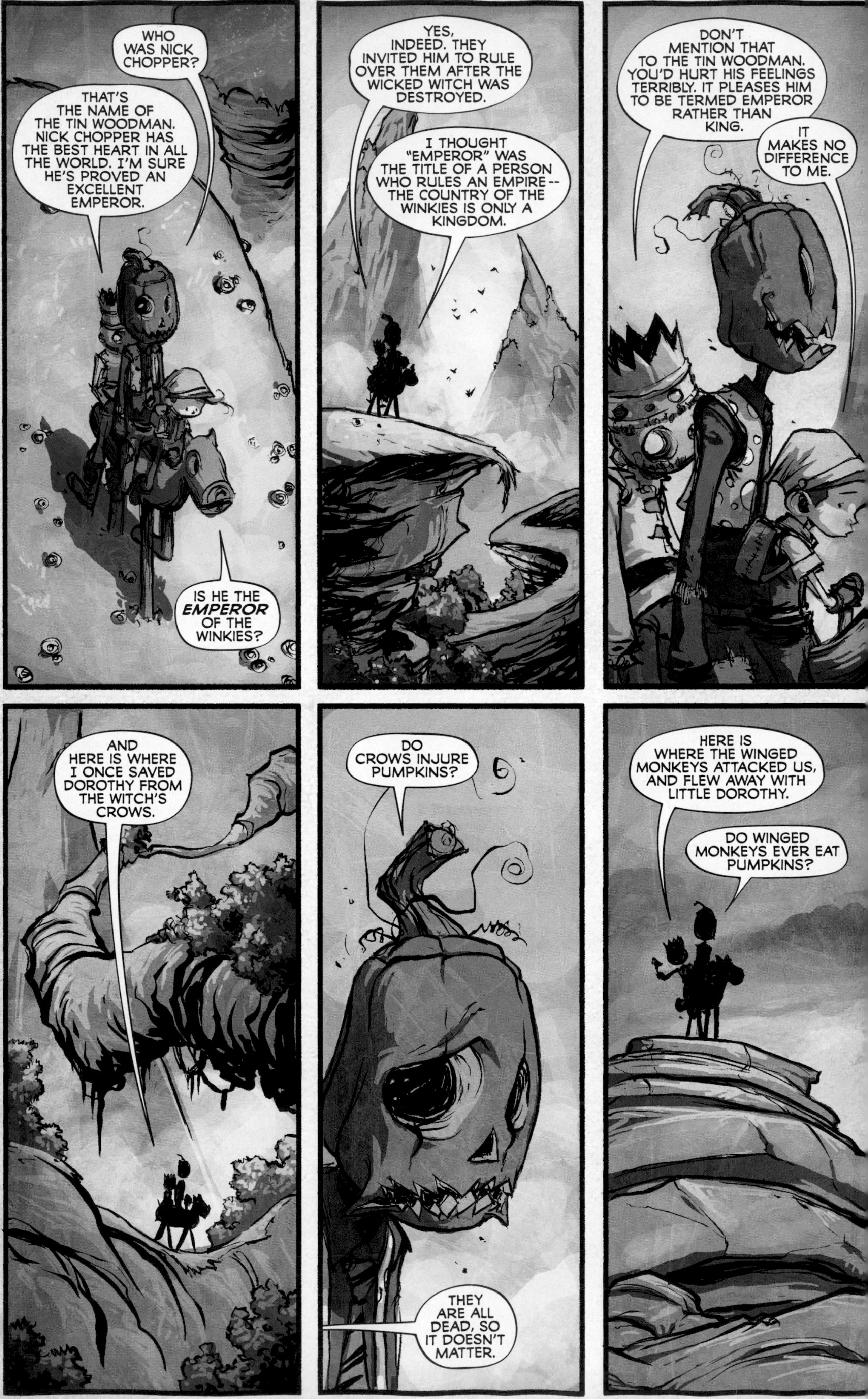
WHO WAS NICK CHOPPER?
THAT'S THE NAME OF THE TIN WOODMAN. NICK CHOPPER HAS THE BEST HEART IN ALL THE WORLD. I'M SURE HE'S PROVED AN EXCELLENT EMPEROR.
IS HE THE *EMPEROR* OF THE WINKIES?
YES, INDEED. THEY INVITED HIM TO RULE OVER THEM AFTER THE WICKED WITCH WAS DESTROYED.
I THOUGHT "EMPEROR" WAS THE TITLE OF A PERSON WHO RULES AN EMPIRE-- THE COUNTRY OF THE WINKIES IS ONLY A KINGDOM.
DON'T MENTION THAT TO THE TIN WOODMAN. YOU'D HURT HIS FEELINGS TERRIBLY. IT PLEASES HIM TO BE TERMED EMPEROR RATHER THAN KING.
IT MAKES NO DIFFERENCE TO ME.
AND HERE IS WHERE I ONCE SAVED DOROTHY FROM THE WITCH'S CROWS.
DO CROWS INJURE PUMPKINS?
THEY ARE ALL DEAD, SO IT DOESN'T MATTER.
HERE IS WHERE THE WINGED MONKEYS ATTACKED US, AND FLEW AWAY WITH LITTLE DOROTHY.
DO WINGED MONKEYS EVER EAT PUMPKINS?

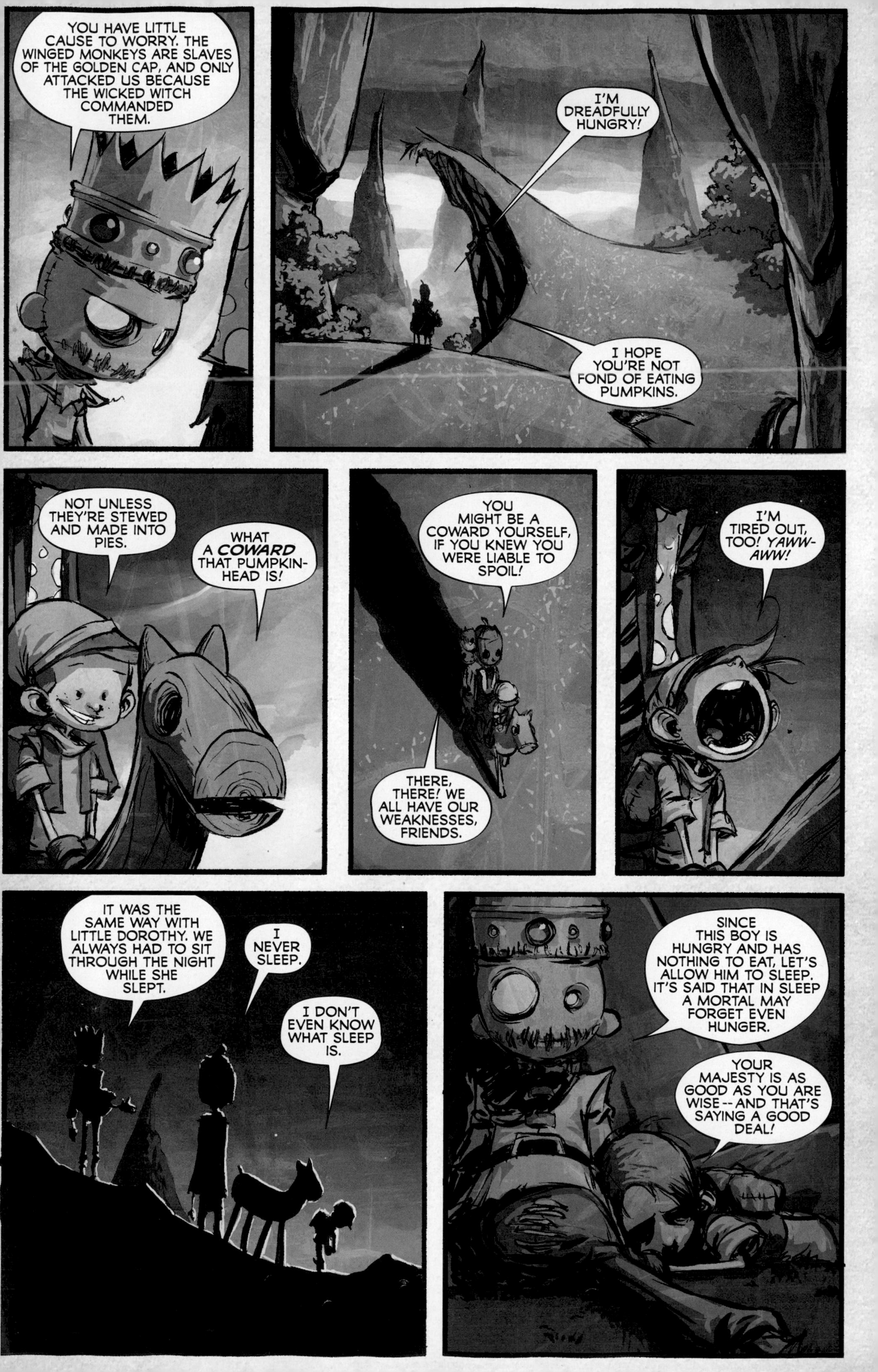
YOU HAVE LITTLE CAUSE TO WORRY. THE WINGED MONKEYS ARE SLAVES OF THE GOLDEN CAP, AND ONLY ATTACKED US BECAUSE THE WICKED WITCH COMMANDED THEM.
I'M DREADFULLY HUNGRY!
I HOPE YOU'RE NOT FOND OF EATING PUMPKINS.
NOT UNLESS THEY'RE STEWED AND MADE INTO PIES.
WHAT A COWARD THAT PUMPKIN-HEAD IS!
YOU MIGHT BE A COWARD YOURSELF, IF YOU KNEW YOU WERE LIABLE TO SPOIL!
THERE, THERE! WE ALL HAVE OUR WEAKNESSES, FRIENDS.
I'M TIRED OUT, TOO! YAWW-AWW!
IT WAS THE SAME WAY WITH LITTLE DOROTHY. WE ALWAYS HAD TO SIT THROUGH THE NIGHT WHILE SHE SLEPT.
I NEVER SLEEP.
I DON'T EVEN KNOW WHAT SLEEP IS.
SINCE THIS BOY IS HUNGRY AND HAS NOTHING TO EAT, LET'S ALLOW HIM TO SLEEP. IT'S SAID THAT IN SLEEP A MORTAL MAY FORGET EVEN HUNGER.
YOUR MAJESTY IS AS GOOD AS YOU ARE WISE--AND THAT'S SAYING A GOOD DEAL!

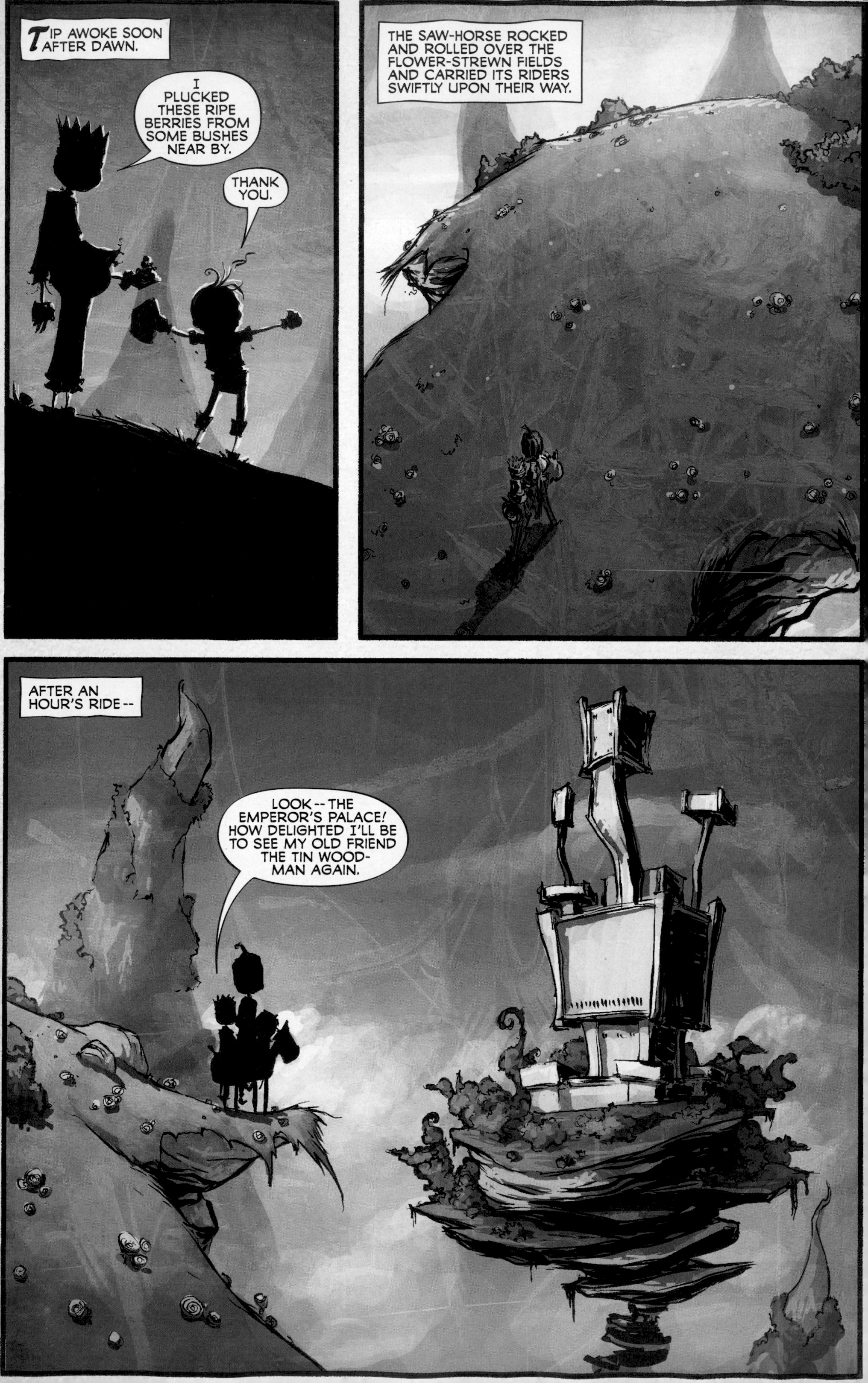
TIP AWOKE SOON AFTER DAWN.
I PLUCKED THESE RIPE BERRIES FROM SOME BUSHES NEAR BY.
THANK YOU.
THE SAW-HORSE ROCKED AND ROLLED OVER THE FLOWER-STREWN FIELDS AND CARRIED ITS RIDERS SWIFTLY UPON THEIR WAY.
AFTER AN HOUR'S RIDE--
LOOK--THE EMPEROR'S PALACE! HOW DELIGHTED I'LL BE TO SEE MY OLD FRIEND THE TIN WOODMAN AGAIN.

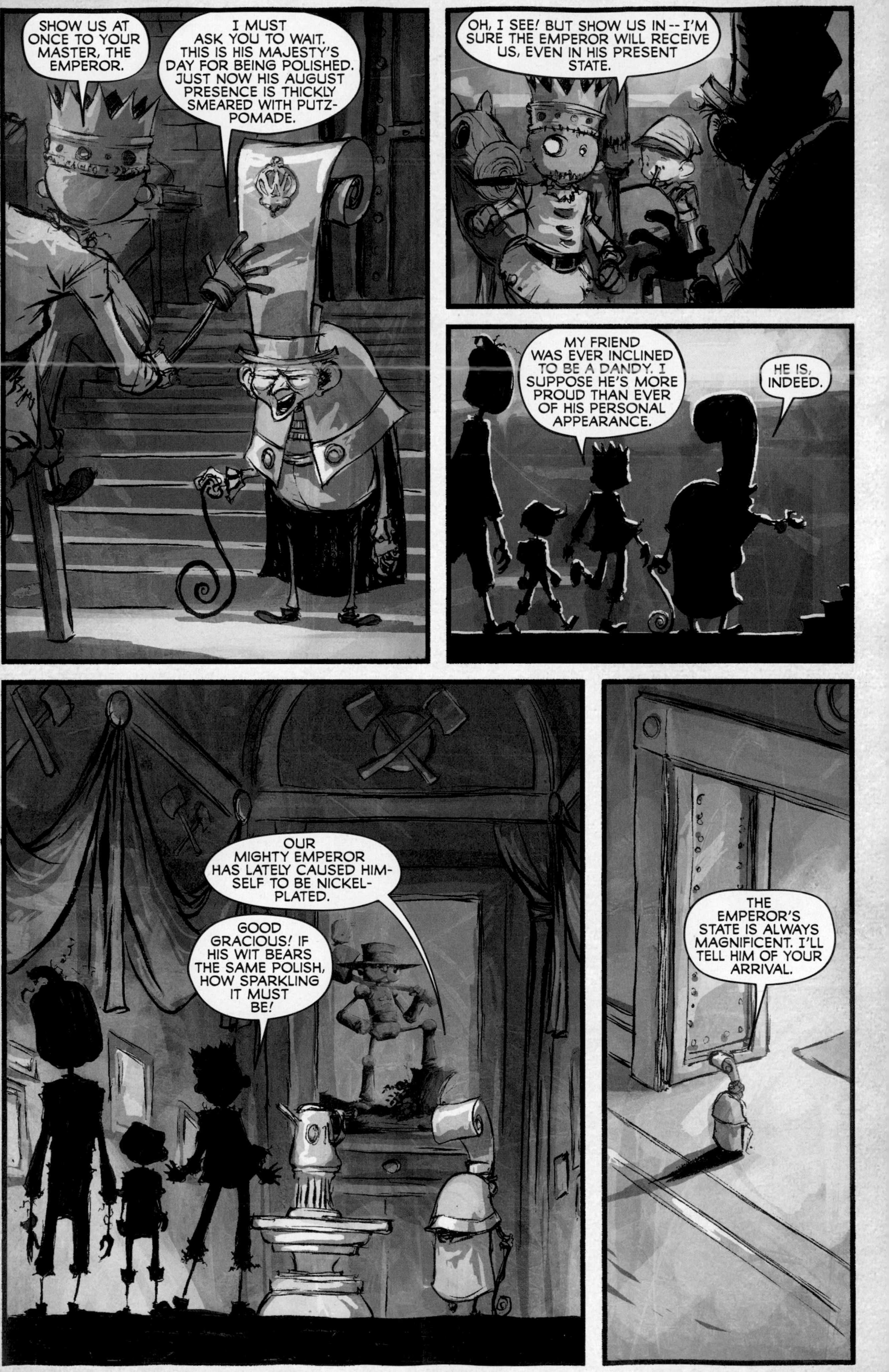
SHOW US AT ONCE TO YOUR MASTER, THE EMPEROR.
I MUST ASK YOU TO WAIT. THIS IS HIS MAJESTY'S DAY FOR BEING POLISHED. JUST NOW HIS AUGUST PRESENCE IS THICKLY SMEARED WITH PUTZ-POMADE.
OH, I SEE! BUT SHOW US IN -- I'M SURE THE EMPEROR WILL RECEIVE US, EVEN IN HIS PRESENT STATE.
MY FRIEND WAS EVER INCLINED TO BE A DANDY. I SUPPOSE HE'S MORE PROUD THAN EVER OF HIS PERSONAL APPEARANCE.
HE IS, INDEED.
OUR MIGHTY EMPEROR HAS LATELY CAUSED HIMSELF TO BE NICKEL-PLATED.
GOOD GRACIOUS! IF HIS WIT BEARS THE SAME POLISH, HOW SPARKLING IT MUST BE!
THE EMPEROR'S STATE IS ALWAYS MAGNIFICENT. I'LL TELL HIM OF YOUR ARRIVAL.

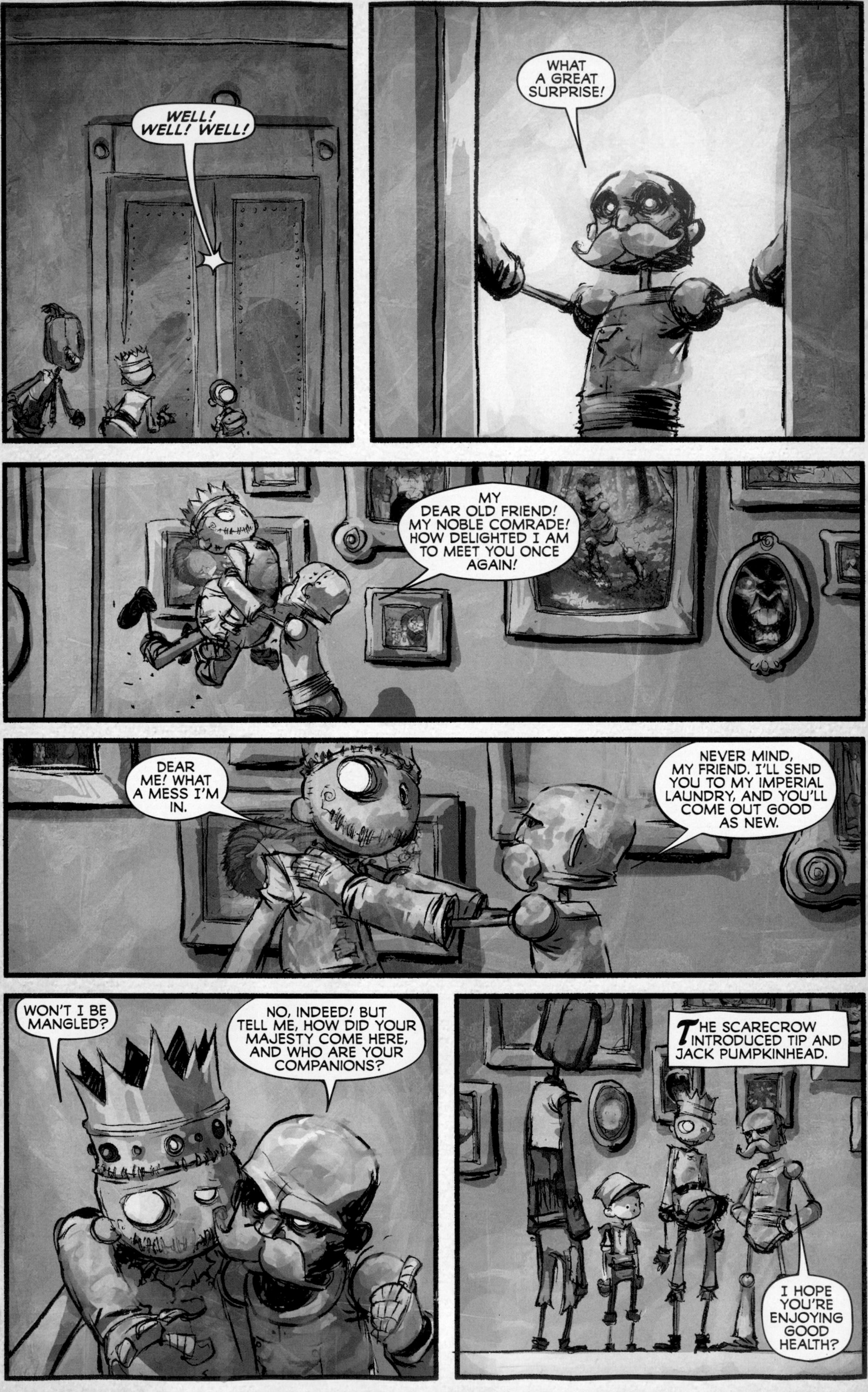
WELL! WELL! WELL!
WHAT A GREAT SURPRISE!
MY DEAR OLD FRIEND! MY NOBLE COMRADE! HOW DELIGHTED I AM TO MEET YOU ONCE AGAIN!
DEAR ME! WHAT A MESS I'M IN.
NEVER MIND, MY FRIEND. I'LL SEND YOU TO MY IMPERIAL LAUNDRY, AND YOU'LL COME OUT GOOD AS NEW.
WON'T I BE MANGLED?
NO, INDEED! BUT TELL ME, HOW DID YOUR MAJESTY COME HERE, AND WHO ARE YOUR COMPANIONS?
THE SCARECROW INTRODUCED TIP AND JACK PUMPKINHEAD.
I HOPE YOU'RE ENJOYING GOOD HEALTH?

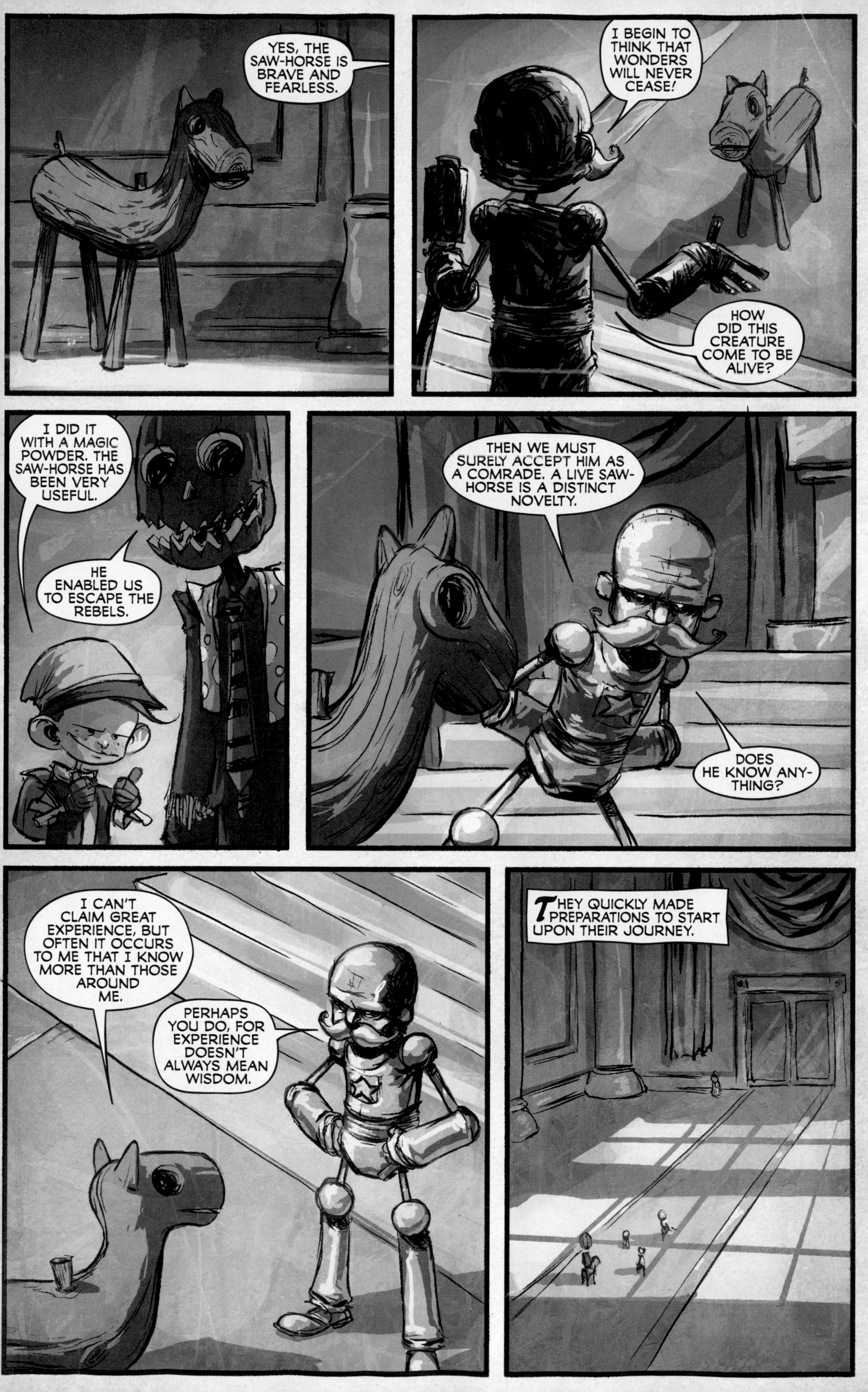
YES, THE SAW-HORSE IS BRAVE AND FEARLESS.
I BEGIN TO THINK THAT WONDERS WILL NEVER CEASE!
HOW DID THIS CREATURE COME TO BE ALIVE?
I DID IT WITH A MAGIC POWDER. THE SAW-HORSE HAS BEEN VERY USEFUL.
HE ENABLED US TO ESCAPE THE REBELS.
THEN WE MUST SURELY ACCEPT HIM AS A COMRADE. A LIVE SAW-HORSE IS A DISTINCT NOVELTY.
DOES HE KNOW ANY-THING?
I CAN'T CLAIM GREAT EXPERIENCE, BUT OFTEN IT OCCURS TO ME THAT I KNOW MORE THAN THOSE AROUND ME.
PERHAPS YOU DO, FOR EXPERIENCE DOESN'T ALWAYS MEAN WISDOM.
THEY QUICKLY MADE PREPARATIONS TO START UPON THEIR JOURNEY.

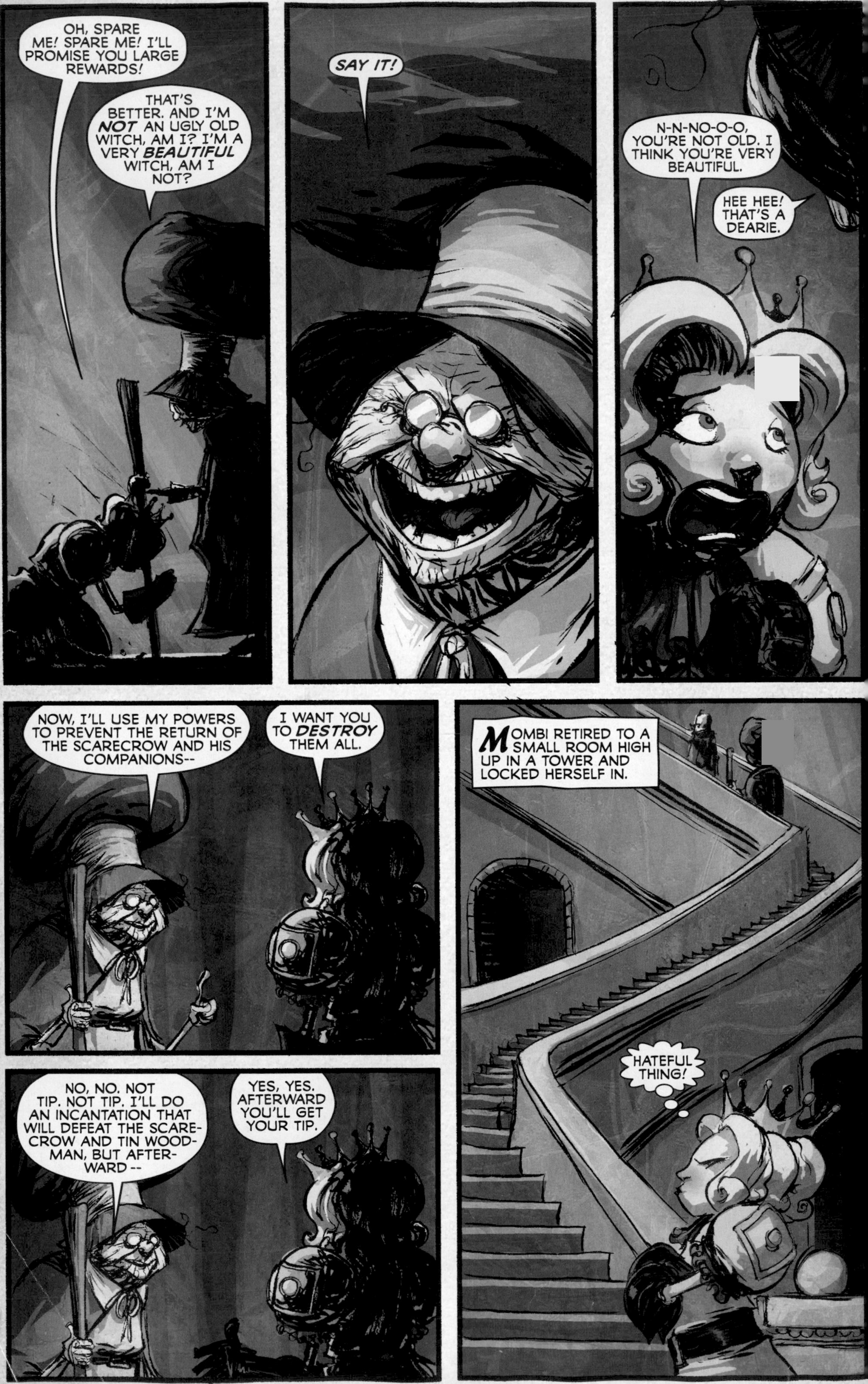

OH, SPARE ME! SPARE ME! I'LL PROMISE YOU LARGE REWARDS!
THAT'S BETTER. AND I'M ***NOT*** AN UGLY OLD WITCH, AM I? I'M A VERY ***BEAUTIFUL*** WITCH, AM I NOT?
SAY IT!
N-N-NO-O-O, YOU'RE NOT OLD. I THINK YOU'RE VERY BEAUTIFUL.
HEE HEE! THAT'S A DEARIE.
NOW, I'LL USE MY POWERS TO PREVENT THE RETURN OF THE SCARECROW AND HIS COMPANIONS--
I WANT YOU TO ***DESTROY*** THEM ALL.
NO, NO. NOT TIP. NOT TIP. I'LL DO AN INCANTATION THAT WILL DEFEAT THE SCARE-CROW AND TIN WOOD-MAN, BUT AFTER-WARD --
YES, YES. AFTERWARD YOU'LL GET YOUR TIP.
MOMBI RETIRED TO A SMALL ROOM HIGH UP IN A TOWER AND LOCKED HERSELF IN.
HATEFUL THING!

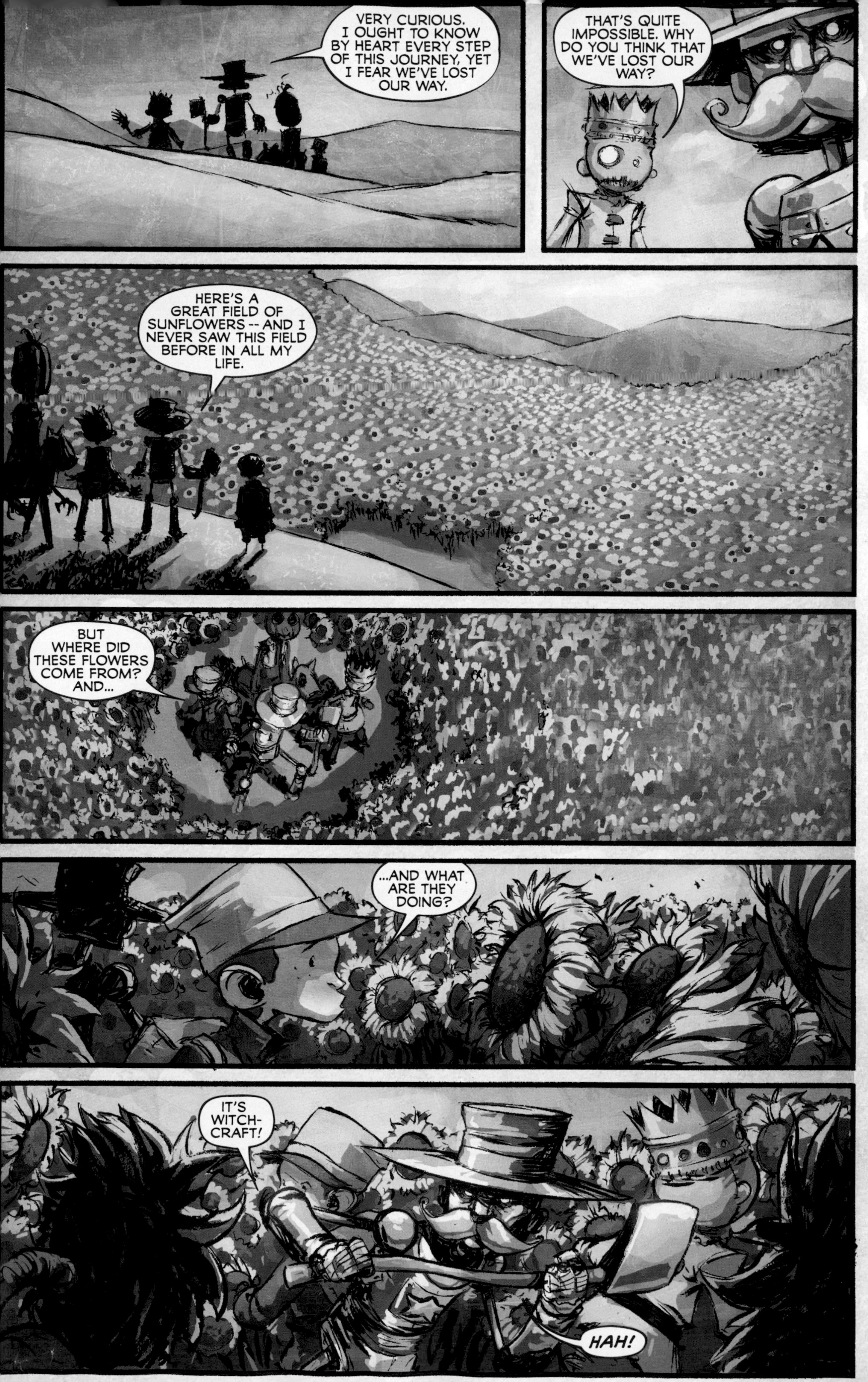
VERY CURIOUS. I OUGHT TO KNOW BY HEART EVERY STEP OF THIS JOURNEY, YET I FEAR WE'VE LOST OUR WAY.
THAT'S QUITE IMPOSSIBLE. WHY DO YOU THINK THAT WE'VE LOST OUR WAY?
HERE'S A GREAT FIELD OF SUNFLOWERS -- AND I NEVER SAW THIS FIELD BEFORE IN ALL MY LIFE.
BUT WHERE DID THESE FLOWERS COME FROM? AND...
...AND WHAT ARE THEY DOING?
IT'S WITCH-CRAFT!
HAH!

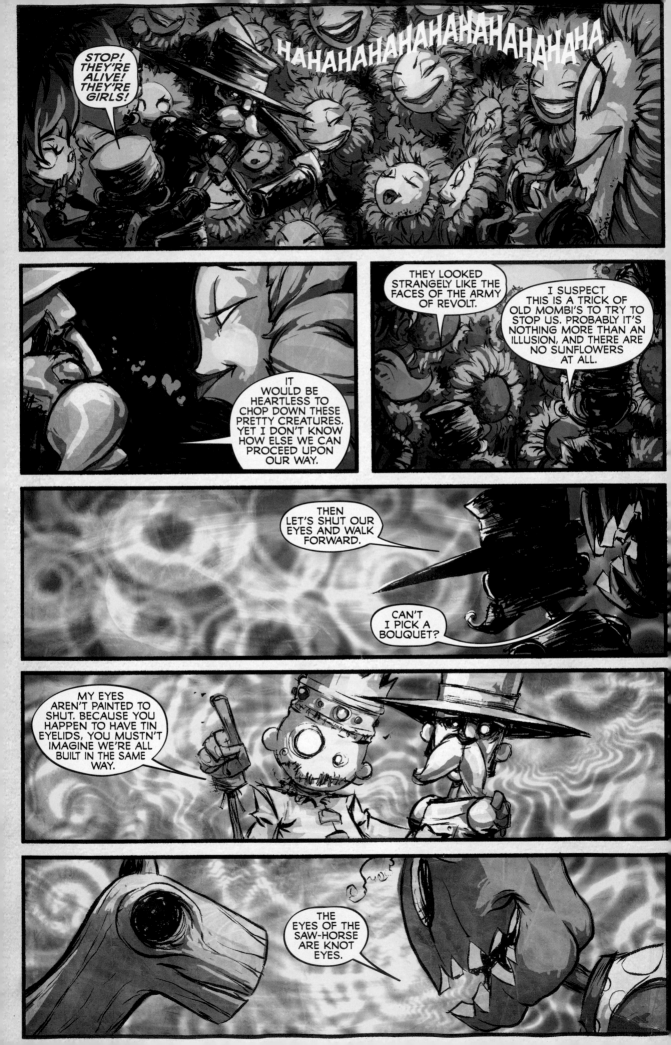

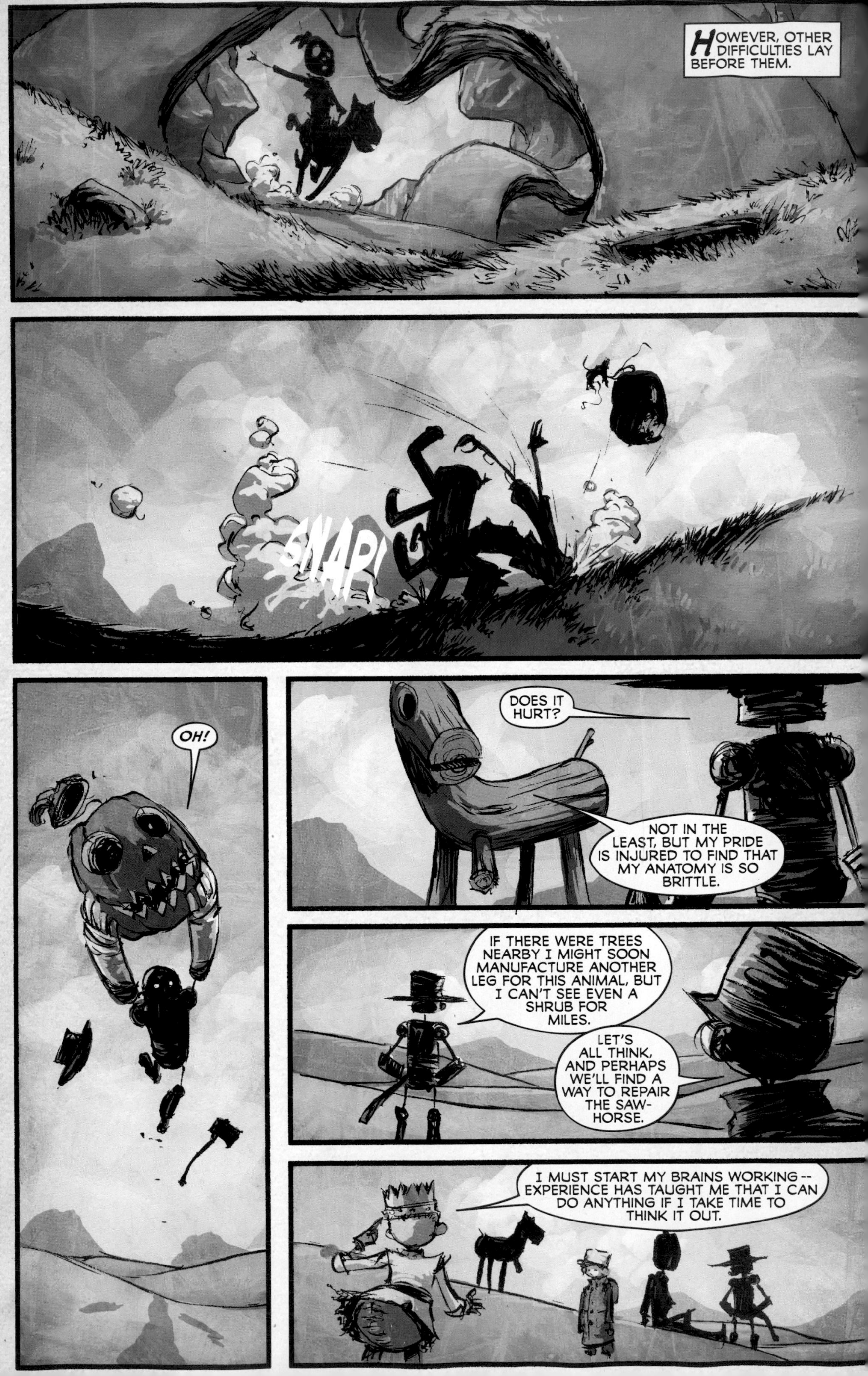
HOWEVER, OTHER DIFFICULTIES LAY BEFORE THEM.
SNAP!
OH!
DOES IT HURT?
NOT IN THE LEAST, BUT MY PRIDE IS INJURED TO FIND THAT MY ANATOMY IS SO BRITTLE.
IF THERE WERE TREES NEARBY I MIGHT SOON MANUFACTURE ANOTHER LEG FOR THIS ANIMAL, BUT I CAN'T SEE EVEN A SHRUB FOR MILES.
LET'S ALL THINK, AND PERHAPS WE'LL FIND A WAY TO REPAIR THE SAW-HORSE.
I MUST START MY BRAINS WORKING -- EXPERIENCE HAS TAUGHT ME THAT I CAN DO ANYTHING IF I TAKE TIME TO THINK IT OUT.

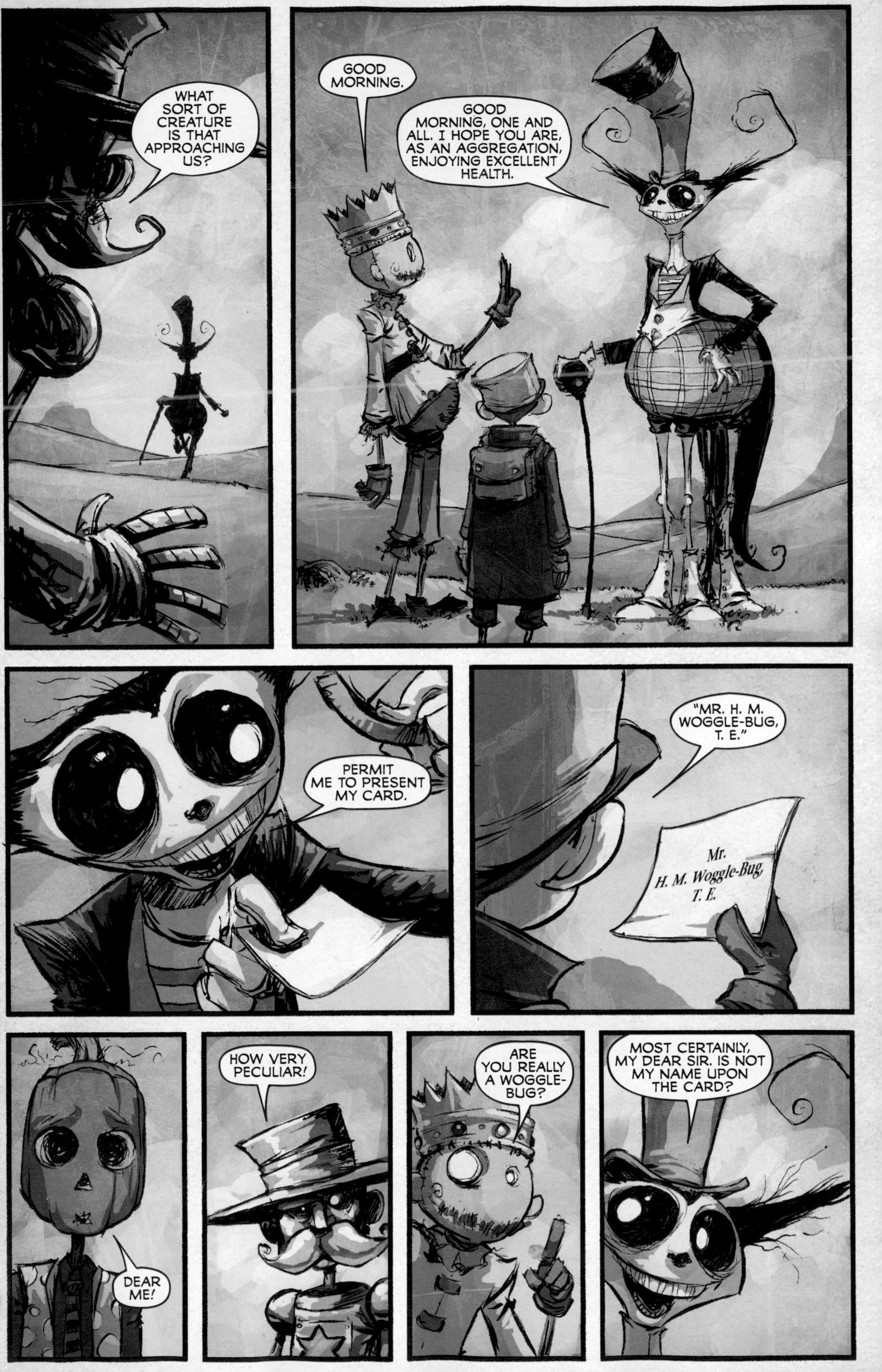
WHAT SORT OF CREATURE IS THAT APPROACHING US?
GOOD MORNING.
GOOD MORNING, ONE AND ALL. I HOPE YOU ARE, AS AN AGGREGATION, ENJOYING EXCELLENT HEALTH.
PERMIT ME TO PRESENT MY CARD.
"MR. H. M. WOGGLE-BUG, T. E."
Mr. H. M. Woggle-Bug, T. E.
DEAR ME!
HOW VERY PECULIAR!
ARE YOU REALLY A WOGGLE-BUG?
MOST CERTAINLY, MY DEAR SIR. IS NOT MY NAME UPON THE CARD?

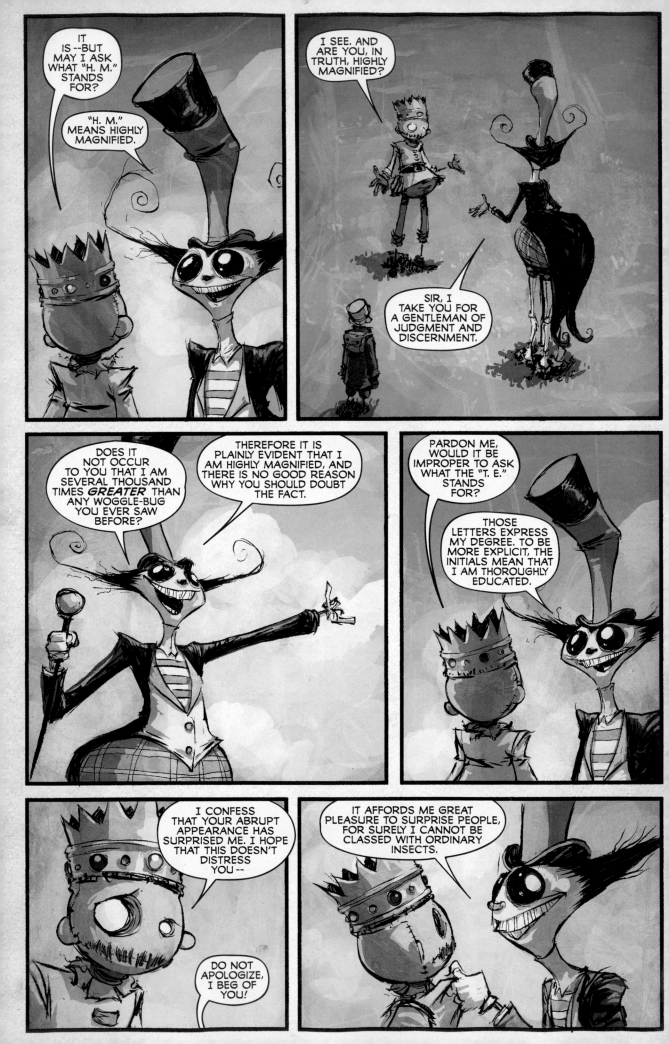

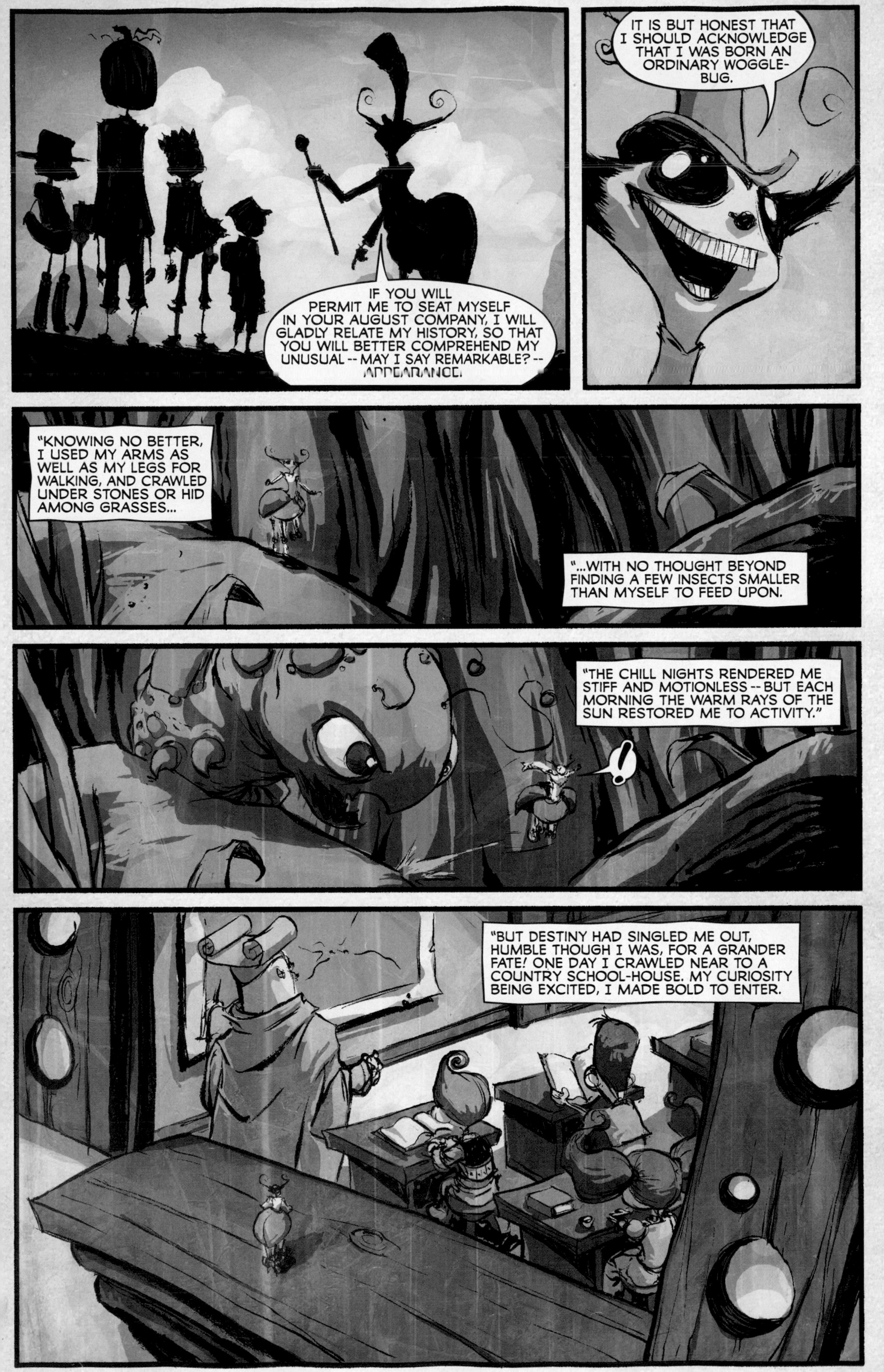
IF YOU WILL PERMIT ME TO SEAT MYSELF IN YOUR AUGUST COMPANY, I WILL GLADLY RELATE MY HISTORY, SO THAT YOU WILL BETTER COMPREHEND MY UNUSUAL -- MAY I SAY REMARKABLE? -- APPEARANCE.
IT IS BUT HONEST THAT I SHOULD ACKNOWLEDGE THAT I WAS BORN AN ORDINARY WOGGLE-BUG.
"KNOWING NO BETTER, I USED MY ARMS AS WELL AS MY LEGS FOR WALKING, AND CRAWLED UNDER STONES OR HID AMONG GRASSES...
"...WITH NO THOUGHT BEYOND FINDING A FEW INSECTS SMALLER THAN MYSELF TO FEED UPON.
"THE CHILL NIGHTS RENDERED ME STIFF AND MOTIONLESS -- BUT EACH MORNING THE WARM RAYS OF THE SUN RESTORED ME TO ACTIVITY."
!
"BUT DESTINY HAD SINGLED ME OUT, HUMBLE THOUGH I WAS, FOR A GRANDER FATE! ONE DAY I CRAWLED NEAR TO A COUNTRY SCHOOL-HOUSE. MY CURIOSITY BEING EXCITED, I MADE BOLD TO ENTER.

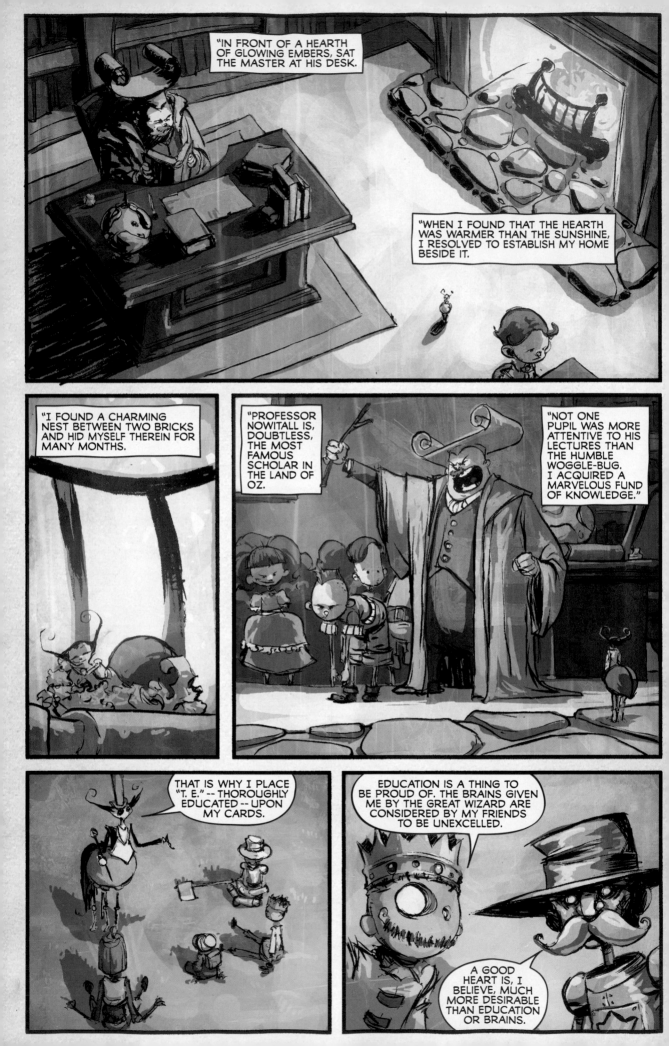

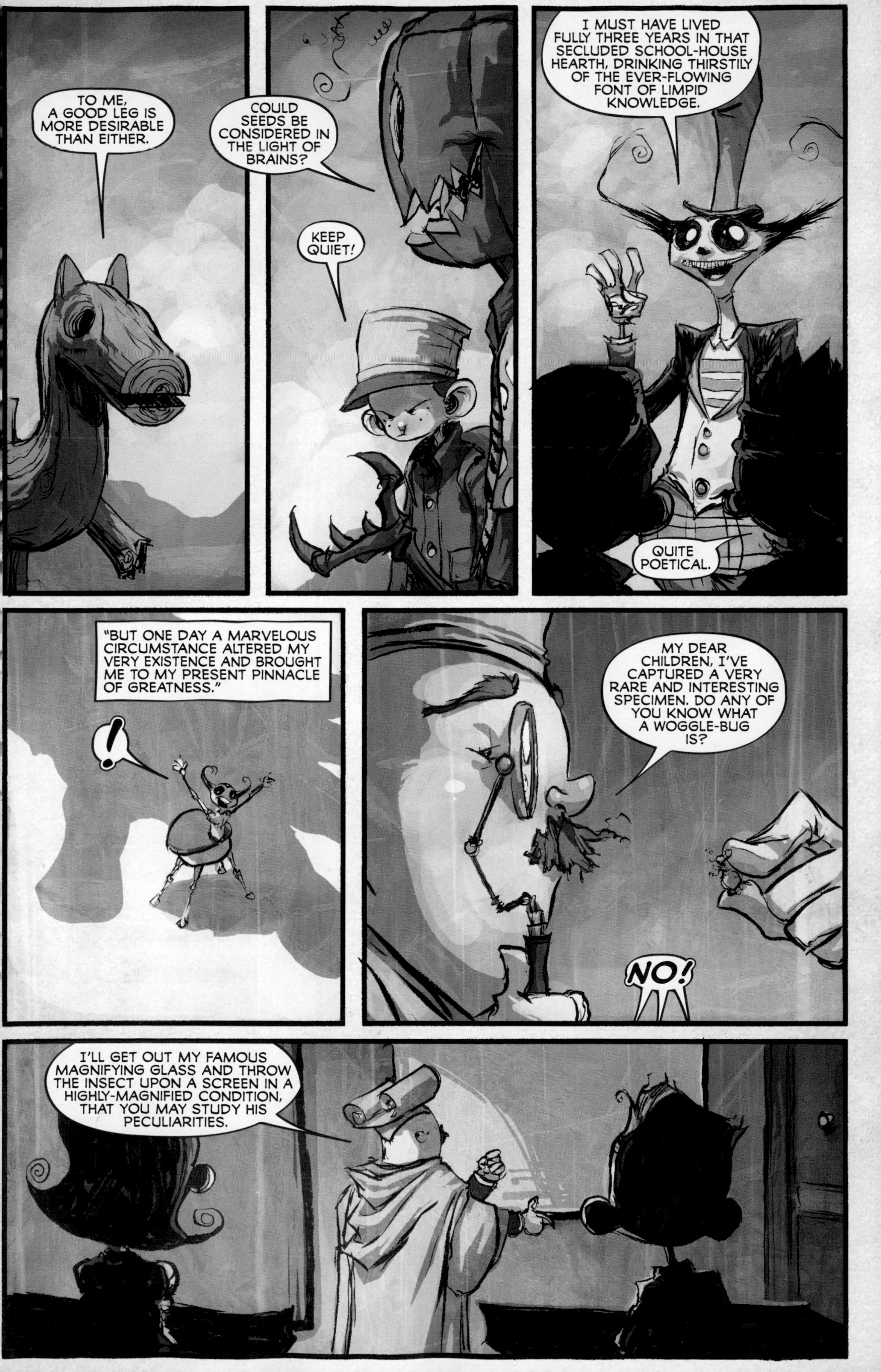
TO ME, A GOOD LEG IS MORE DESIRABLE THAN EITHER.
COULD SEEDS BE CONSIDERED IN THE LIGHT OF BRAINS?
KEEP QUIET!
I MUST HAVE LIVED FULLY THREE YEARS IN THAT SECLUDED SCHOOL-HOUSE HEARTH, DRINKING THIRSTILY OF THE EVER-FLOWING FONT OF LIMPID KNOWLEDGE.
QUITE POETICAL.
"BUT ONE DAY A MARVELOUS CIRCUMSTANCE ALTERED MY VERY EXISTENCE AND BROUGHT ME TO MY PRESENT PINNACLE OF GREATNESS."
!
MY DEAR CHILDREN, I'VE CAPTURED A VERY RARE AND INTERESTING SPECIMEN. DO ANY OF YOU KNOW WHAT A WOGGLE-BUG IS?
NO!
I'LL GET OUT MY FAMOUS MAGNIFYING GLASS AND THROW THE INSECT UPON A SCREEN IN A HIGHLY-MAGNIFIED CONDITION, THAT YOU MAY STUDY HIS PECULIARITIES.

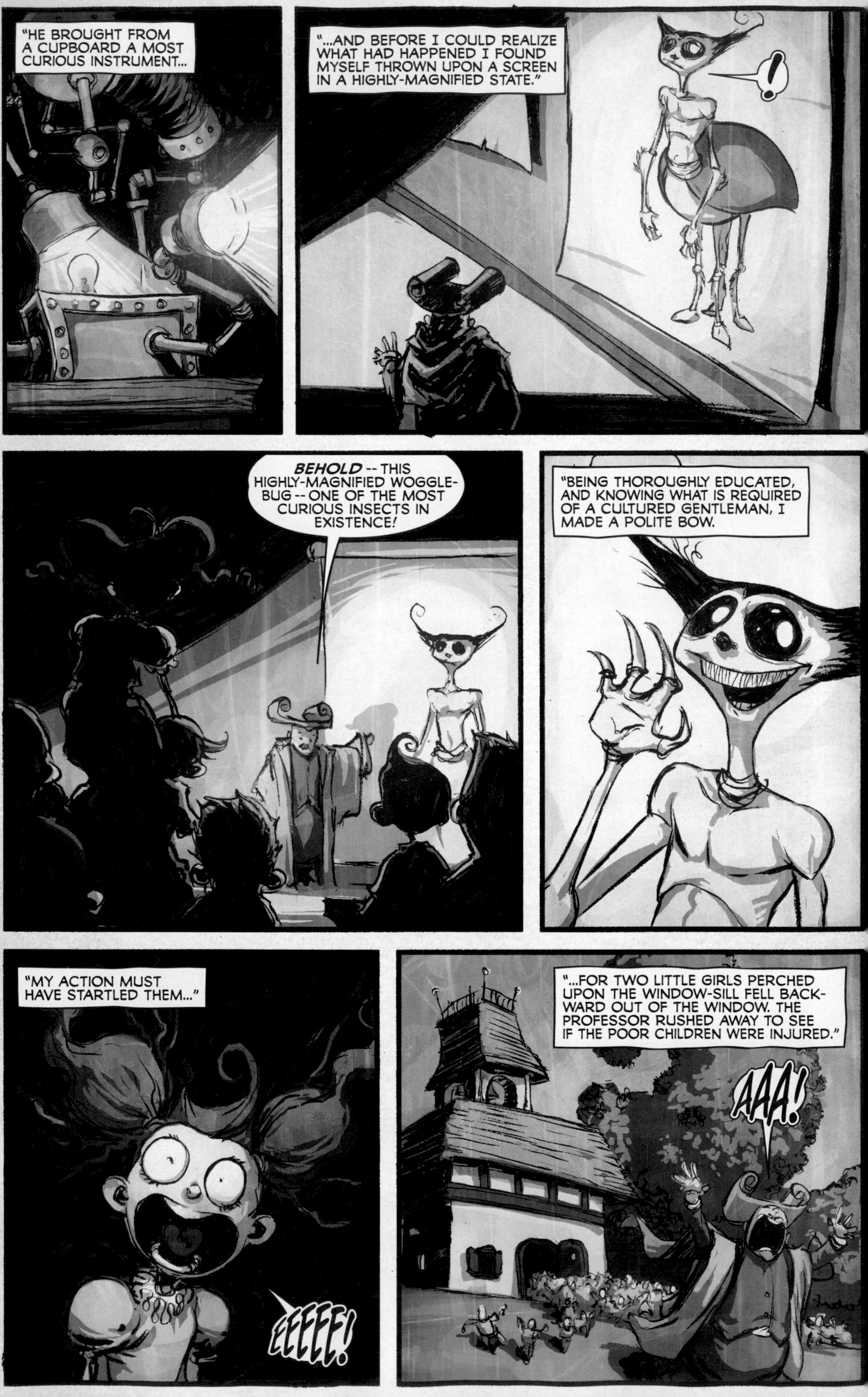
"HE BROUGHT FROM A CUPBOARD A MOST CURIOUS INSTRUMENT...
"...AND BEFORE I COULD REALIZE WHAT HAD HAPPENED I FOUND MYSELF THROWN UPON A SCREEN IN A HIGHLY-MAGNIFIED STATE."
!
BEHOLD -- THIS HIGHLY-MAGNIFIED WOGGLE-BUG -- ONE OF THE MOST CURIOUS INSECTS IN EXISTENCE!
"BEING THOROUGHLY EDUCATED, AND KNOWING WHAT IS REQUIRED OF A CULTURED GENTLEMAN, I MADE A POLITE BOW.
"MY ACTION MUST HAVE STARTLED THEM..."
EEEEE!
"...FOR TWO LITTLE GIRLS PERCHED UPON THE WINDOW-SILL FELL BACKWARD OUT OF THE WINDOW. THE PROFESSOR RUSHED AWAY TO SEE IF THE POOR CHILDREN WERE INJURED."
AAA!

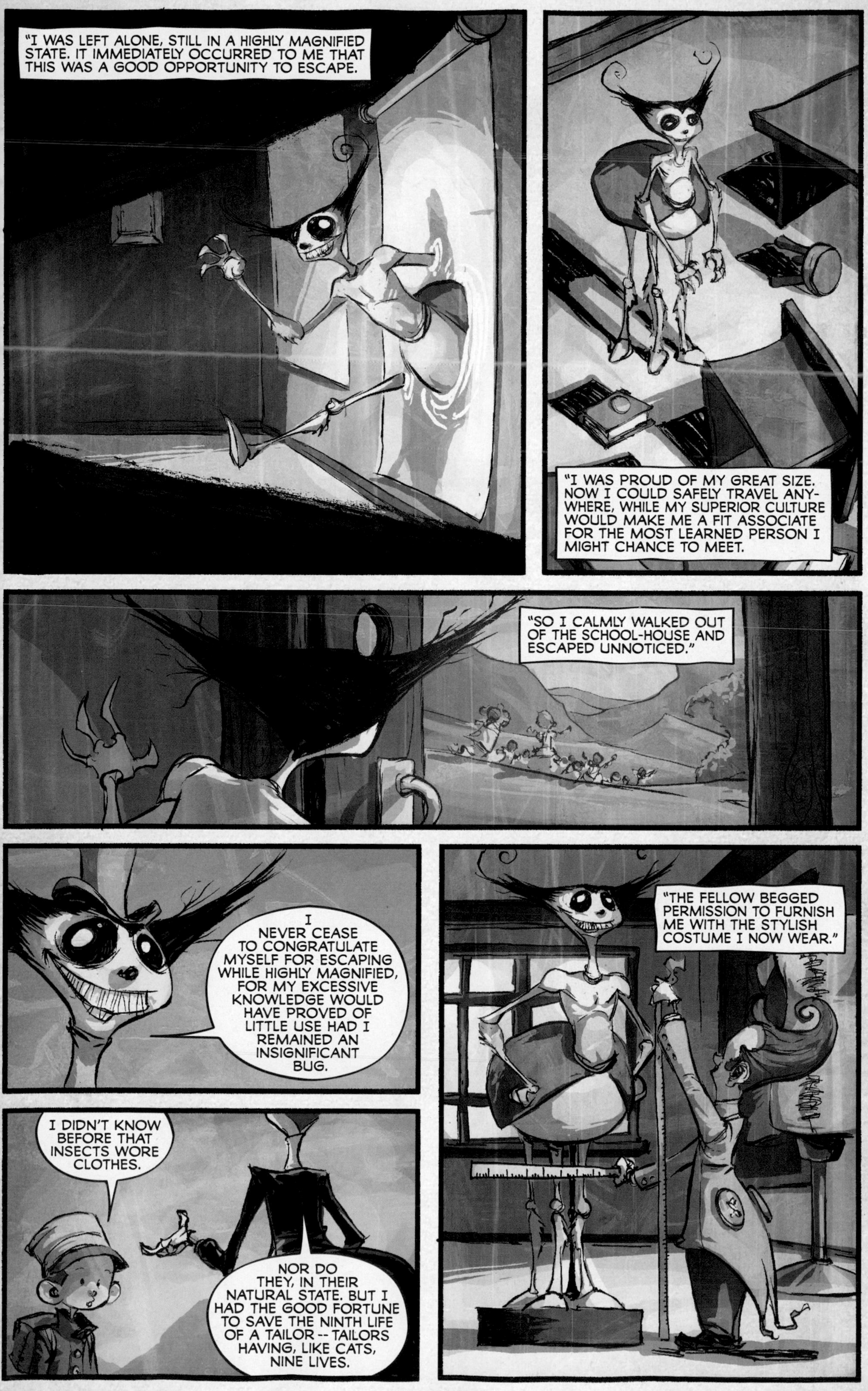
"I WAS LEFT ALONE, STILL IN A HIGHLY MAGNIFIED STATE. IT IMMEDIATELY OCCURRED TO ME THAT THIS WAS A GOOD OPPORTUNITY TO ESCAPE.
"I WAS PROUD OF MY GREAT SIZE. NOW I COULD SAFELY TRAVEL ANY-WHERE, WHILE MY SUPERIOR CULTURE WOULD MAKE ME A FIT ASSOCIATE FOR THE MOST LEARNED PERSON I MIGHT CHANCE TO MEET.
"SO I CALMLY WALKED OUT OF THE SCHOOL-HOUSE AND ESCAPED UNNOTICED."
I NEVER CEASE TO CONGRATULATE MYSELF FOR ESCAPING WHILE HIGHLY MAGNIFIED, FOR MY EXCESSIVE KNOWLEDGE WOULD HAVE PROVED OF LITTLE USE HAD I REMAINED AN INSIGNIFICANT BUG.
I DIDN'T KNOW BEFORE THAT INSECTS WORE CLOTHES.
NOR DO THEY, IN THEIR NATURAL STATE. BUT I HAD THE GOOD FORTUNE TO SAVE THE NINTH LIFE OF A TAILOR -- TAILORS HAVING, LIKE CATS, NINE LIVES.
"THE FELLOW BEGGED PERMISSION TO FURNISH ME WITH THE STYLISH COSTUME I NOW WEAR."

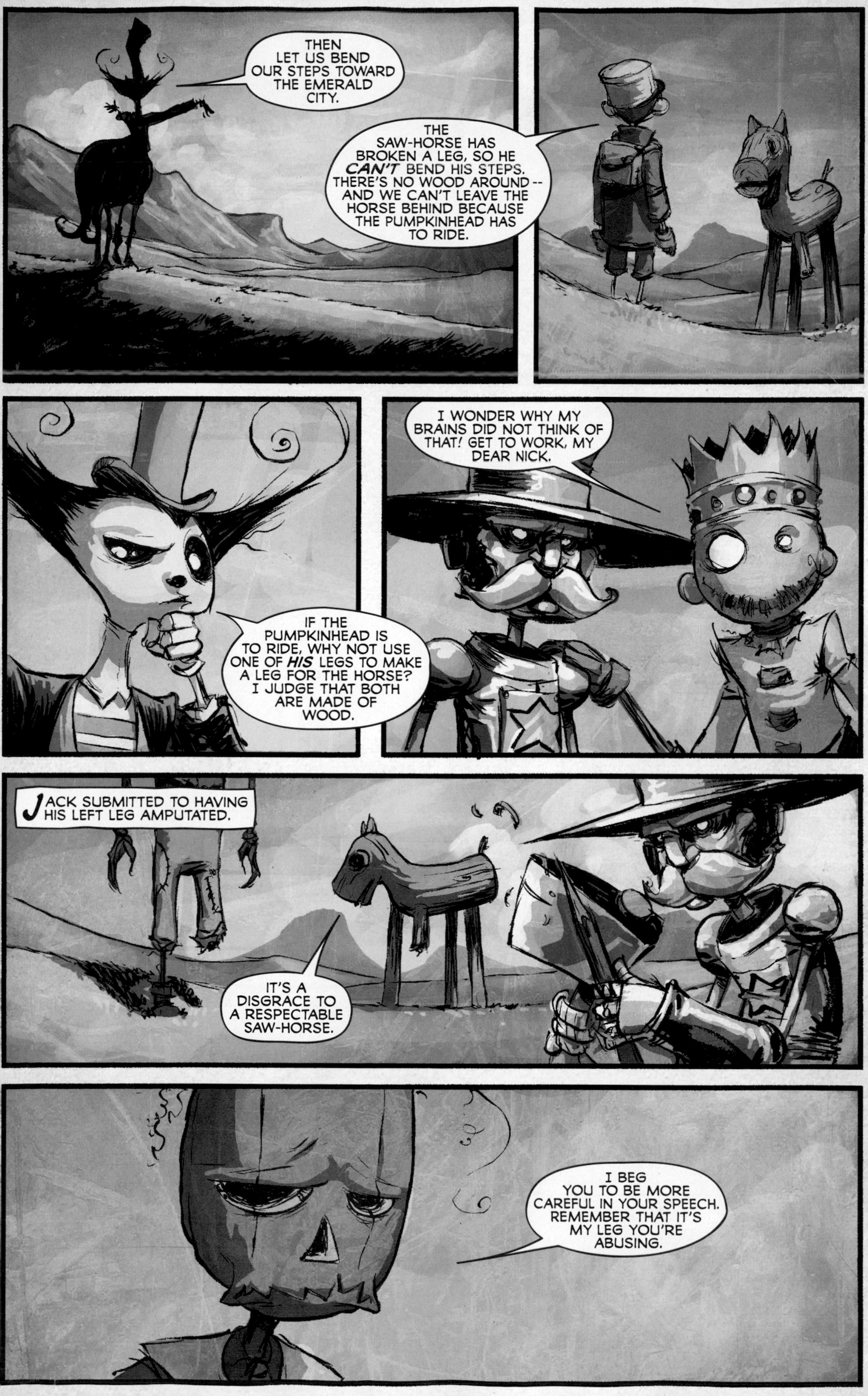
THEN LET US BEND OUR STEPS TOWARD THE EMERALD CITY.
THE SAW-HORSE HAS BROKEN A LEG, SO HE CAN'T BEND HIS STEPS. THERE'S NO WOOD AROUND -- AND WE CAN'T LEAVE THE HORSE BEHIND BECAUSE THE PUMPKINHEAD HAS TO RIDE.
IF THE PUMPKINHEAD IS TO RIDE, WHY NOT USE ONE OF HIS LEGS TO MAKE A LEG FOR THE HORSE? I JUDGE THAT BOTH ARE MADE OF WOOD.
I WONDER WHY MY BRAINS DID NOT THINK OF THAT! GET TO WORK, MY DEAR NICK.
JACK SUBMITTED TO HAVING HIS LEFT LEG AMPUTATED.
IT'S A DISGRACE TO A RESPECTABLE SAW-HORSE.
I BEG YOU TO BE MORE CAREFUL IN YOUR SPEECH. REMEMBER THAT IT'S MY LEG YOU'RE ABUSING.

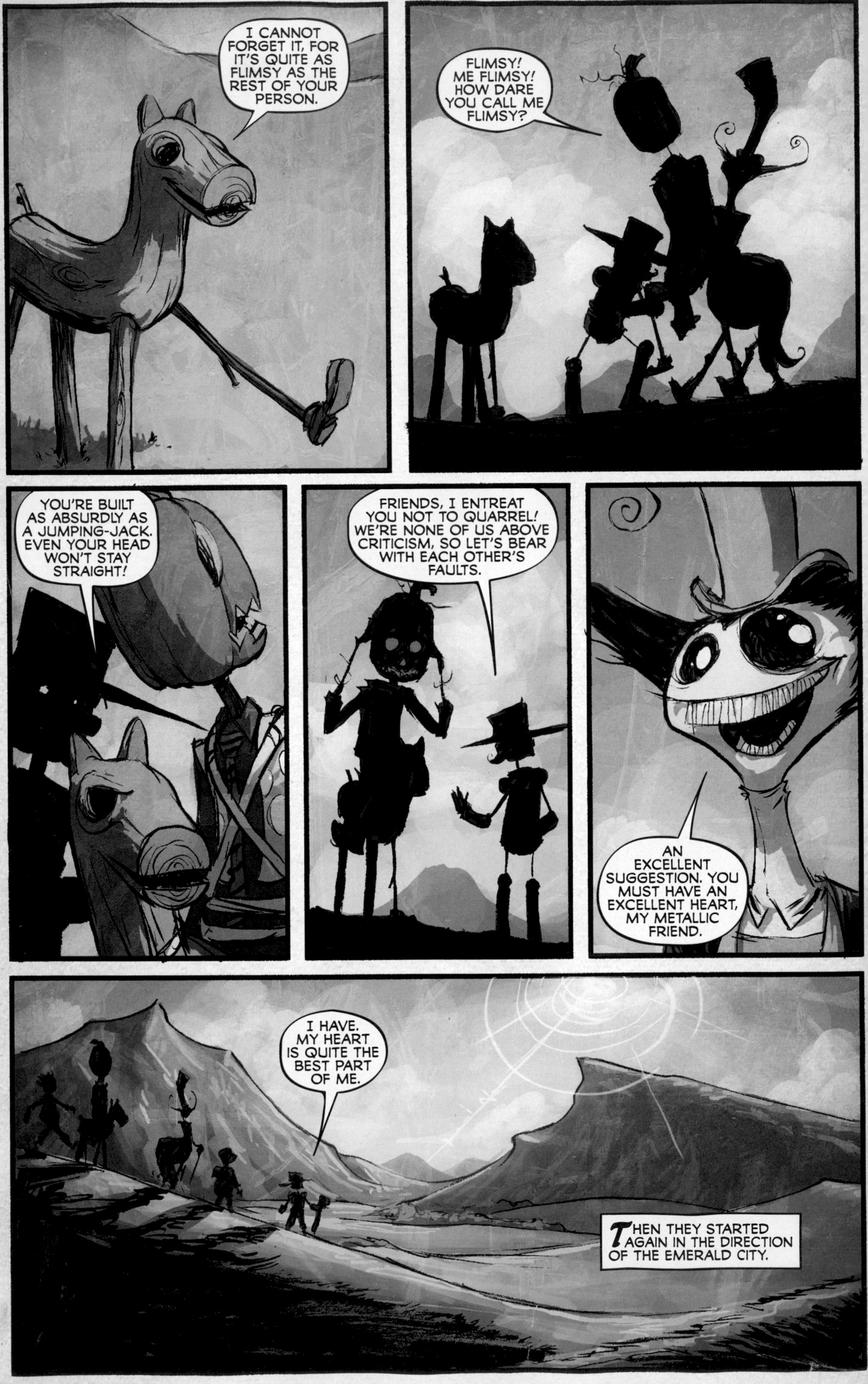
I CANNOT FORGET IT, FOR IT'S QUITE AS FLIMSY AS THE REST OF YOUR PERSON.
FLIMSY! ME FLIMSY! HOW DARE YOU CALL ME FLIMSY?
YOU'RE BUILT AS ABSURDLY AS A JUMPING-JACK. EVEN YOUR HEAD WON'T STAY STRAIGHT!
FRIENDS, I ENTREAT YOU NOT TO QUARREL! WE'RE NONE OF US ABOVE CRITICISM, SO LET'S BEAR WITH EACH OTHER'S FAULTS.
AN EXCELLENT SUGGESTION. YOU MUST HAVE AN EXCELLENT HEART, MY METALLIC FRIEND.
I HAVE. MY HEART IS QUITE THE BEST PART OF ME.
THEN THEY STARTED AGAIN IN THE DIRECTION OF THE EMERALD CITY.

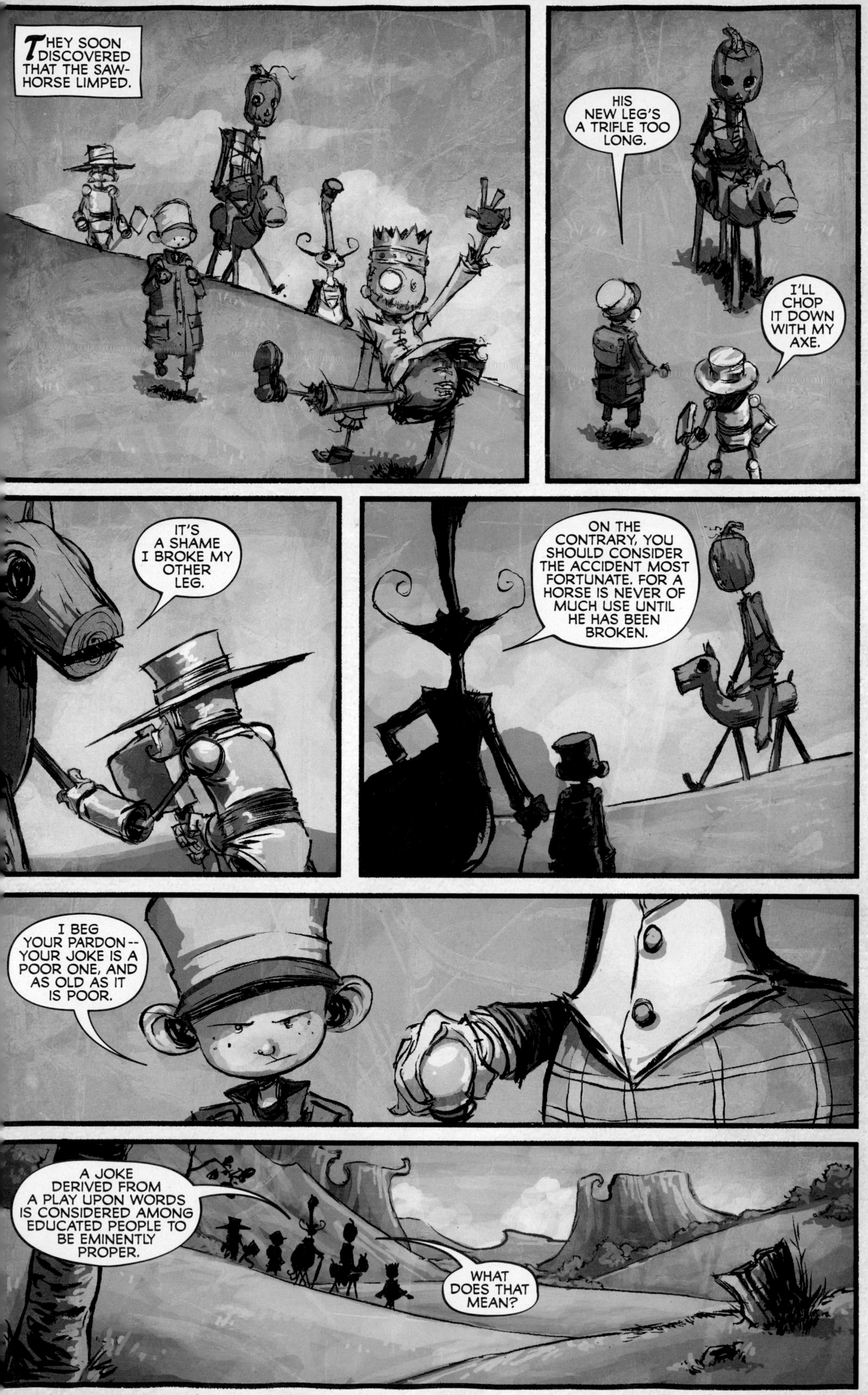
THEY SOON DISCOVERED THAT THE SAW-HORSE LIMPED.
HIS NEW LEG'S A TRIFLE TOO LONG.
I'LL CHOP IT DOWN WITH MY AXE.
IT'S A SHAME I BROKE MY OTHER LEG.
ON THE CONTRARY, YOU SHOULD CONSIDER THE ACCIDENT MOST FORTUNATE. FOR A HORSE IS NEVER OF MUCH USE UNTIL HE HAS BEEN BROKEN.
I BEG YOUR PARDON-- YOUR JOKE IS A POOR ONE, AND AS OLD AS IT IS POOR.
A JOKE DERIVED FROM A PLAY UPON WORDS IS CONSIDERED AMONG EDUCATED PEOPLE TO BE EMINENTLY PROPER.
WHAT DOES THAT MEAN?

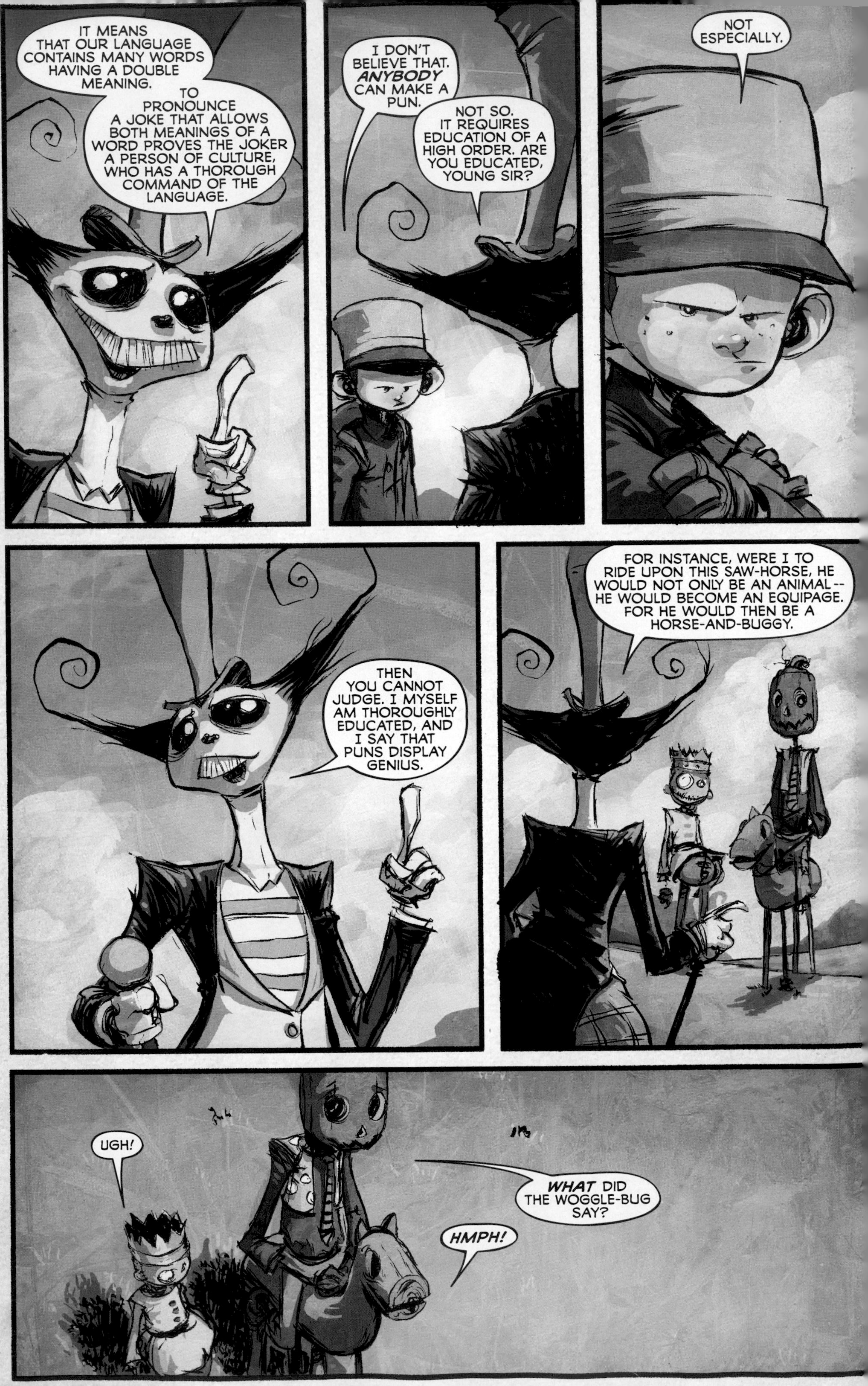
IT MEANS THAT OUR LANGUAGE CONTAINS MANY WORDS HAVING A DOUBLE MEANING.
TO PRONOUNCE A JOKE THAT ALLOWS BOTH MEANINGS OF A WORD PROVES THE JOKER A PERSON OF CULTURE, WHO HAS A THOROUGH COMMAND OF THE LANGUAGE.
I DON'T BELIEVE THAT. ANYBODY CAN MAKE A PUN.
NOT SO. IT REQUIRES EDUCATION OF A HIGH ORDER. ARE YOU EDUCATED, YOUNG SIR?
NOT ESPECIALLY.
THEN YOU CANNOT JUDGE. I MYSELF AM THOROUGHLY EDUCATED, AND I SAY THAT PUNS DISPLAY GENIUS.
FOR INSTANCE, WERE I TO RIDE UPON THIS SAW-HORSE, HE WOULD NOT ONLY BE AN ANIMAL-- HE WOULD BECOME AN EQUIPAGE. FOR HE WOULD THEN BE A HORSE-AND-BUGGY.
UGH!
WHAT DID THE WOGGLE-BUG SAY?
HMPH!

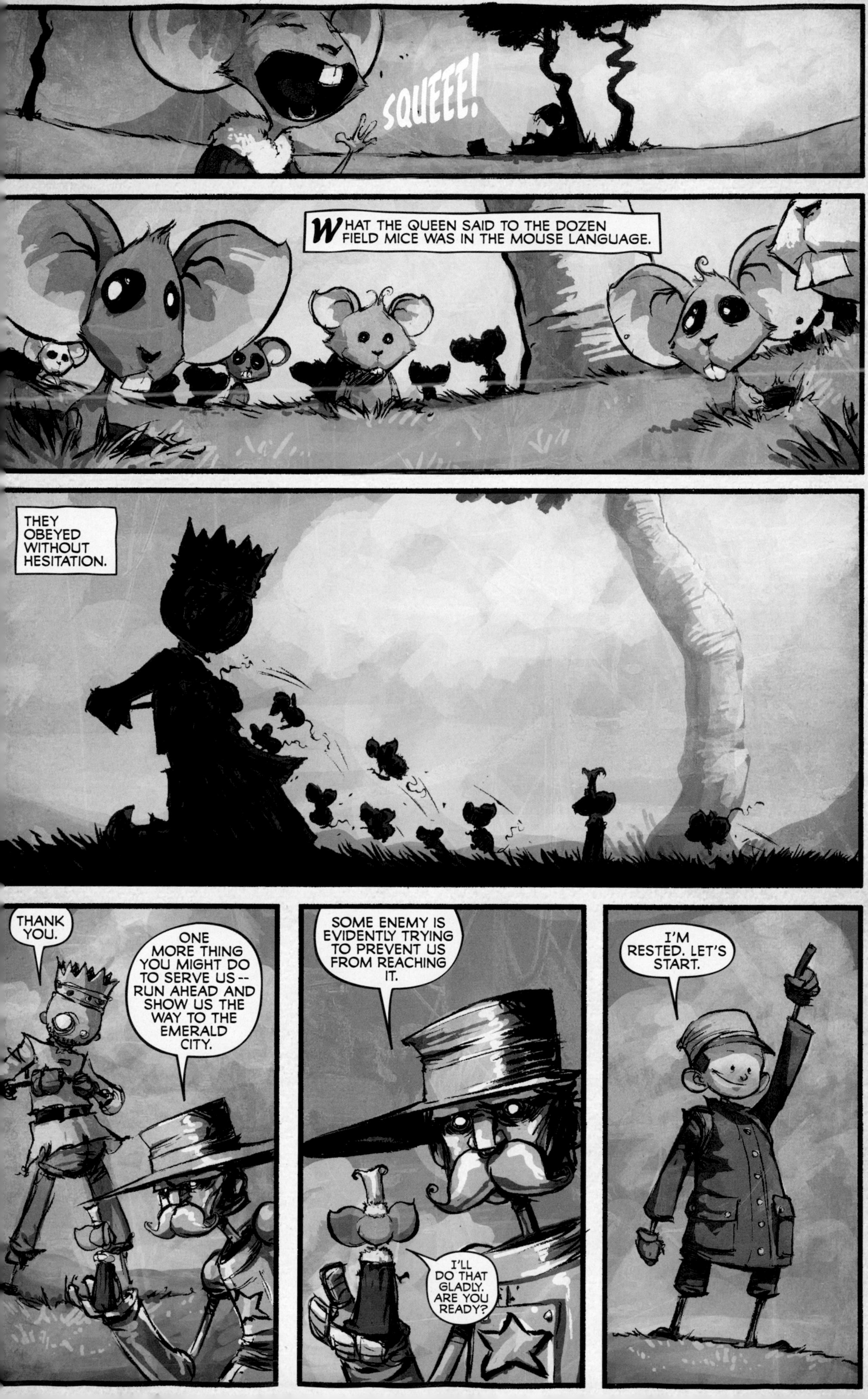
SQUEEEE!
WHAT THE QUEEN SAID TO THE DOZEN FIELD MICE WAS IN THE MOUSE LANGUAGE.
THEY OBEYED WITHOUT HESITATION.
THANK YOU.
ONE MORE THING YOU MIGHT DO TO SERVE US -- RUN AHEAD AND SHOW US THE WAY TO THE EMERALD CITY.
SOME ENEMY IS EVIDENTLY TRYING TO PREVENT US FROM REACHING IT.
I'LL DO THAT GLADLY. ARE YOU READY?
I'M RESTED. LET'S START.

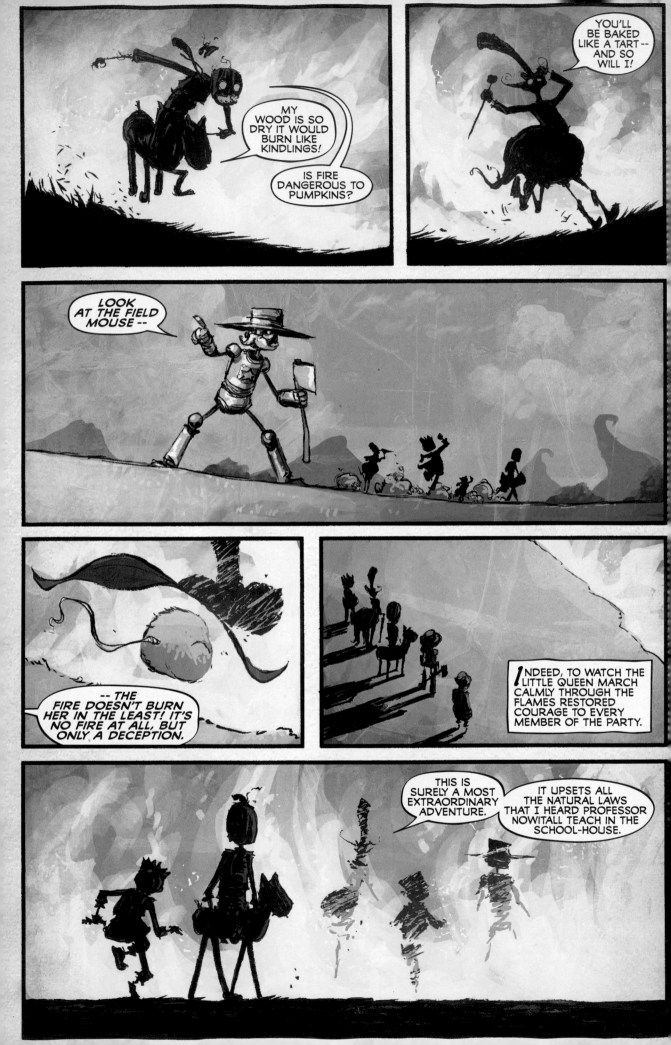

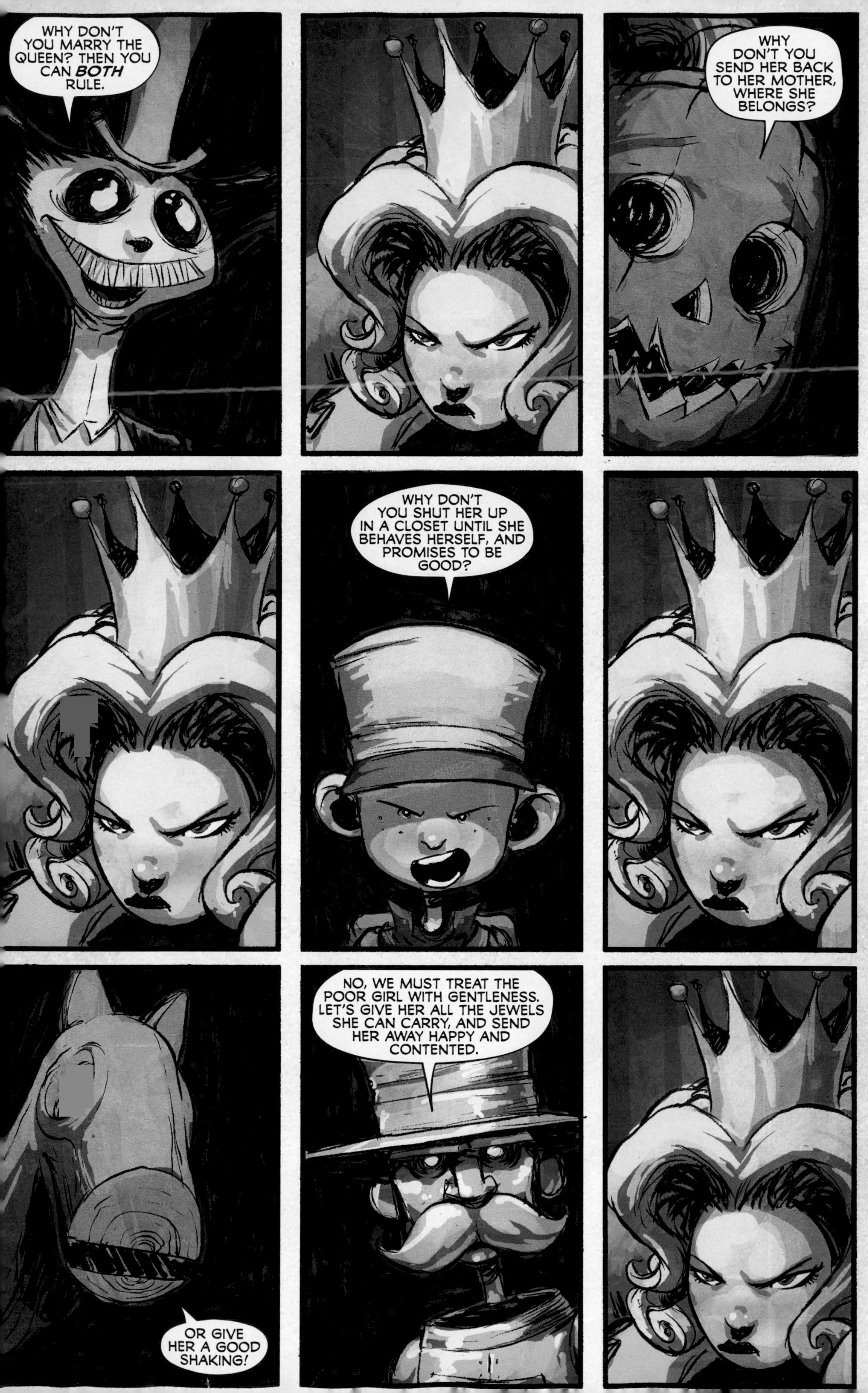
WHY DON'T YOU MARRY THE QUEEN? THEN YOU CAN *BOTH* RULE.
WHY DON'T YOU SEND HER BACK TO HER MOTHER, WHERE SHE BELONGS?
WHY DON'T YOU SHUT HER UP IN A CLOSET UNTIL SHE BEHAVES HERSELF, AND PROMISES TO BE GOOD?
OR GIVE HER A GOOD SHAKING!
NO, WE MUST TREAT THE POOR GIRL WITH GENTLENESS. LET'S GIVE HER ALL THE JEWELS SHE CAN CARRY, AND SEND HER AWAY HAPPY AND CONTENTED.

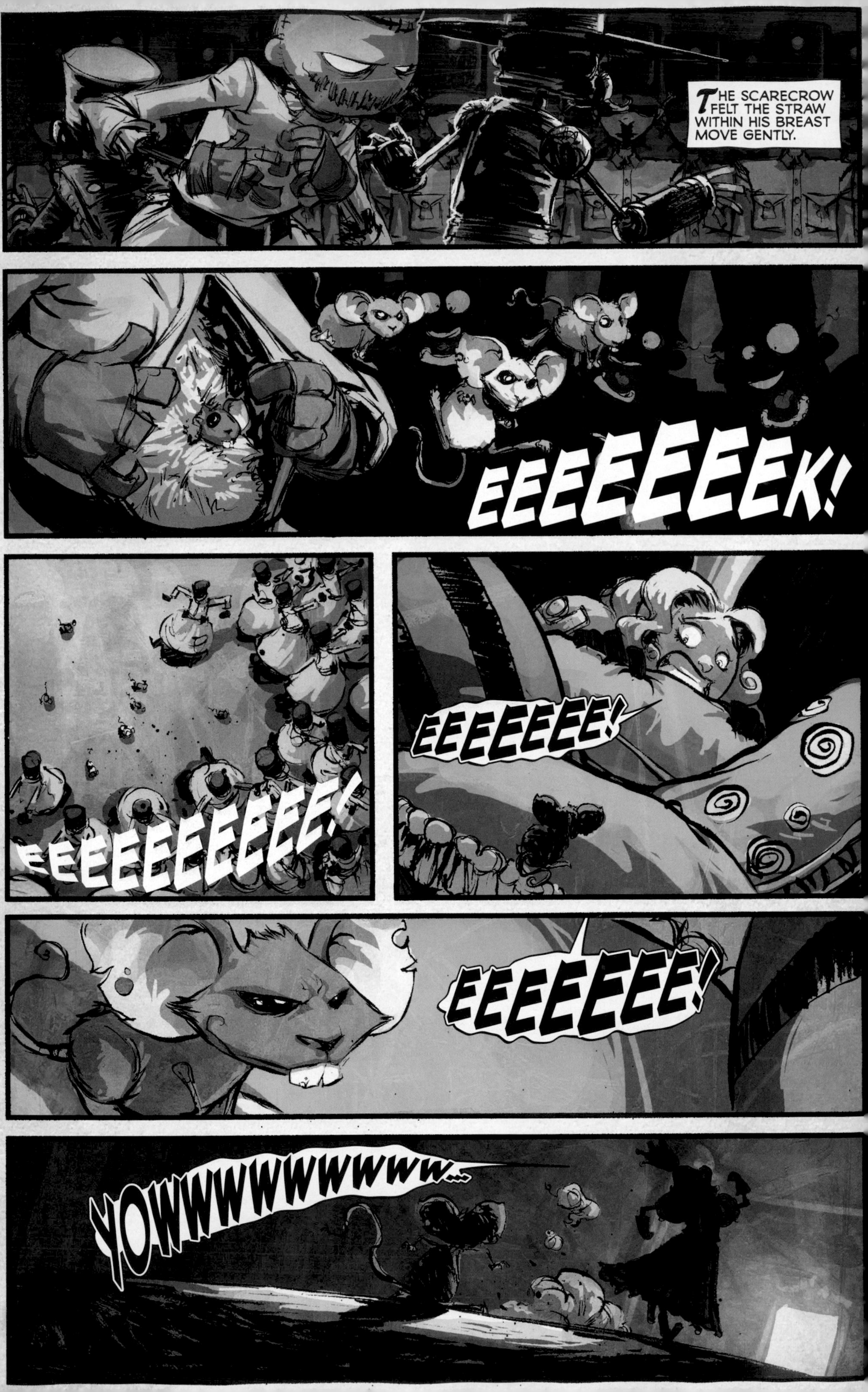
THE SCARECROW FELT THE STRAW WITHIN HIS BREAST MOVE GENTLY.
EEEEEEEEK!
EEEEEEEEEEEE!
EEEEEEE!
EEEEEEE!
YOWWWWWWWWW...

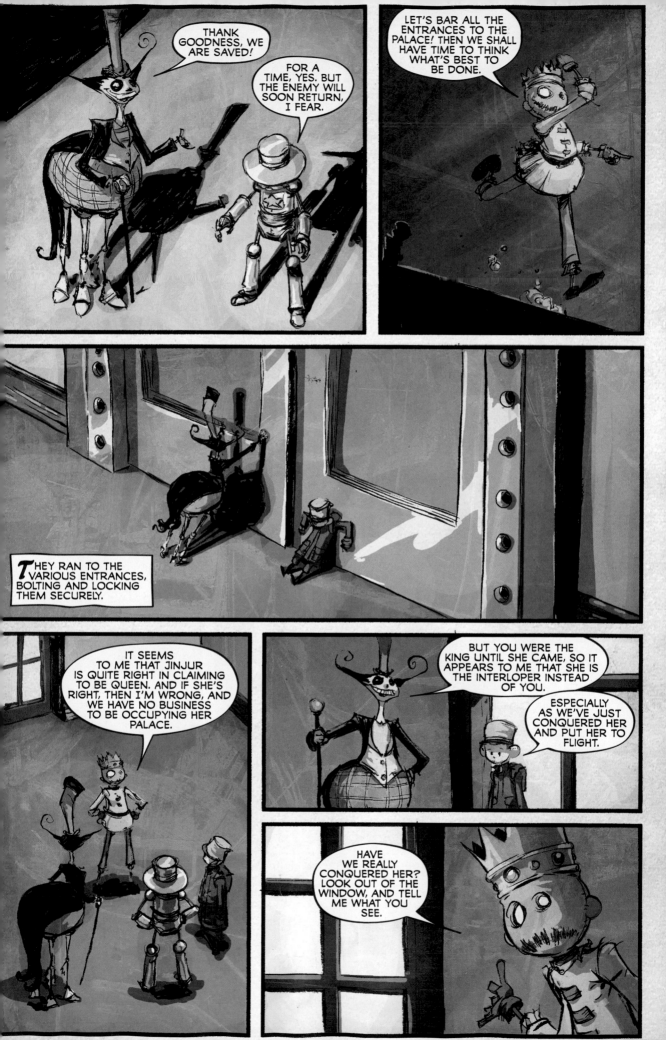

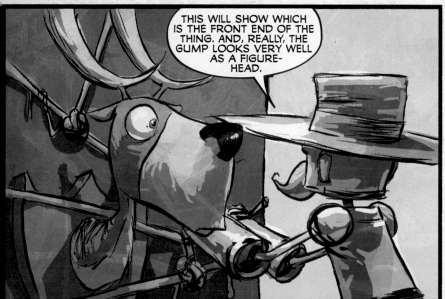

THEY'RE AS STRONG AS ANYTHING WE CAN GET. ALTHOUGH THEY'RE NOT IN PROPORTION TO THE THING'S BODY, WE'RE NOT IN A POSITION TO BE VERY PARTICULAR.

THE THING IS NOW COMPLETE, AND ONLY NEEDS TO BE BROUGHT TO LIFE.

AREN'T YOU GOING TO USE MY BROOM?

WHAT FOR?

FOR A *TAIL!* SURELY YOU WOULDN'T CALL THE THING COMPLETE WITHOUT A TAIL!

HM! I DON'T SEE THE USE OF A TAIL. WE'RE NOT TRYING TO COPY A BEAST OR A FISH OR A BIRD. ALL WE ASK OF THE THING IS TO CARRY US THROUGH THE AIR.

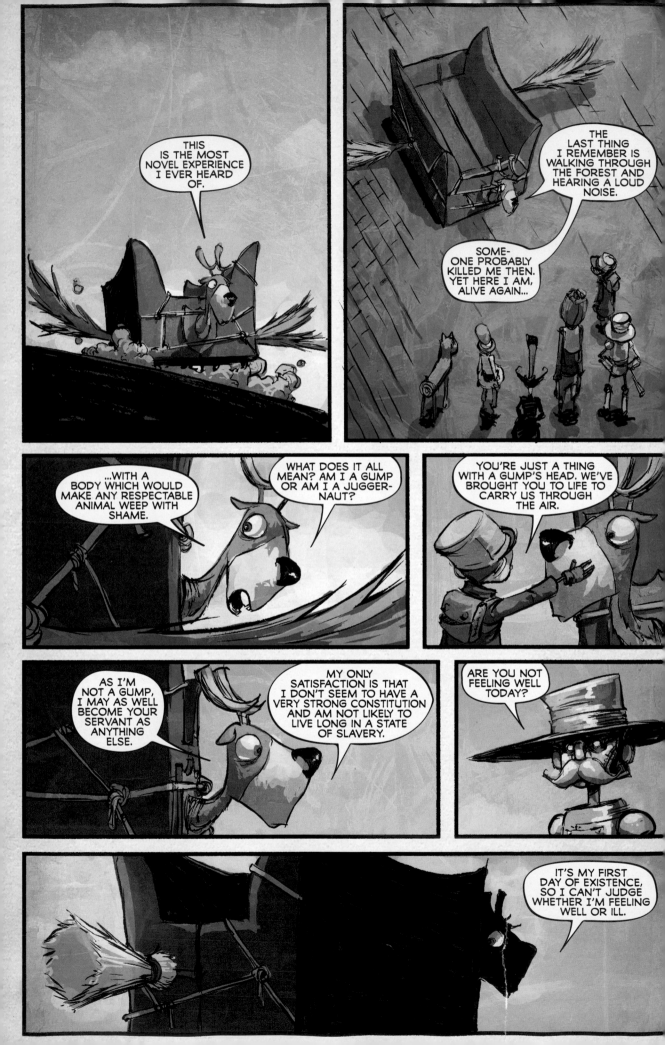

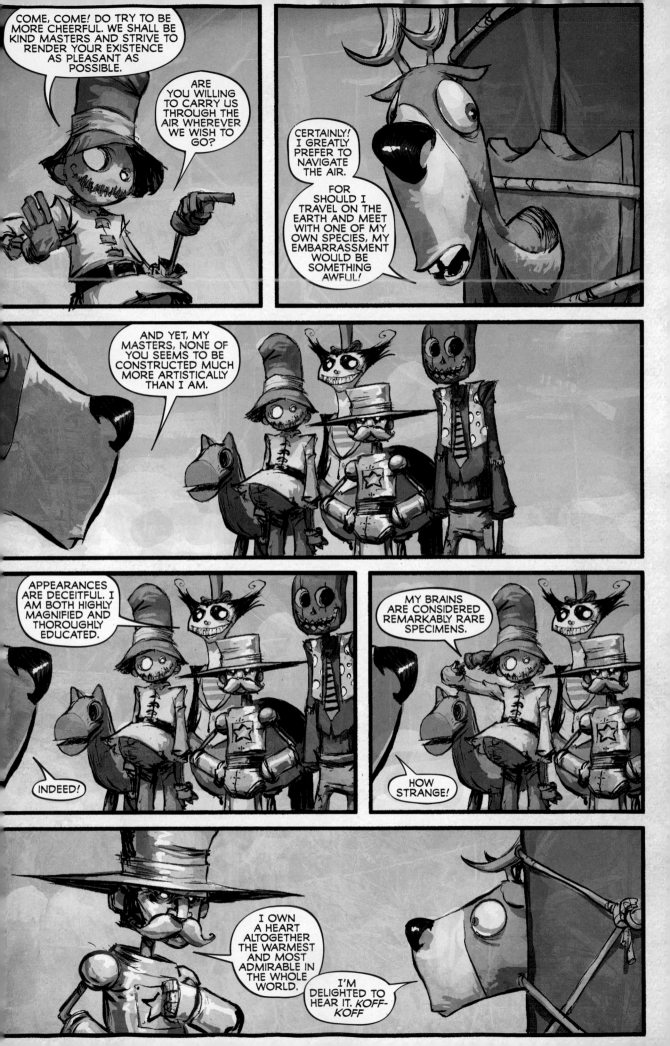

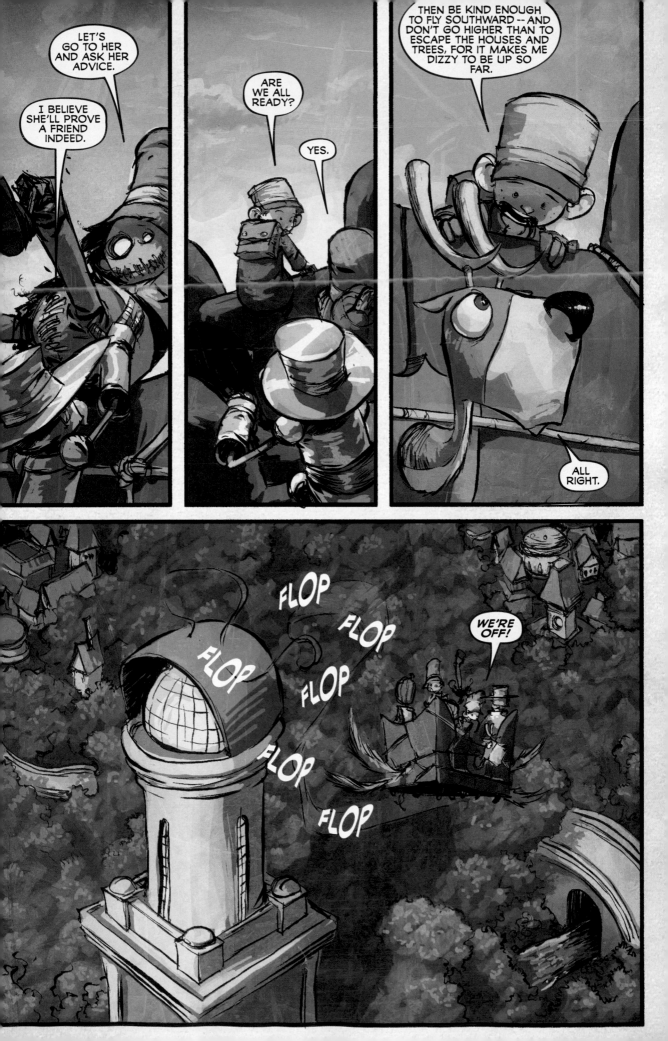

YES, THE THING CERTAINLY HAS A FALSE BOTTOM.

MY FINGERS ARE RATHER STIFF -- PLEASE SEE IF YOU CAN OPEN IT.

*T*IP HAD NO DIFFICULTY IN UNSCREWING THE BOTTOM.

"DR. NIKIDIK'S CELEBRATED WISHING PILLS.

"DIRECTIONS FOR USE: SWALLOW ONE PILL, COUNT SEVENTEEN BY TWOS, THEN MAKE A WISH. THE WISH WILL IMMEDIATELY BE GRANTED.

"CAUTION: KEEP IN A DRY AND DARK PLACE."

WHY, THIS IS A VERY VALUABLE DISCOVERY! THESE PILLS MAY BE OF GREAT USE.

I WONDER IF OLD MOMBI KNEW THEY WERE IN THE BOTTOM OF THE PEPPERBOX. I REMEMBER HEARING HER SAY SHE GOT THE POWDER OF LIFE FROM THIS SAME NIKIDIK.

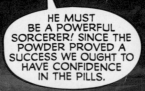

HE MUST BE A POWERFUL SORCERER! SINCE THE POWDER PROVED A SUCCESS WE OUGHT TO HAVE CONFIDENCE IN THE PILLS.

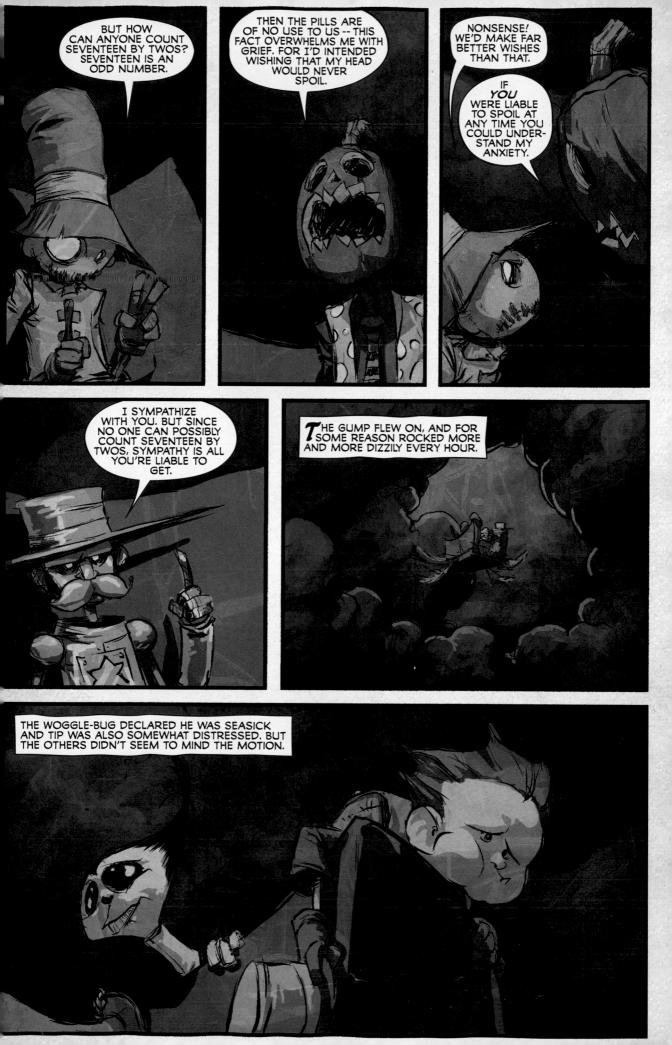

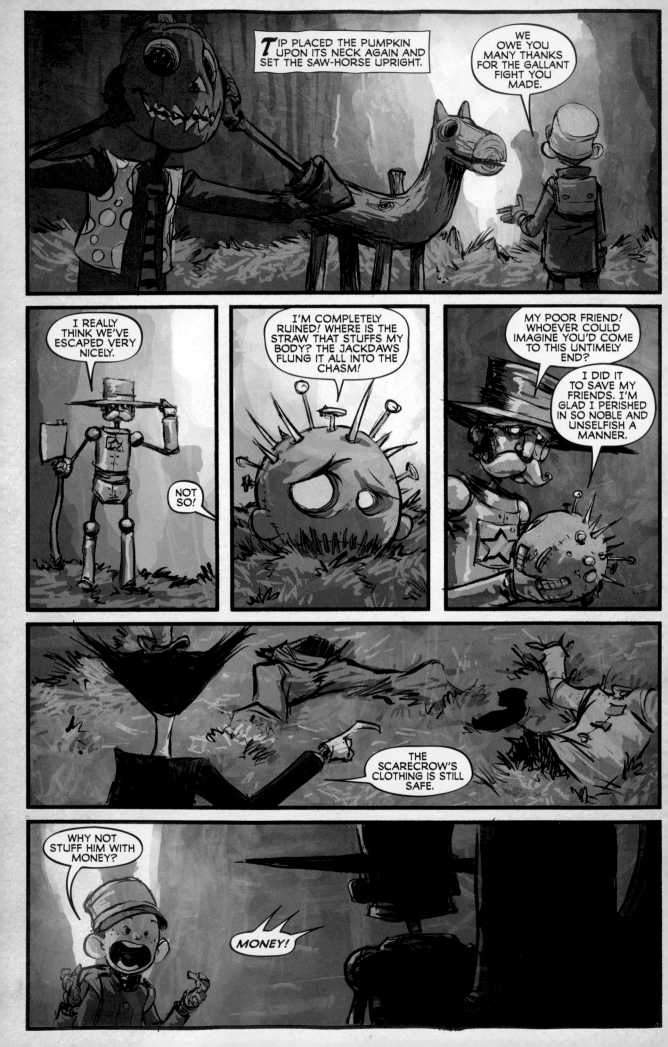

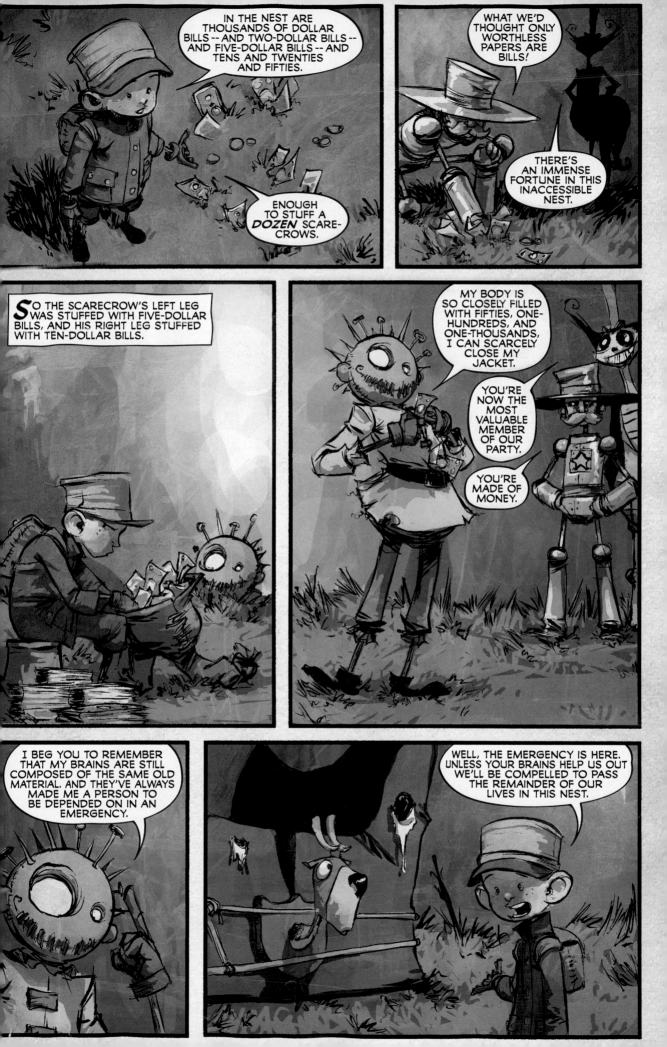

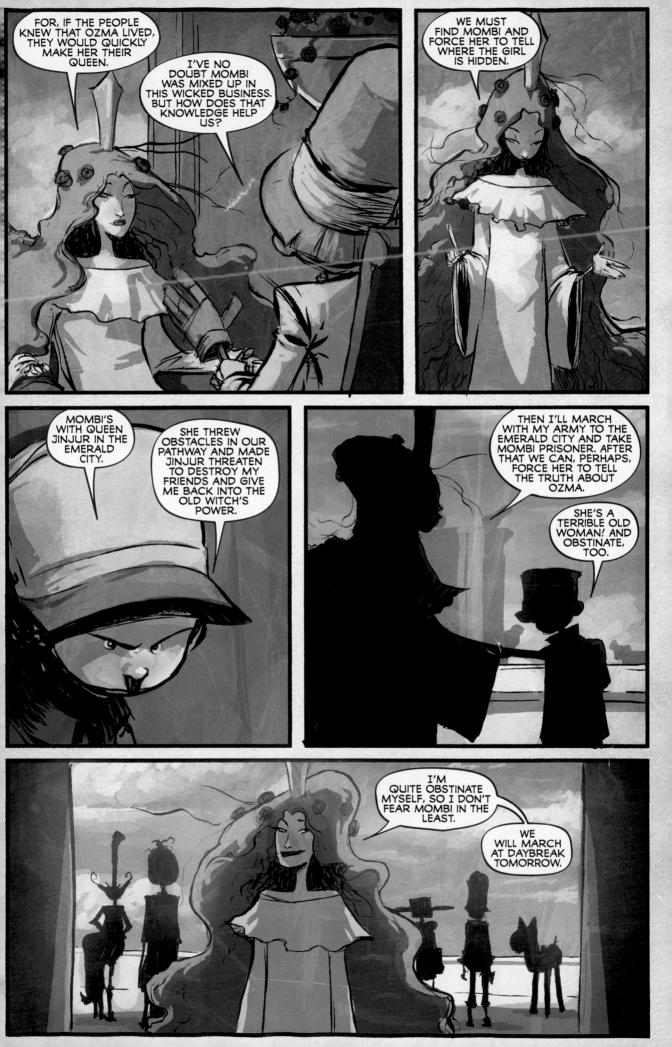

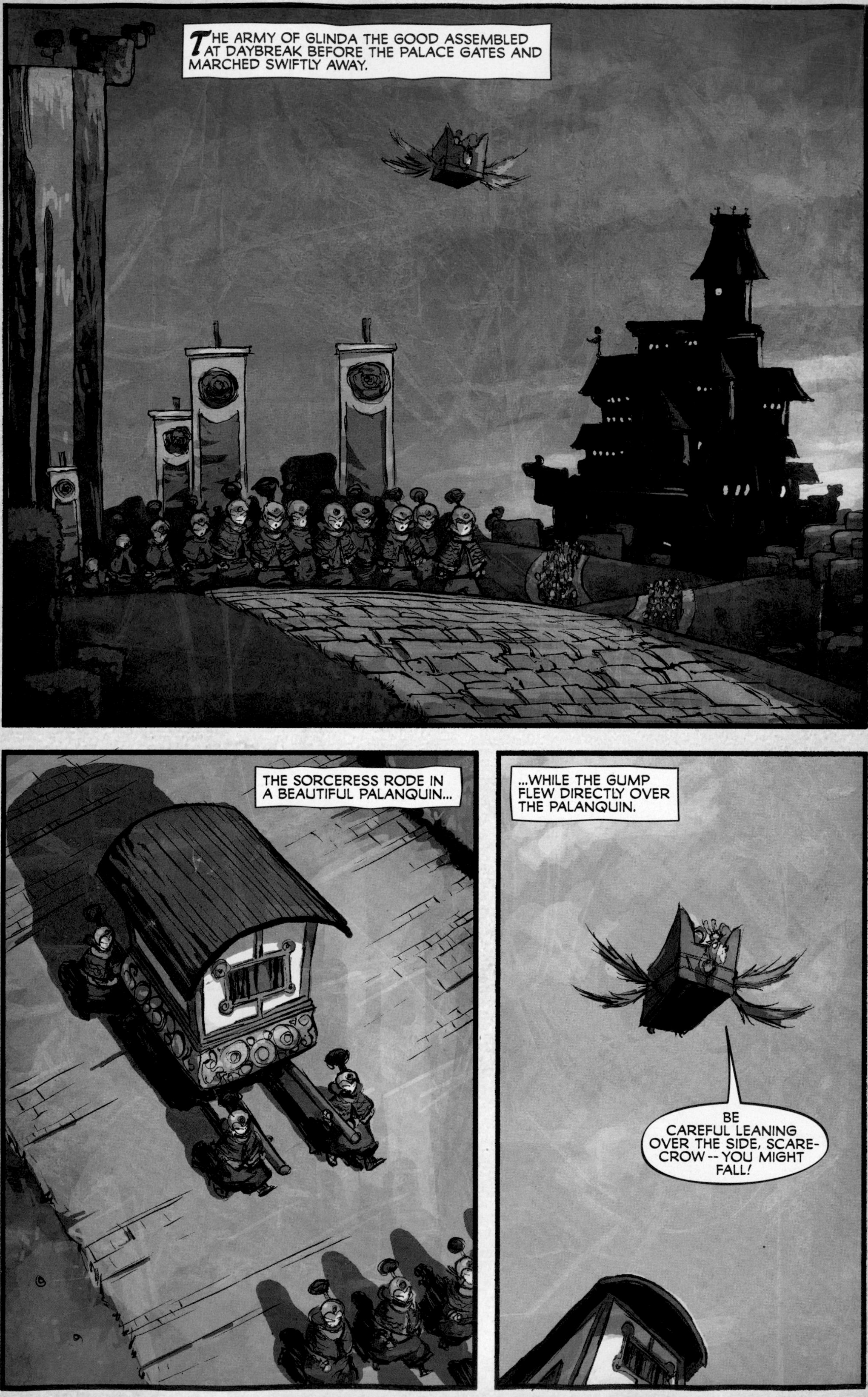
THE ARMY OF GLINDA THE GOOD ASSEMBLED AT DAYBREAK BEFORE THE PALACE GATES AND MARCHED SWIFTLY AWAY.
THE SORCERESS RODE IN A BEAUTIFUL PALANQUIN...
...WHILE THE GUMP FLEW DIRECTLY OVER THE PALANQUIN.
BE CAREFUL LEANING OVER THE SIDE, SCARE-CROW -- YOU MIGHT FALL!

NIGHT HAD FALLEN BEFORE THEY CAME TO THE WALLS OF THE EMERALD CITY.

NEXT MORNING.

WE ARE LOST!

HOW CAN OUR KNITTING-NEEDLES AVAIL AGAINST LONG SPEARS AND TERRIBLE SWORDS?

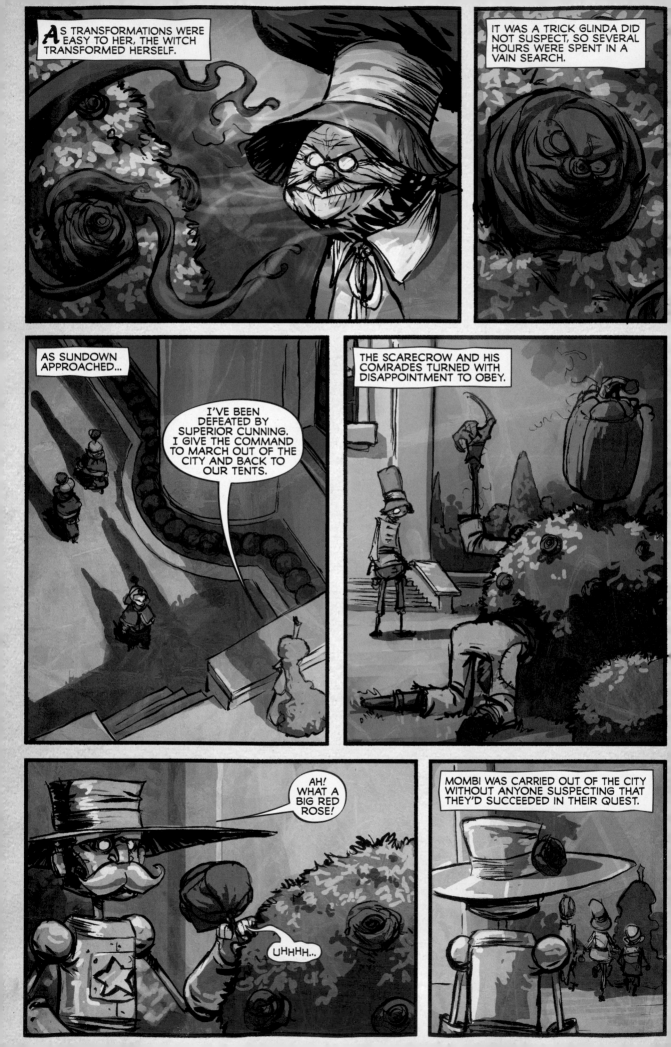

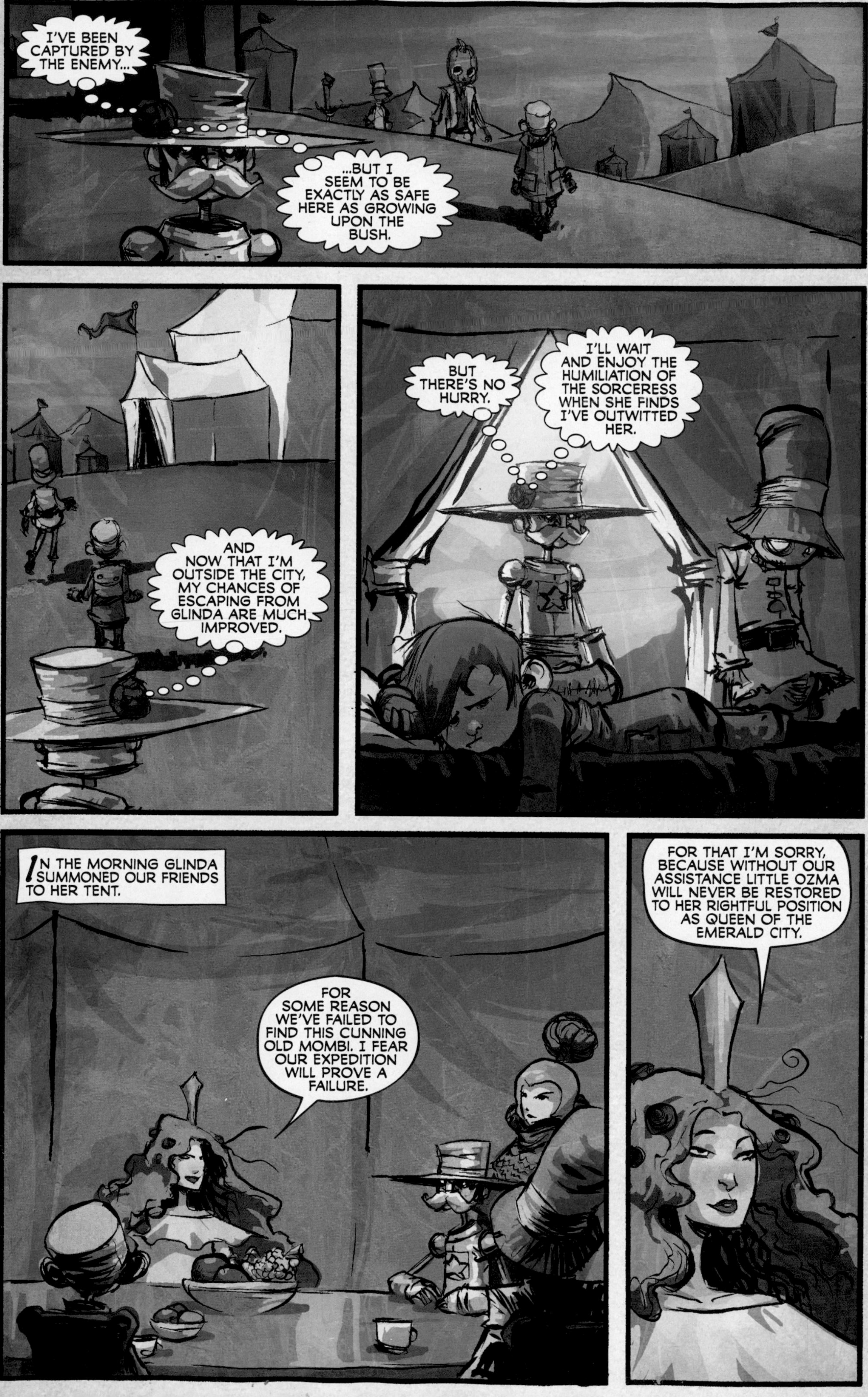
I'VE BEEN CAPTURED BY THE ENEMY...
...BUT I SEEM TO BE EXACTLY AS SAFE HERE AS GROWING UPON THE BUSH.
AND NOW THAT I'M OUTSIDE THE CITY, MY CHANCES OF ESCAPING FROM GLINDA ARE MUCH IMPROVED.
BUT THERE'S NO HURRY.
I'LL WAIT AND ENJOY THE HUMILIATION OF THE SORCERESS WHEN SHE FINDS I'VE OUTWITTED HER.
IN THE MORNING GLINDA SUMMONED OUR FRIENDS TO HER TENT.
FOR SOME REASON WE'VE FAILED TO FIND THIS CUNNING OLD MOMBI. I FEAR OUR EXPEDITION WILL PROVE A FAILURE.
FOR THAT I'M SORRY, BECAUSE WITHOUT OUR ASSISTANCE LITTLE OZMA WILL NEVER BE RESTORED TO HER RIGHTFUL POSITION AS QUEEN OF THE EMERALD CITY.

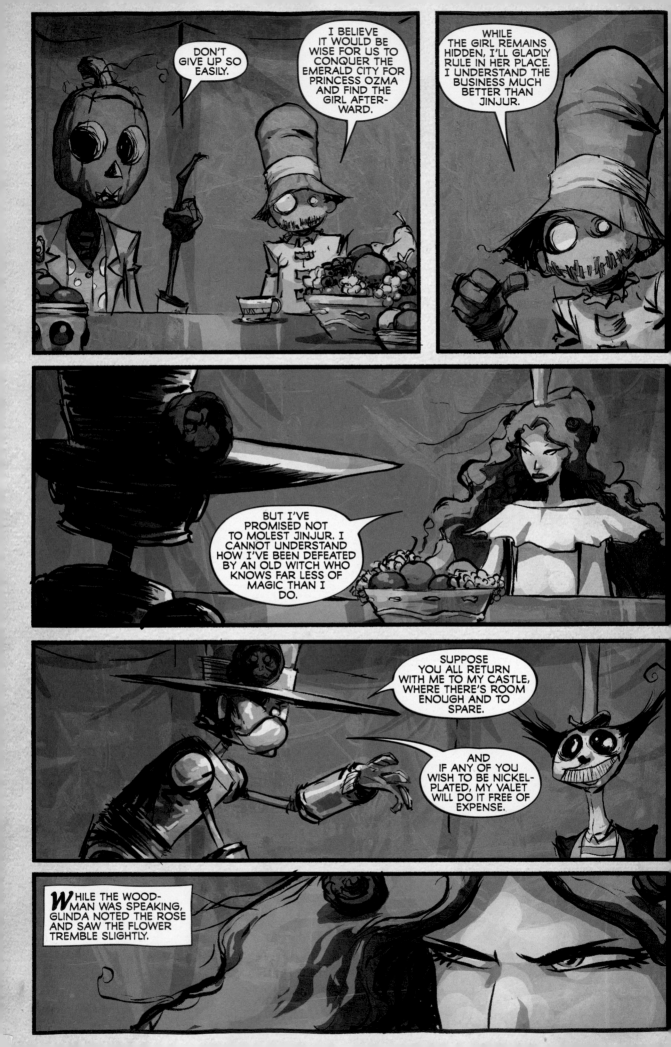

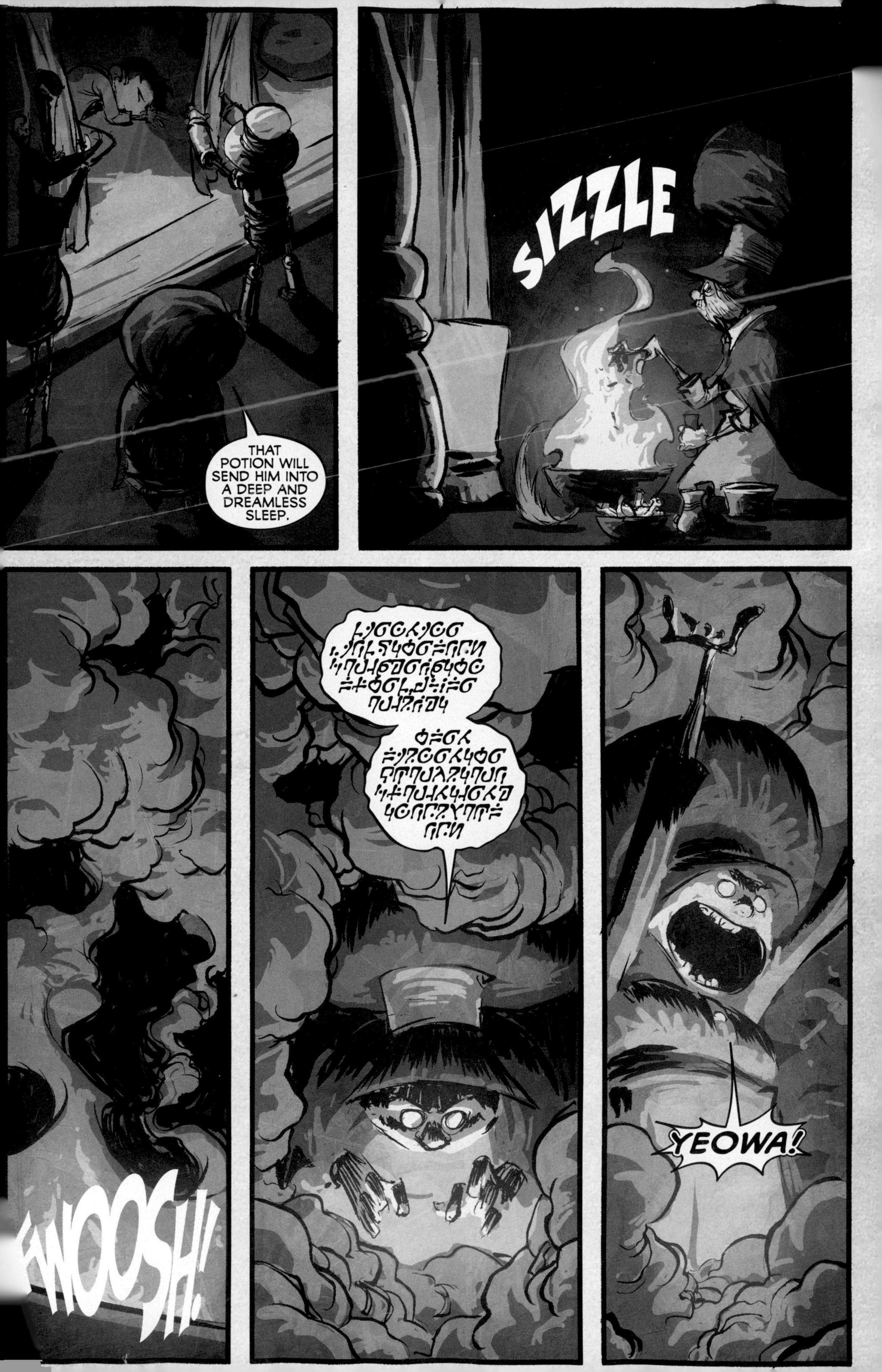
THAT POTION WILL SEND HIM INTO A DEEP AND DREAMLESS SLEEP.
SIZZLE
WOOSH!
YEOWA!

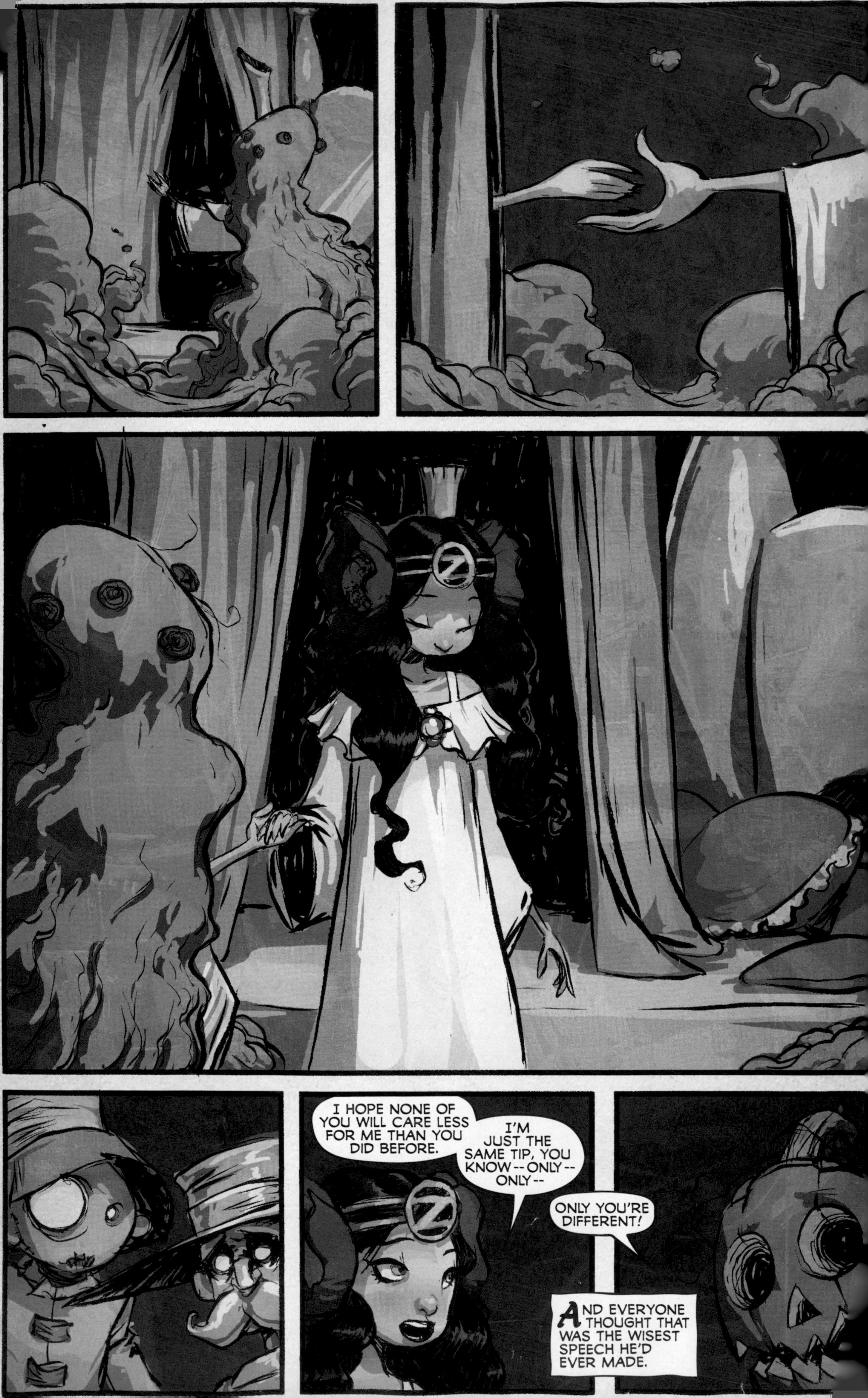
I HOPE NONE OF YOU WILL CARE LESS FOR ME THAN YOU DID BEFORE.
I'M JUST THE SAME TIP, YOU KNOW -- ONLY -- ONLY --
ONLY YOU'RE DIFFERENT!
AND EVERYONE THOUGHT THAT WAS THE WISEST SPEECH HE'D EVER MADE.

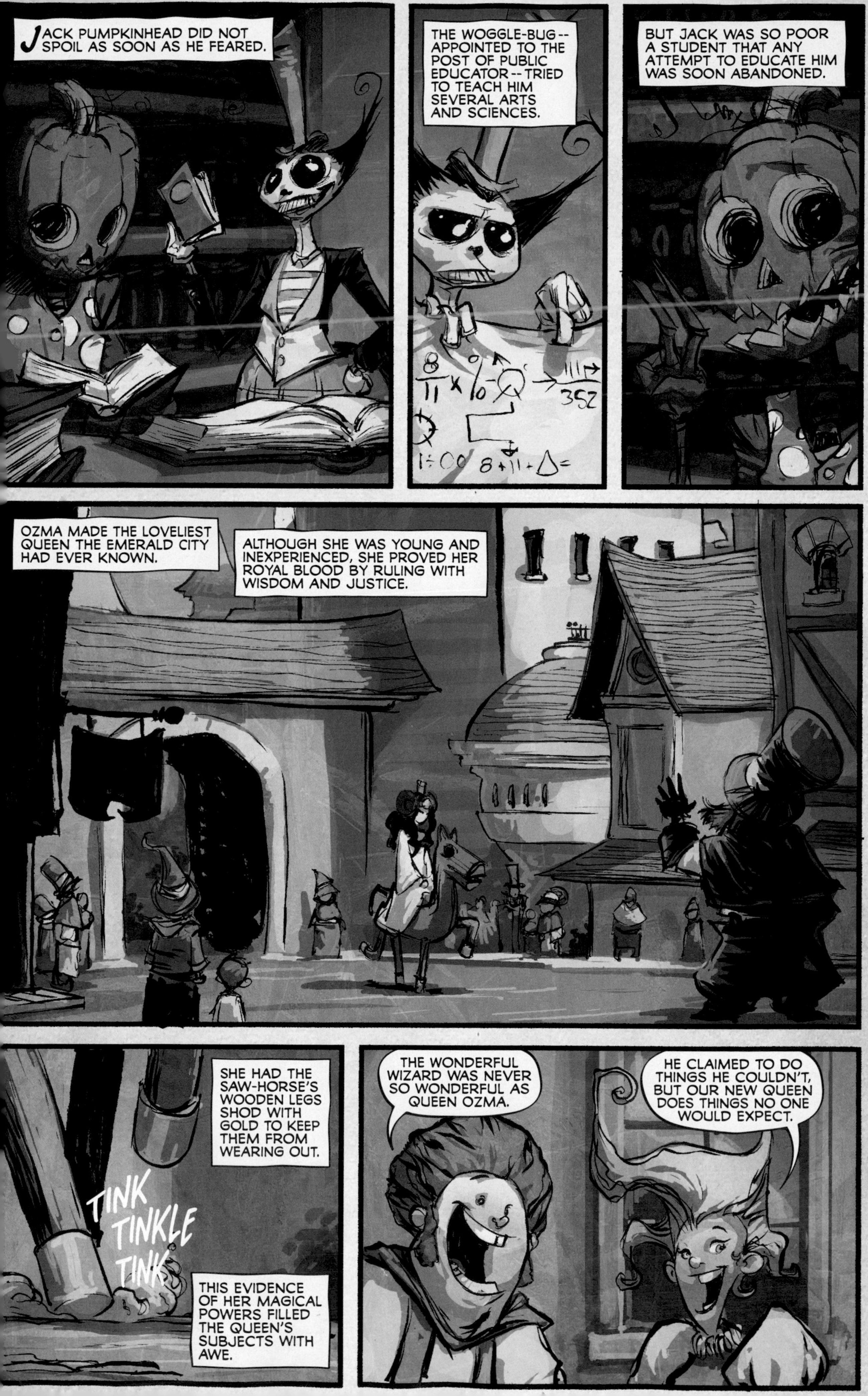

JACK PUMPKINHEAD DID NOT SPOIL AS SOON AS HE FEARED.
THE WOGGLE-BUG -- APPOINTED TO THE POST OF PUBLIC EDUCATOR -- TRIED TO TEACH HIM SEVERAL ARTS AND SCIENCES.
BUT JACK WAS SO POOR A STUDENT THAT ANY ATTEMPT TO EDUCATE HIM WAS SOON ABANDONED.
OZMA MADE THE LOVELIEST QUEEN THE EMERALD CITY HAD EVER KNOWN.
ALTHOUGH SHE WAS YOUNG AND INEXPERIENCED, SHE PROVED HER ROYAL BLOOD BY RULING WITH WISDOM AND JUSTICE.
SHE HAD THE SAW-HORSE'S WOODEN LEGS SHOD WITH GOLD TO KEEP THEM FROM WEARING OUT.
TINK
TINKLE
TINK
THIS EVIDENCE OF HER MAGICAL POWERS FILLED THE QUEEN'S SUBJECTS WITH AWE.
THE WONDERFUL WIZARD WAS NEVER SO WONDERFUL AS QUEEN OZMA.
HE CLAIMED TO DO THINGS HE COULDN'T, BUT OUR NEW QUEEN DOES THINGS NO ONE WOULD EXPECT.

THE STORY CONTINUES IN...

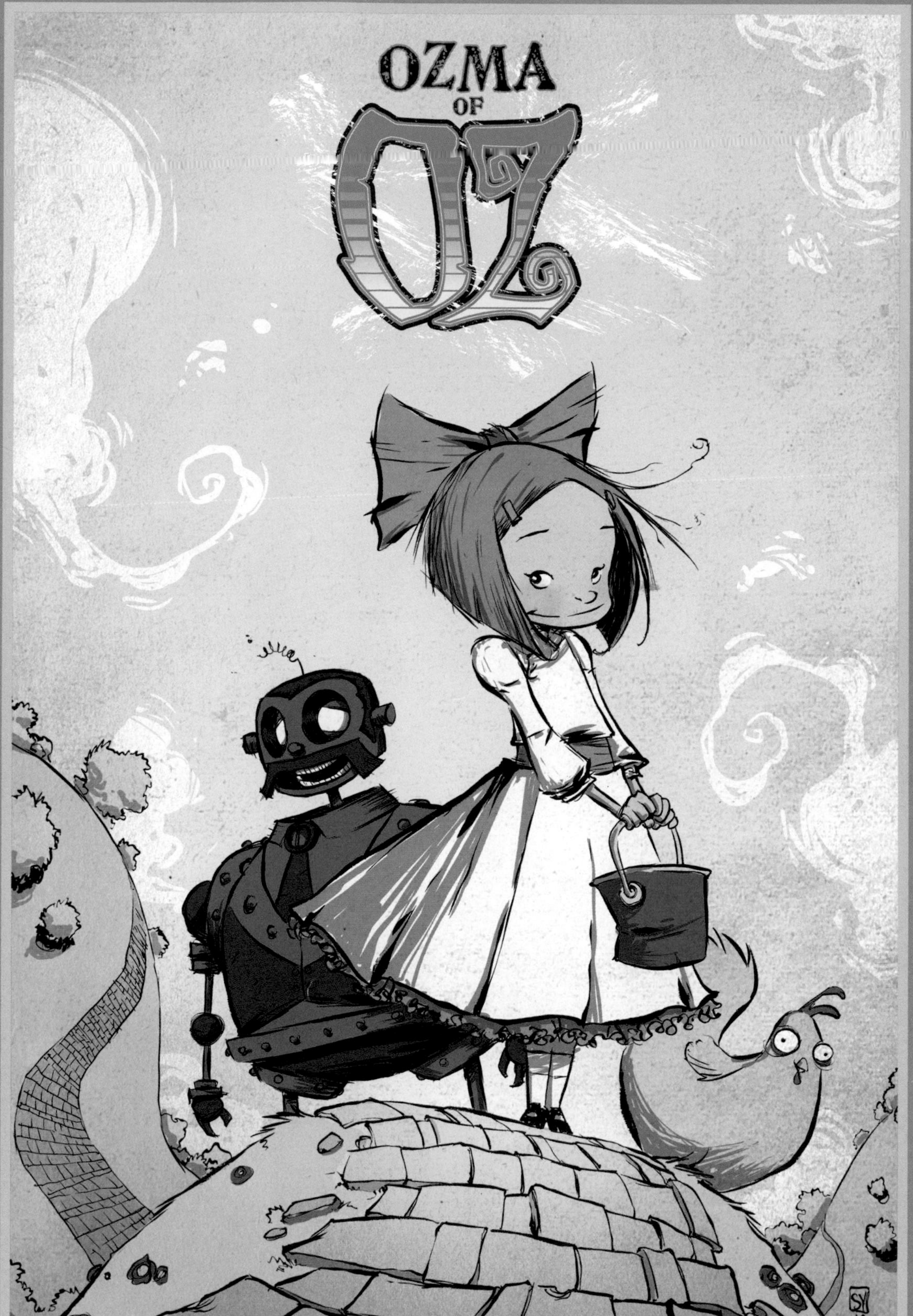
OZMA OF OZ
SY 10

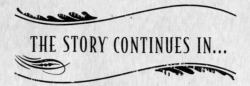

ONE

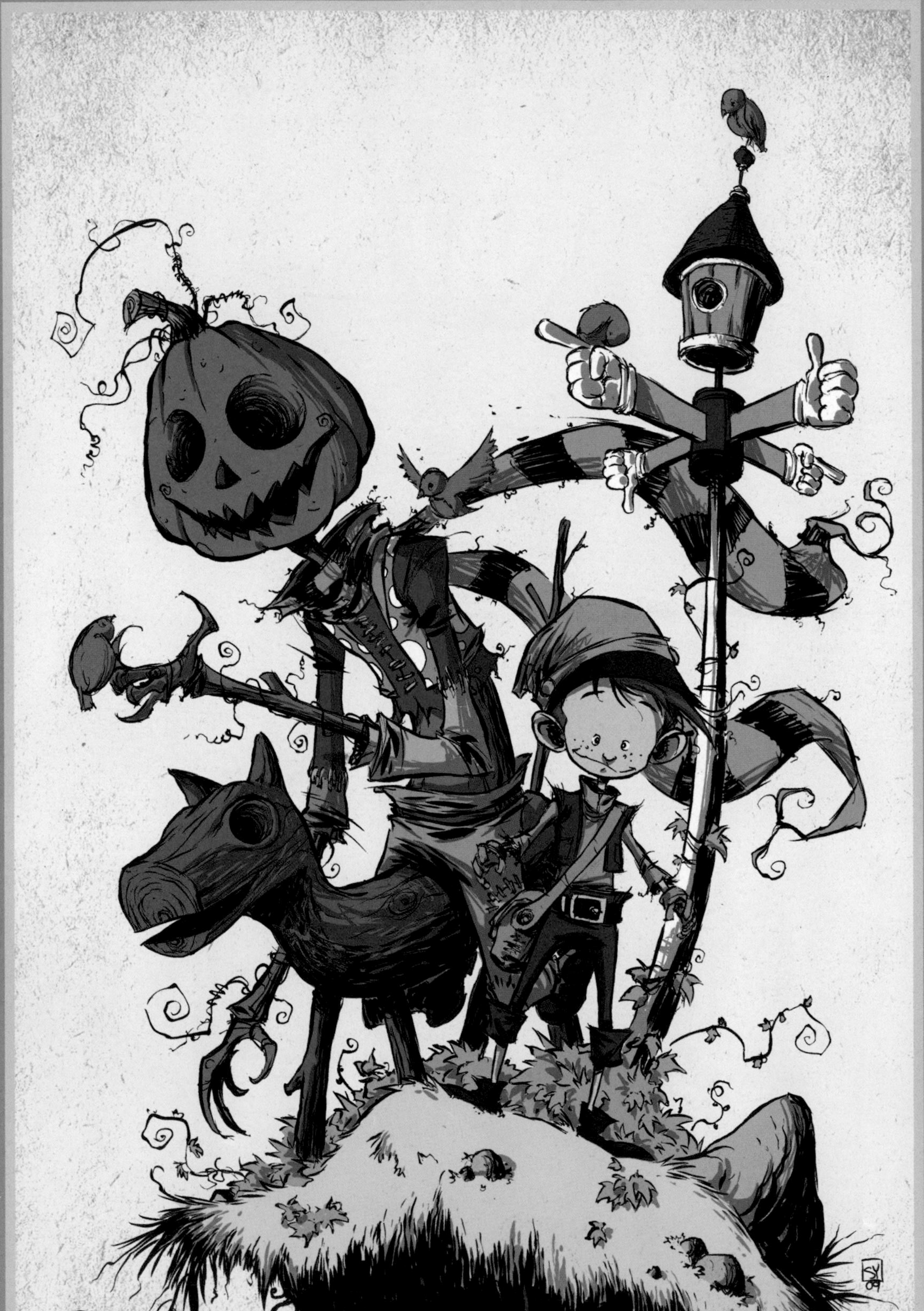

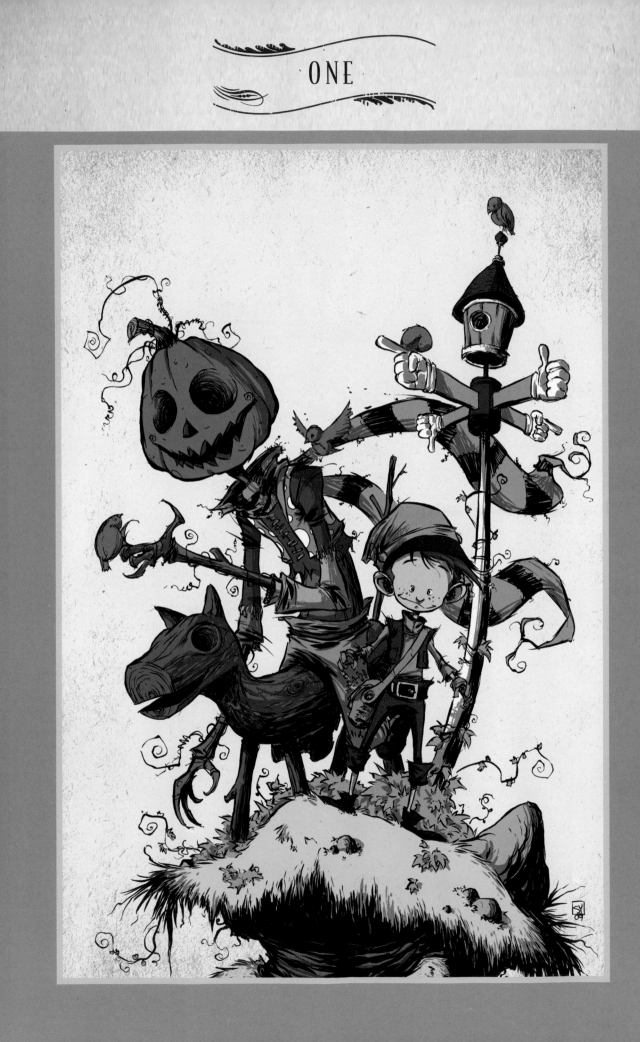

ONE

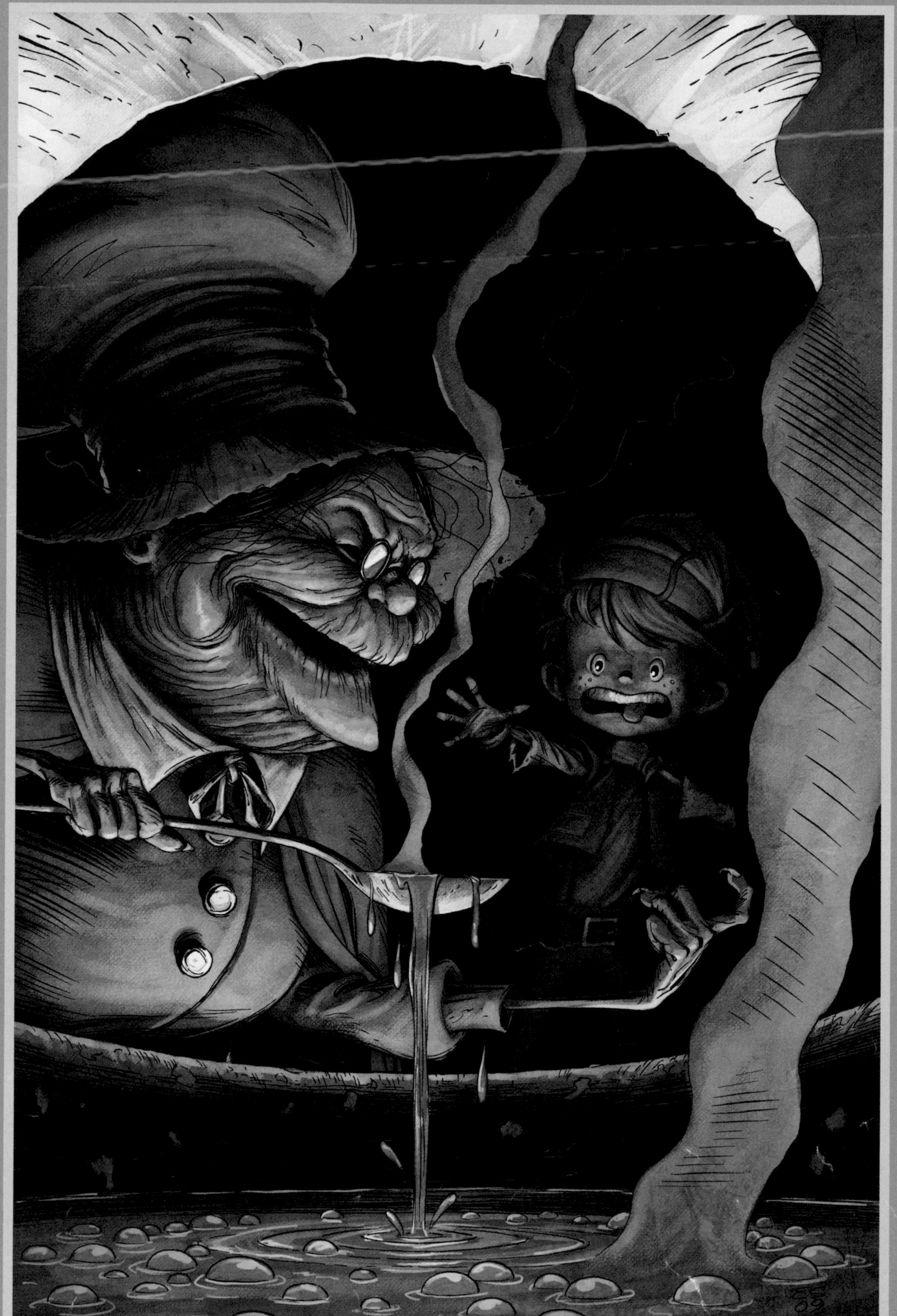

VARIANT COVER BY ERIC SHANOWER

ONE

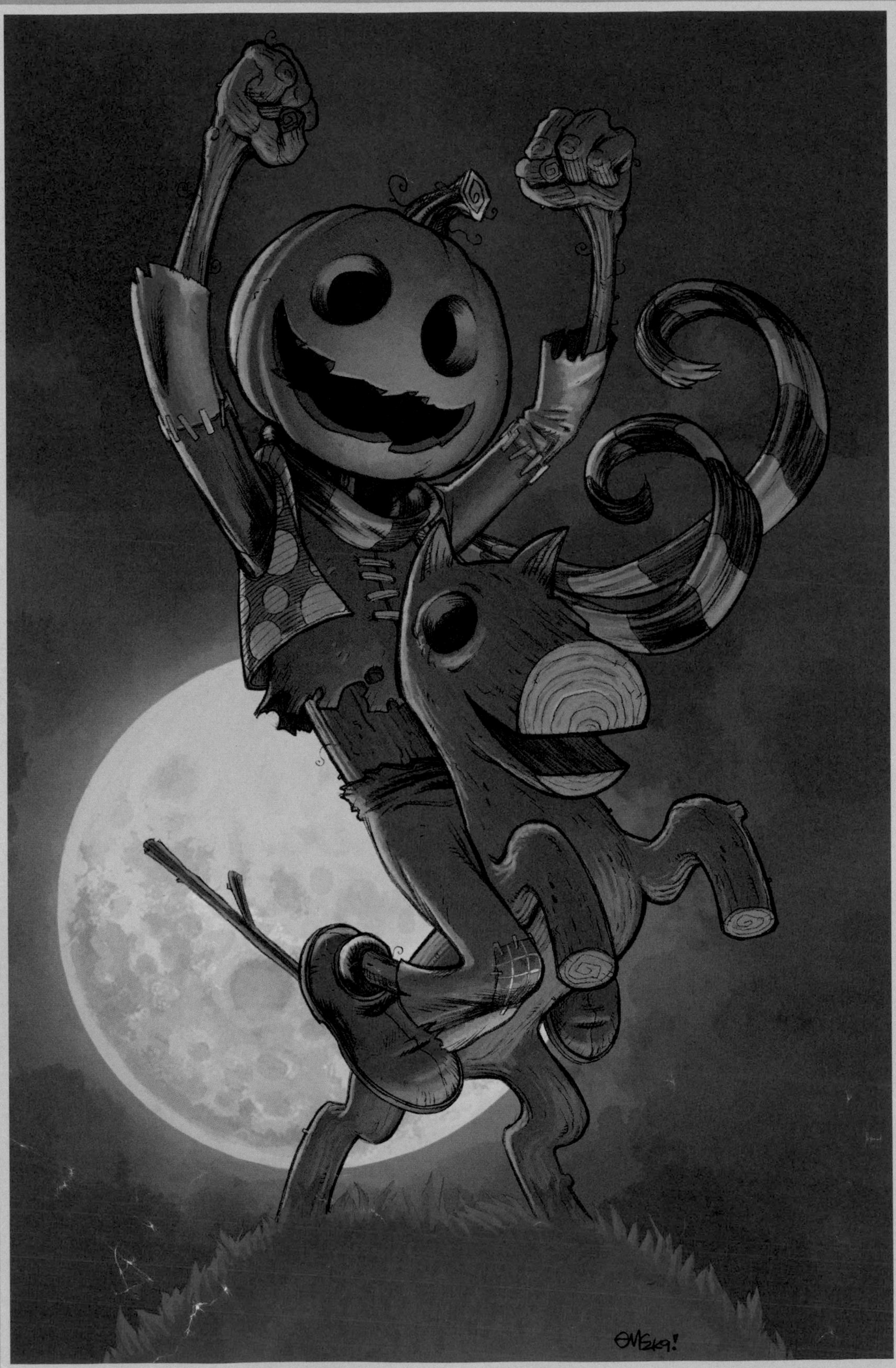

Variant Cover by Ed McGuinness

ONE

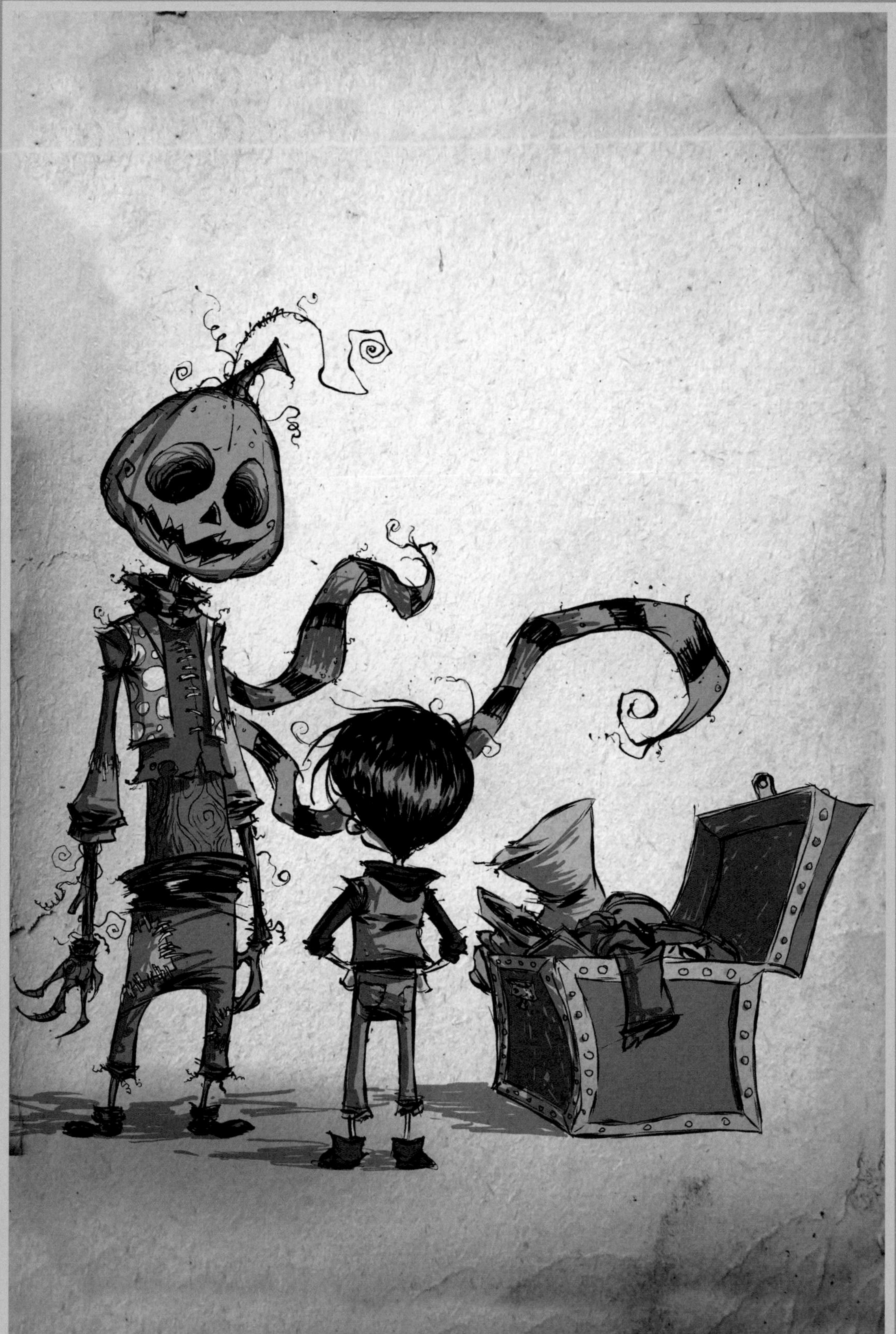

(2nd Printing) Variant Cover by Skottie Young

TWO

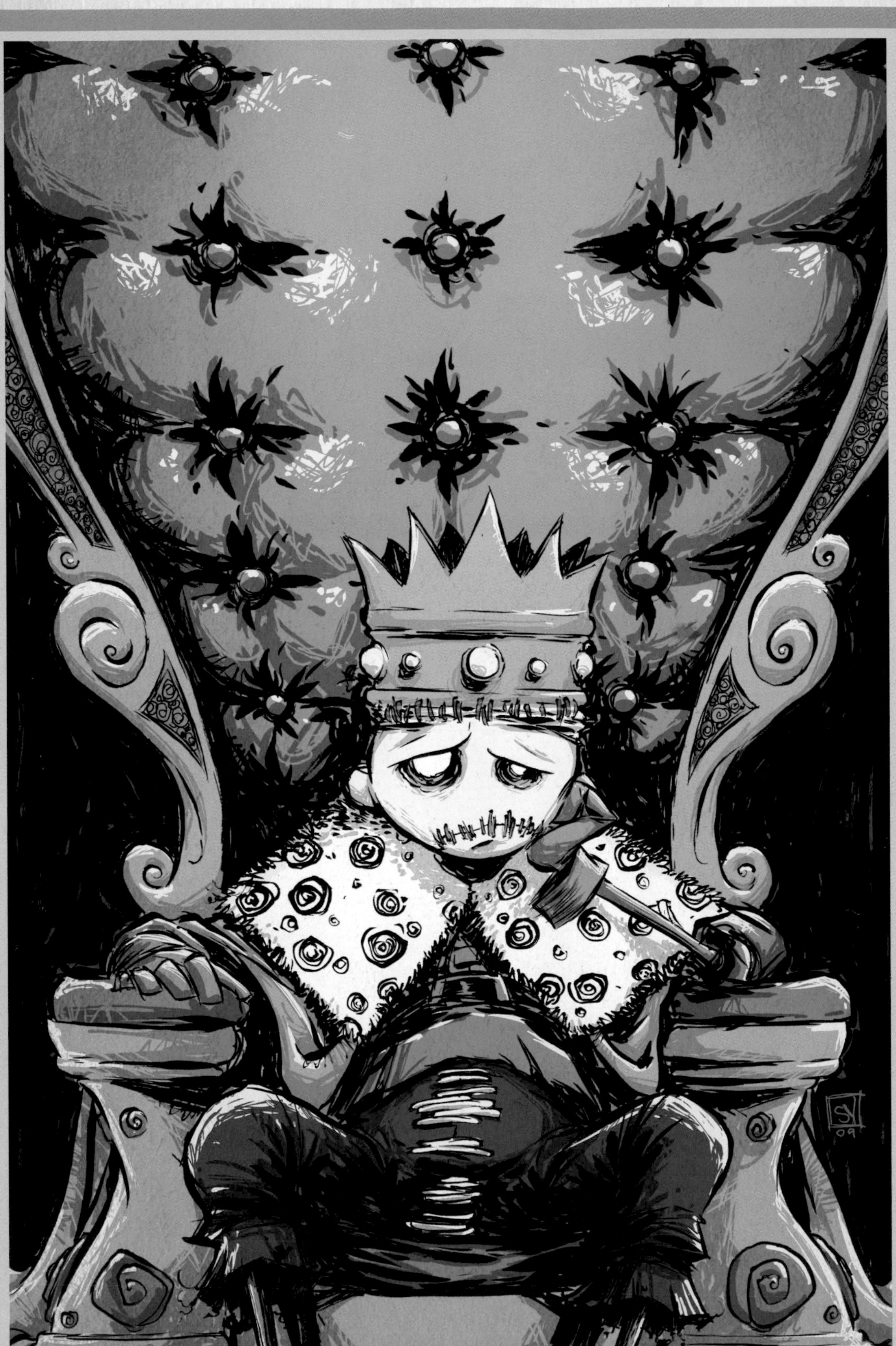

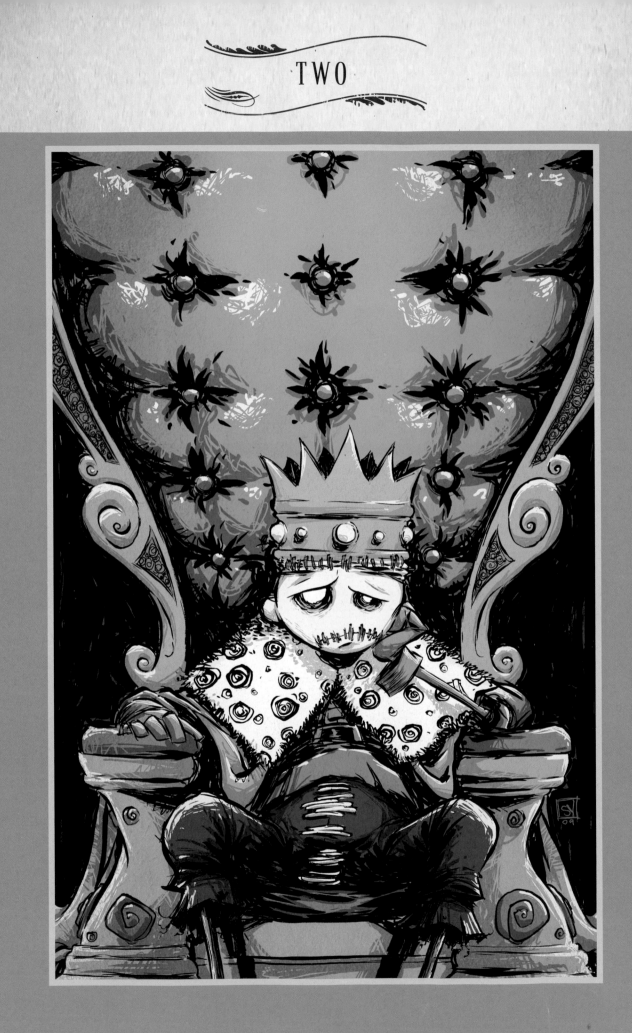

THREE

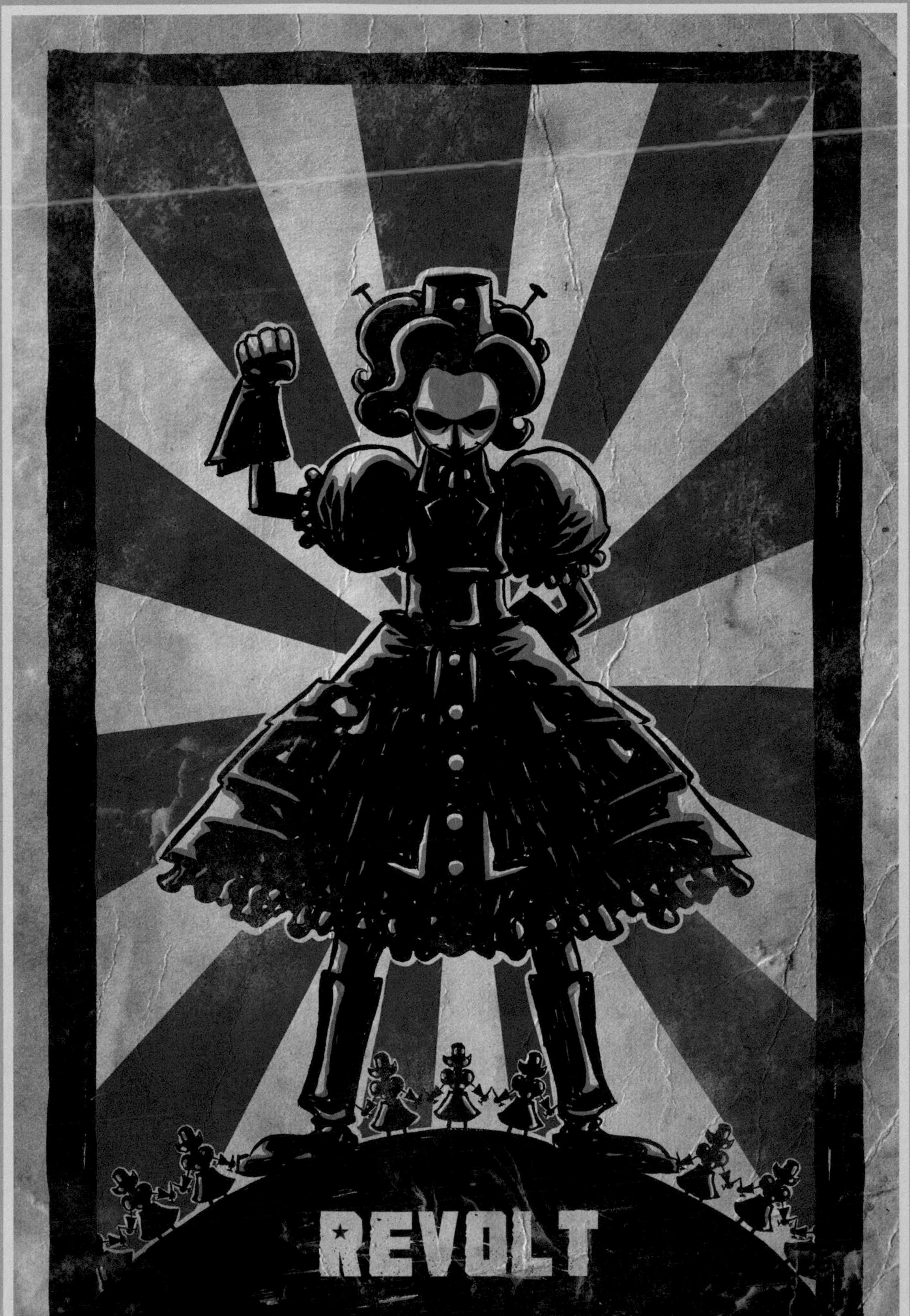
REVOLT

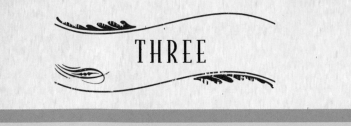

FOUR

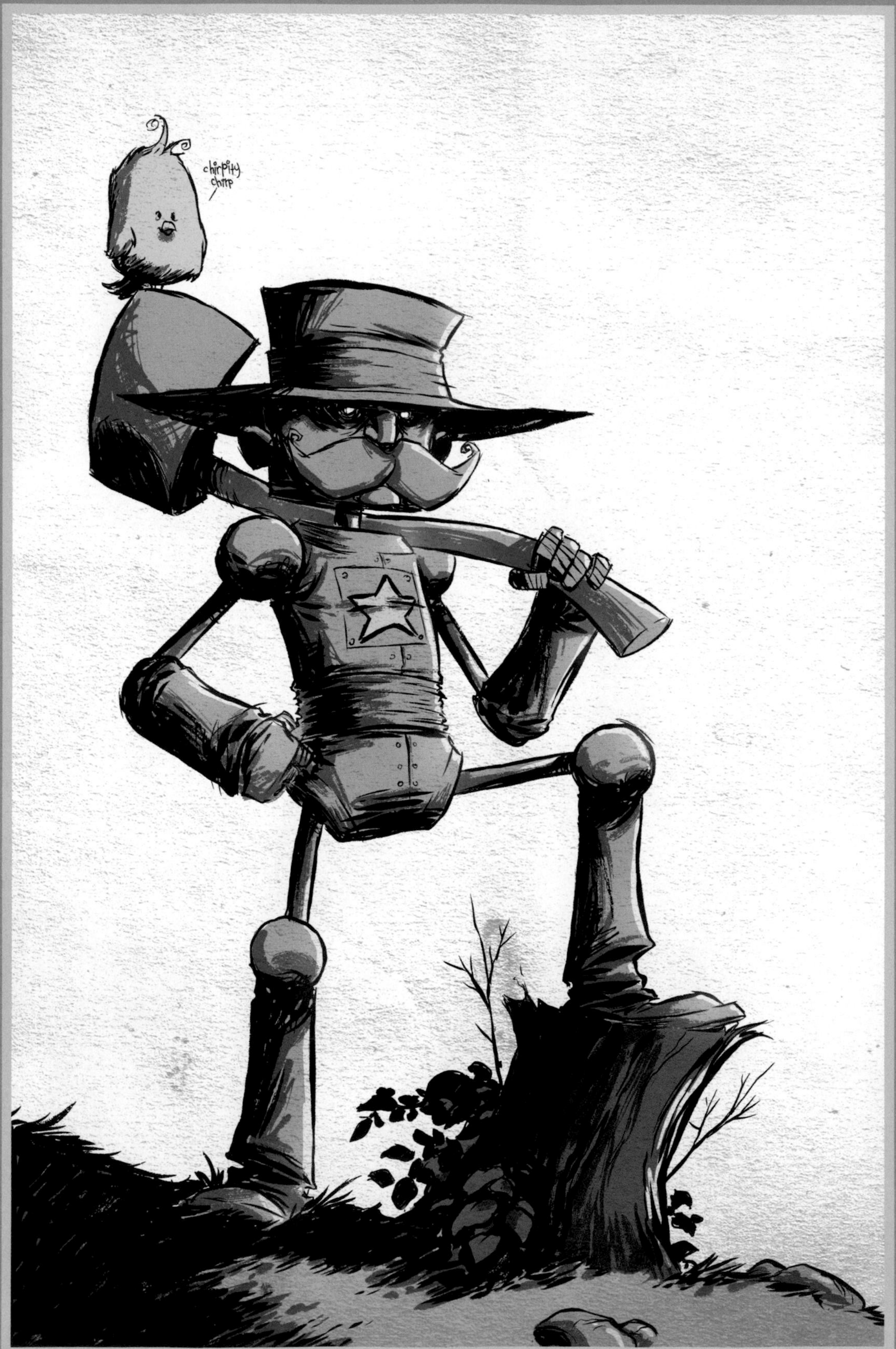
chirpity chirp

FIVE

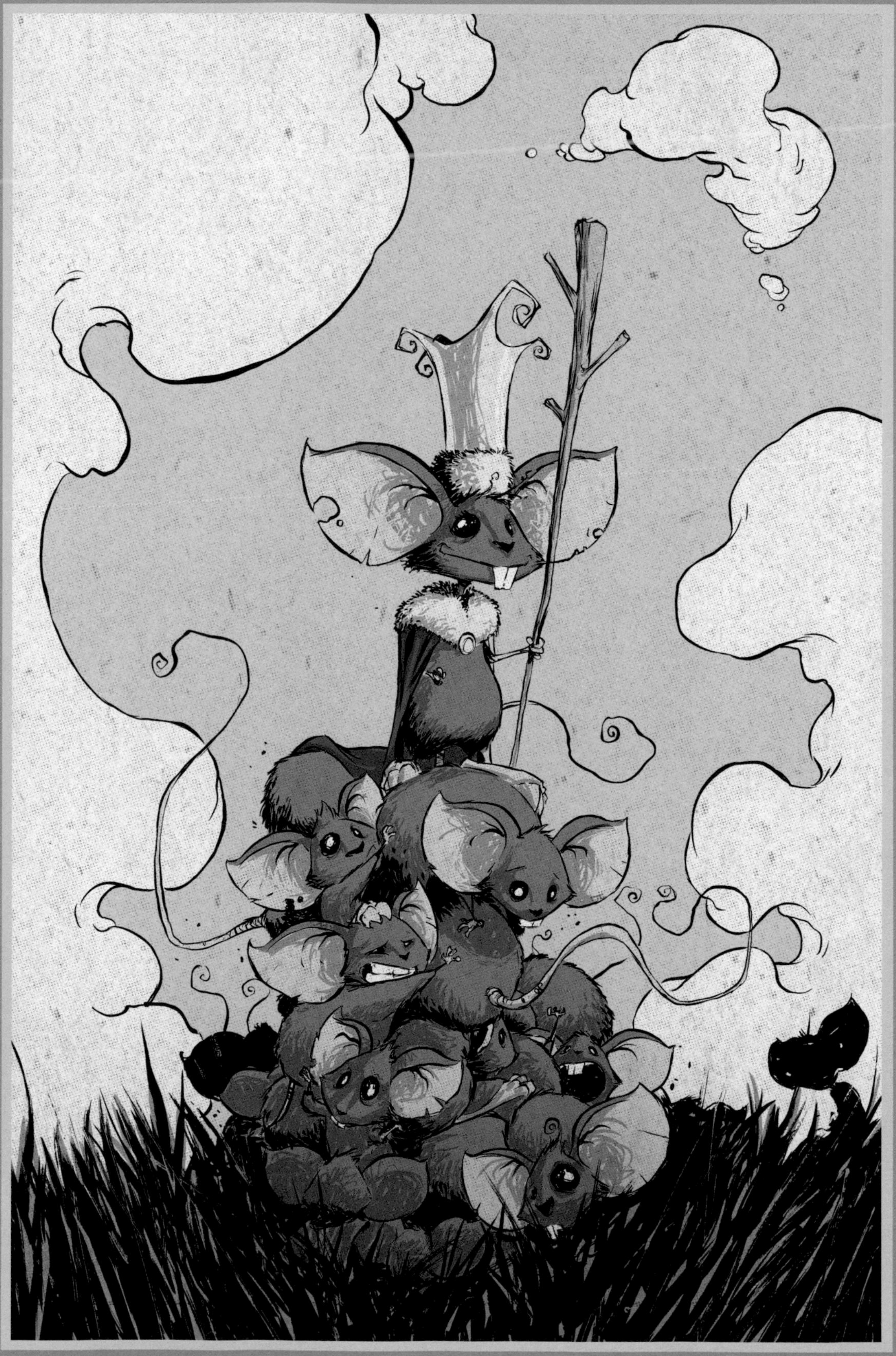

SIX

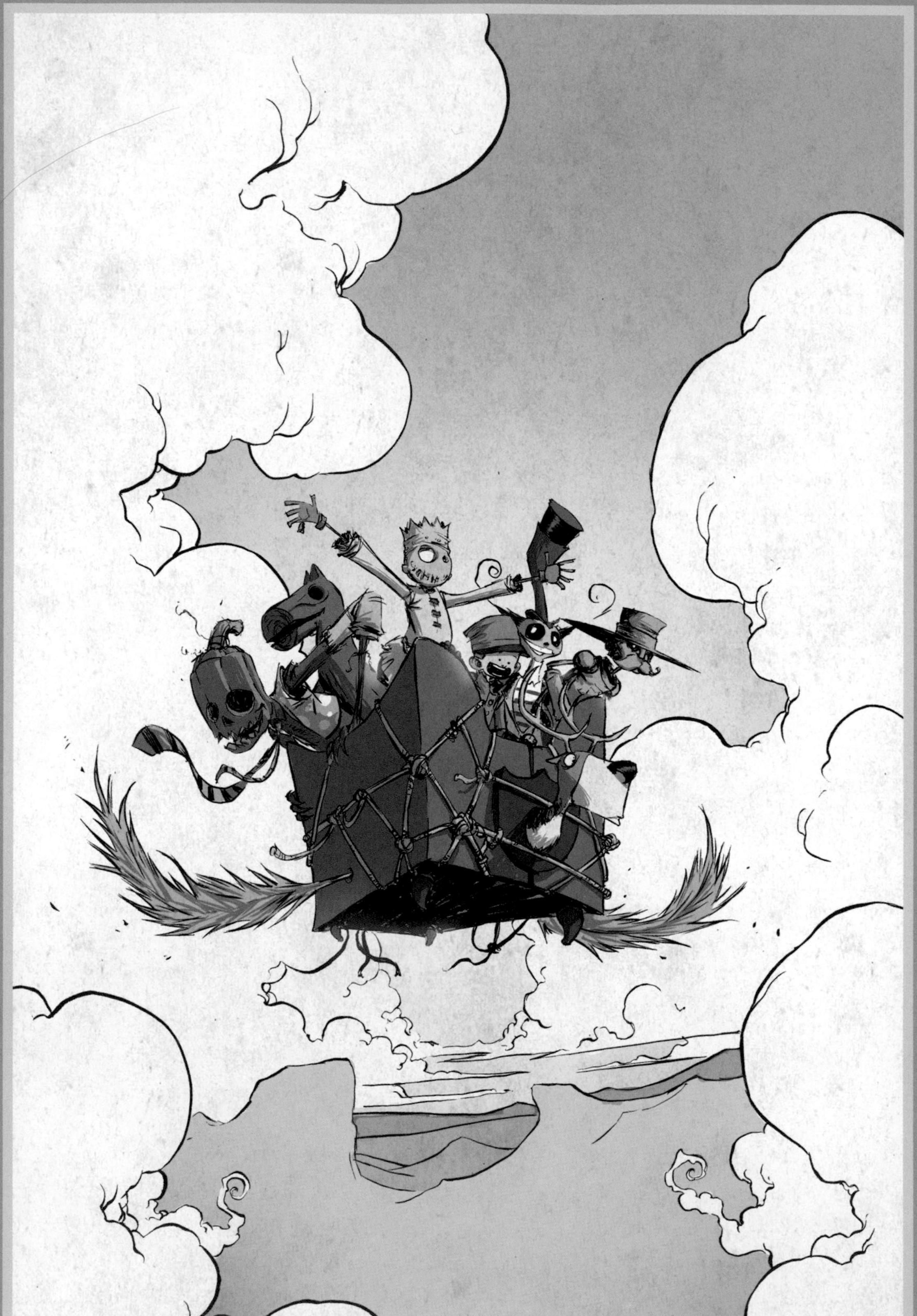

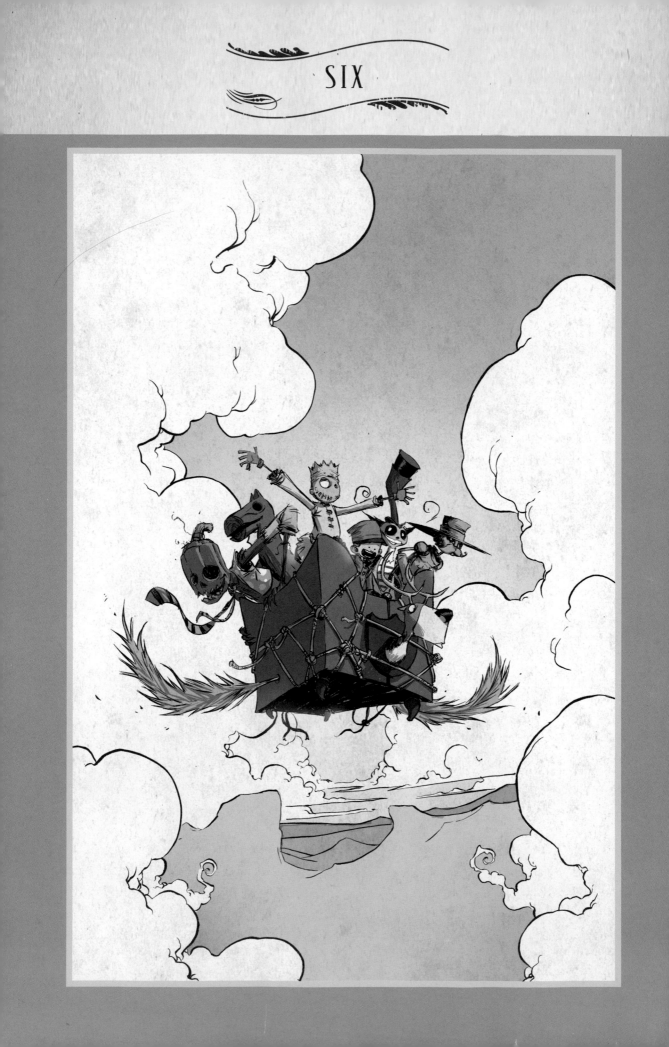

SEVEN

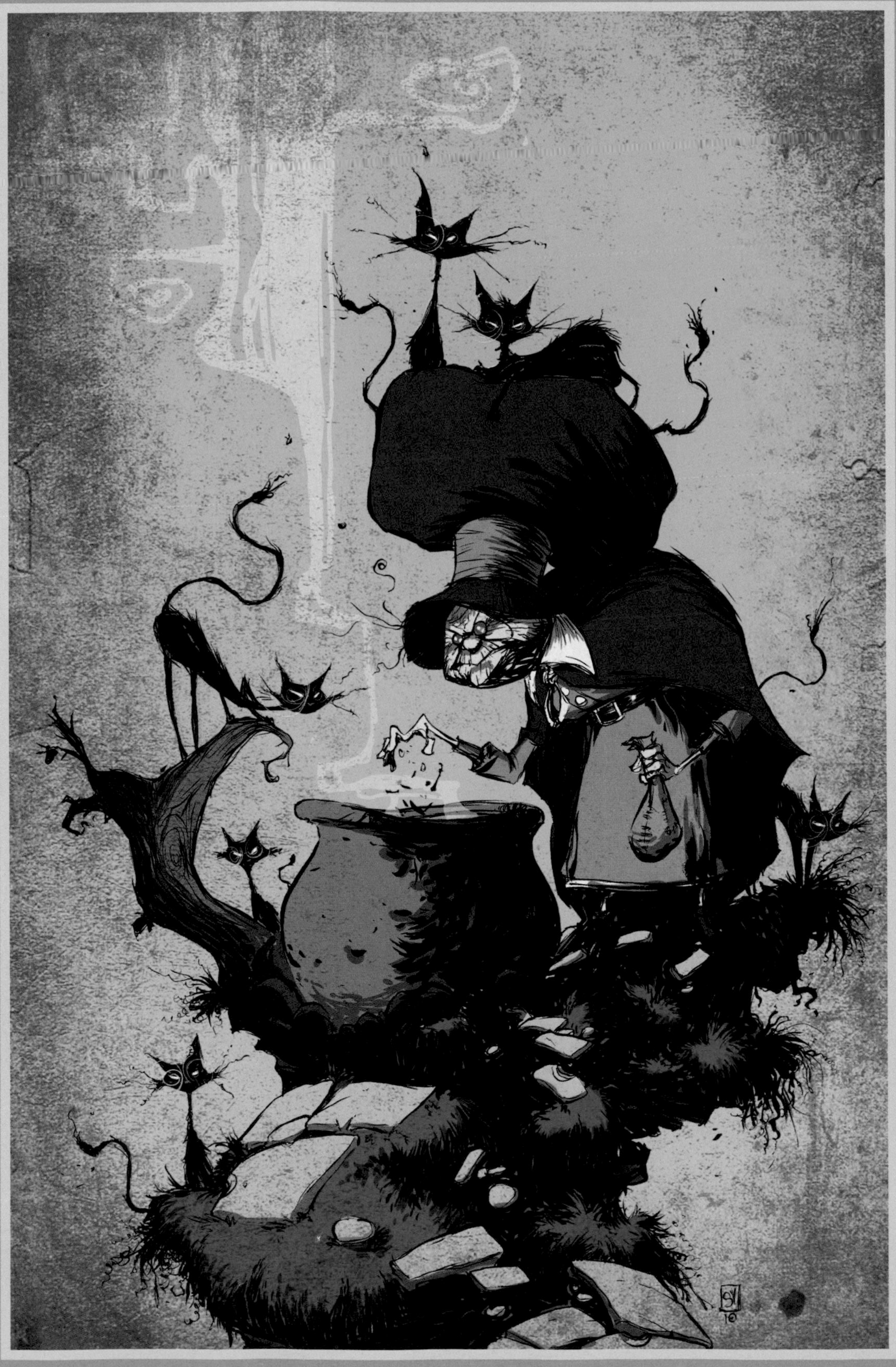

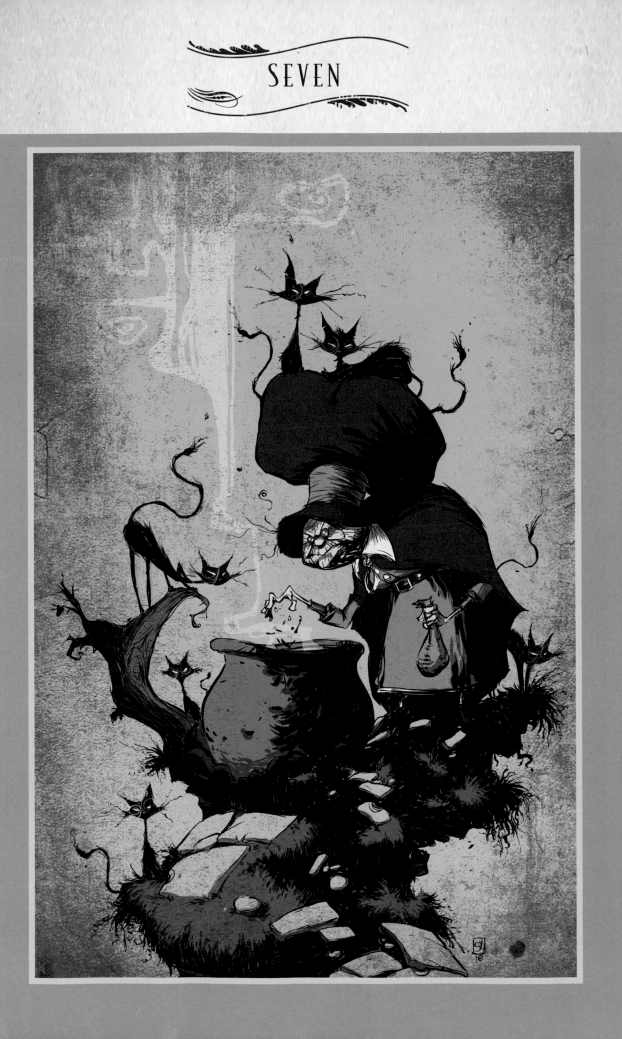

EIGHT

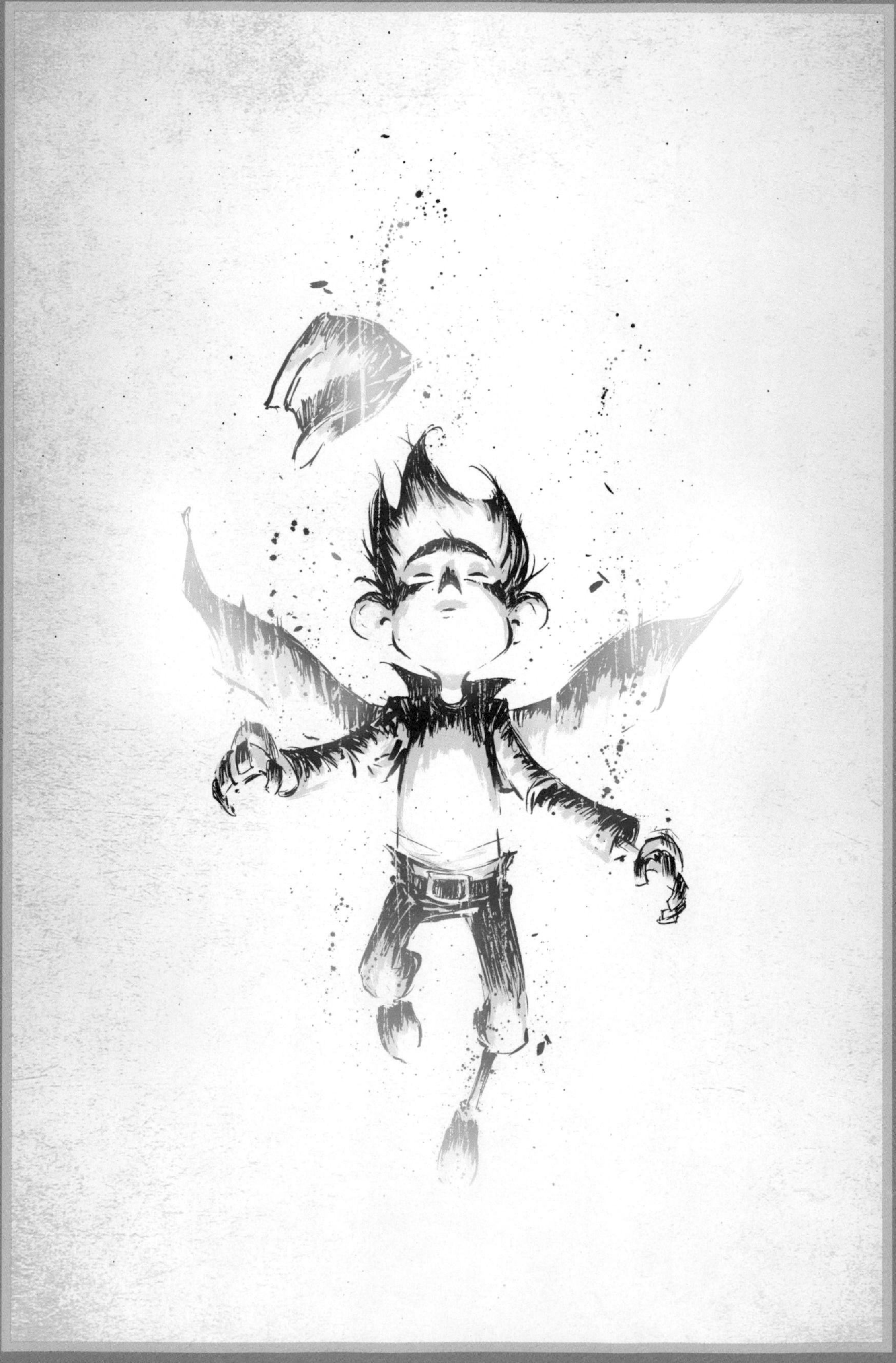

EIGHT

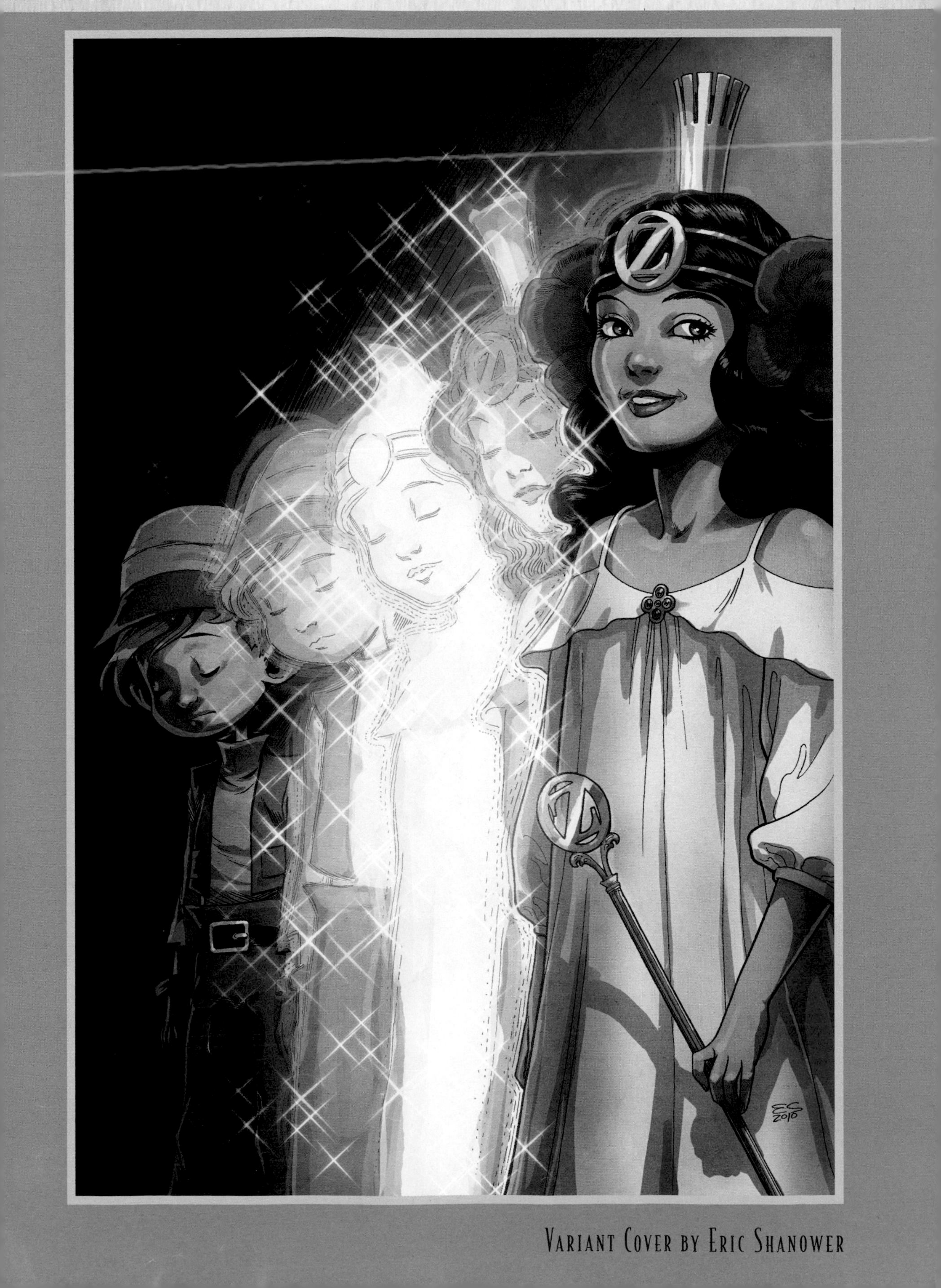

Variant Cover by Eric Shanower

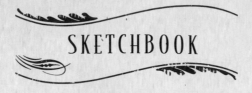

JINJUR

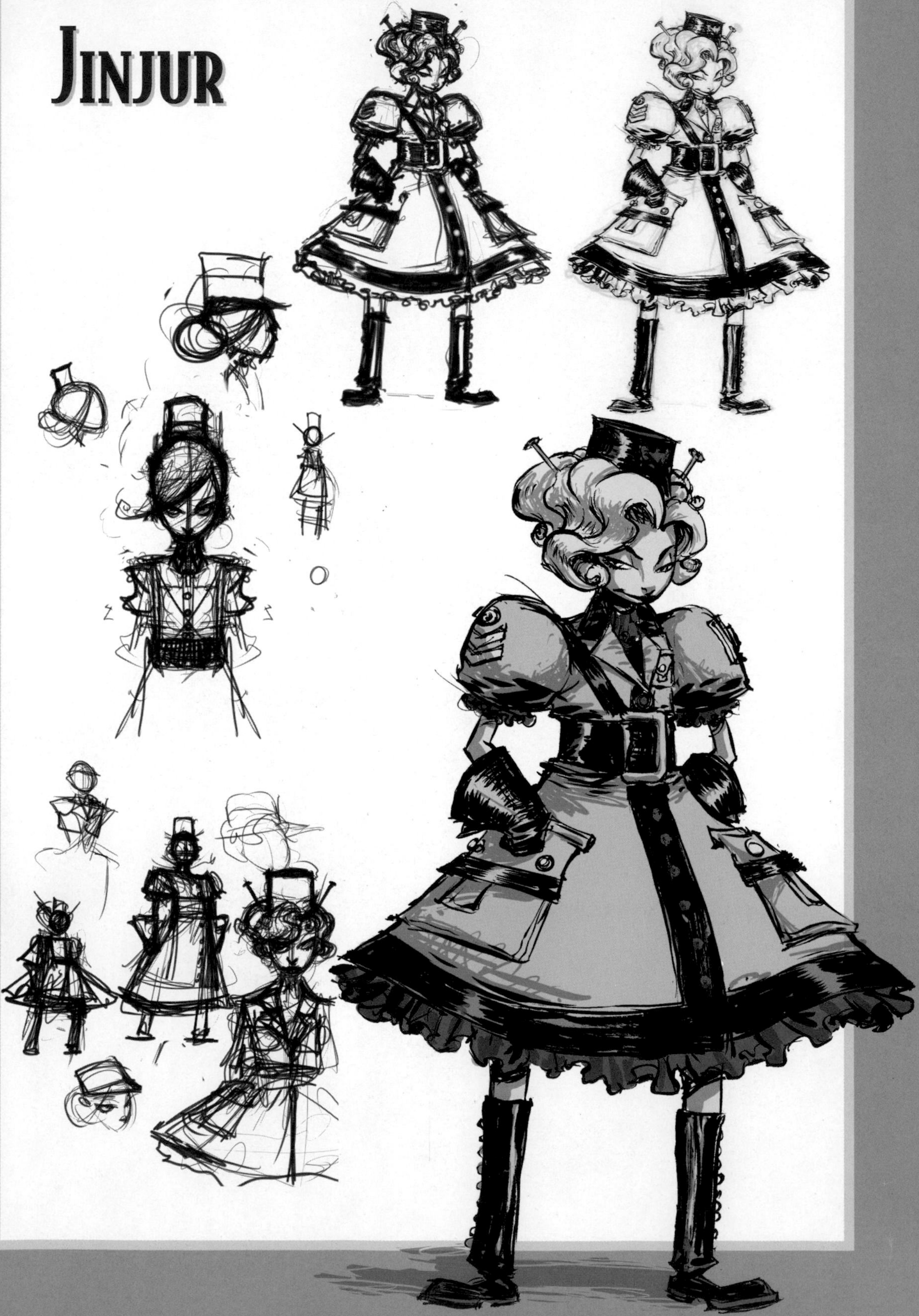

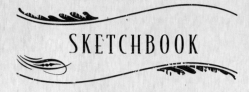

Mombi

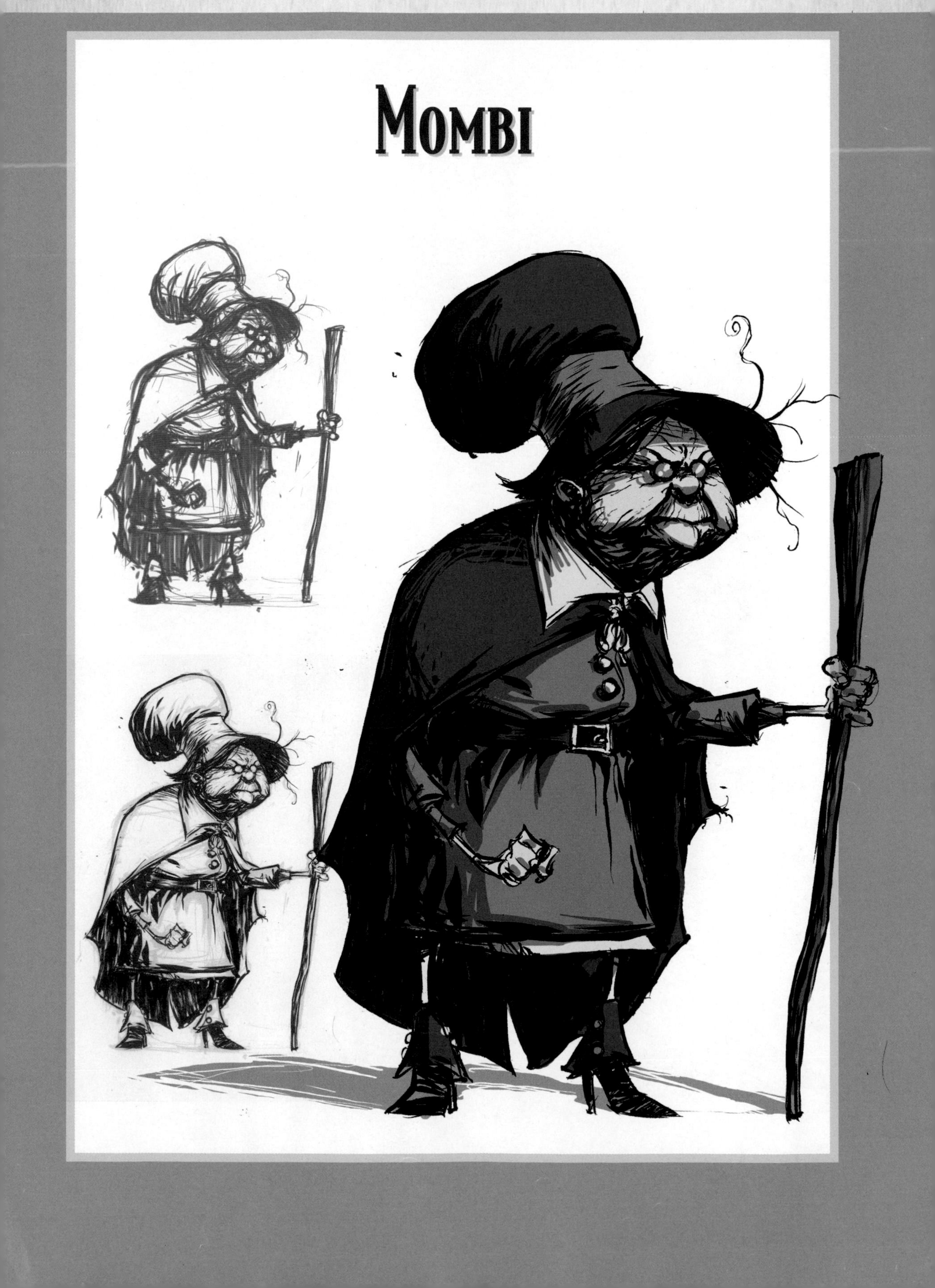

Tip

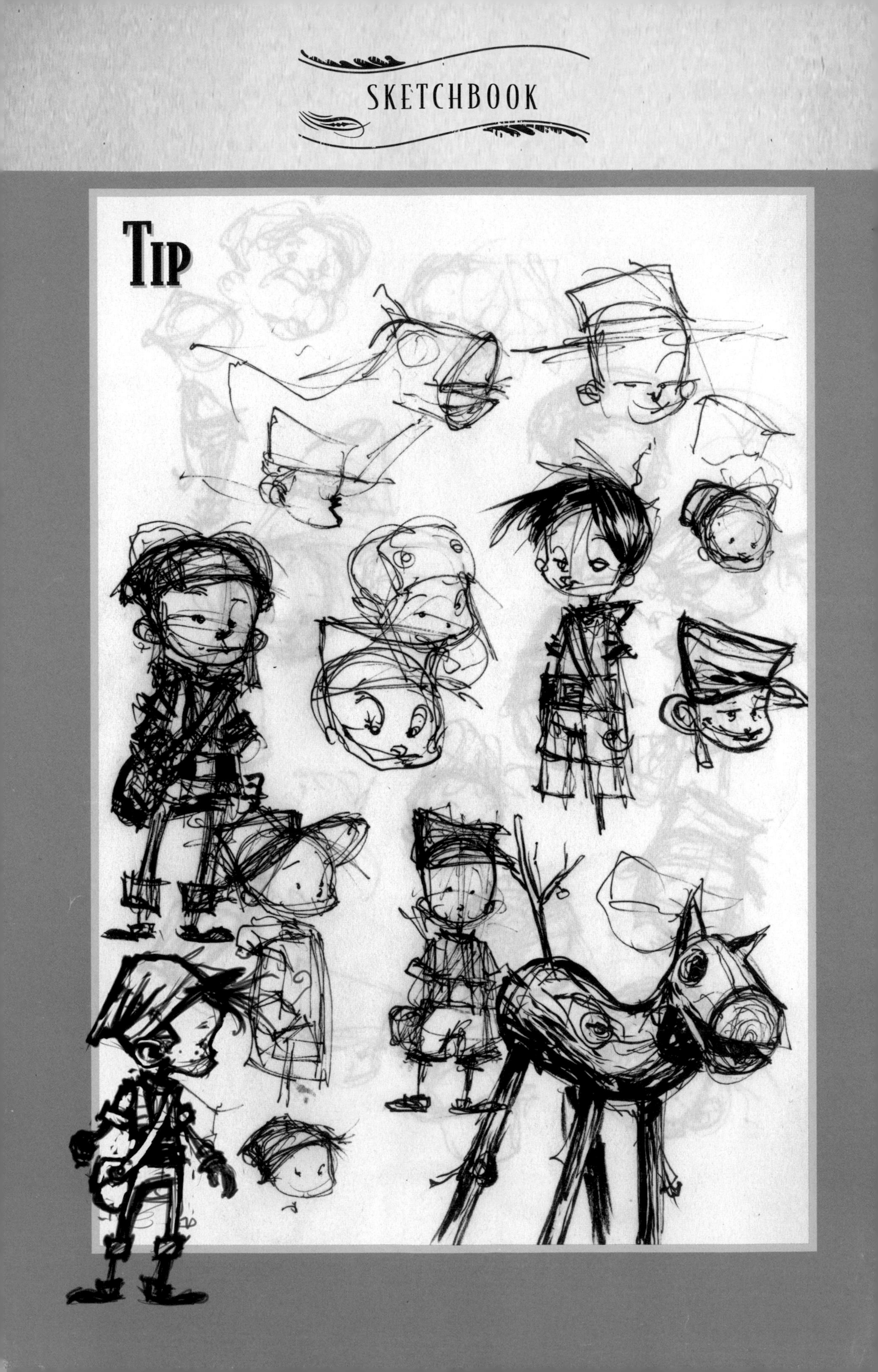

The Woggle-Bug

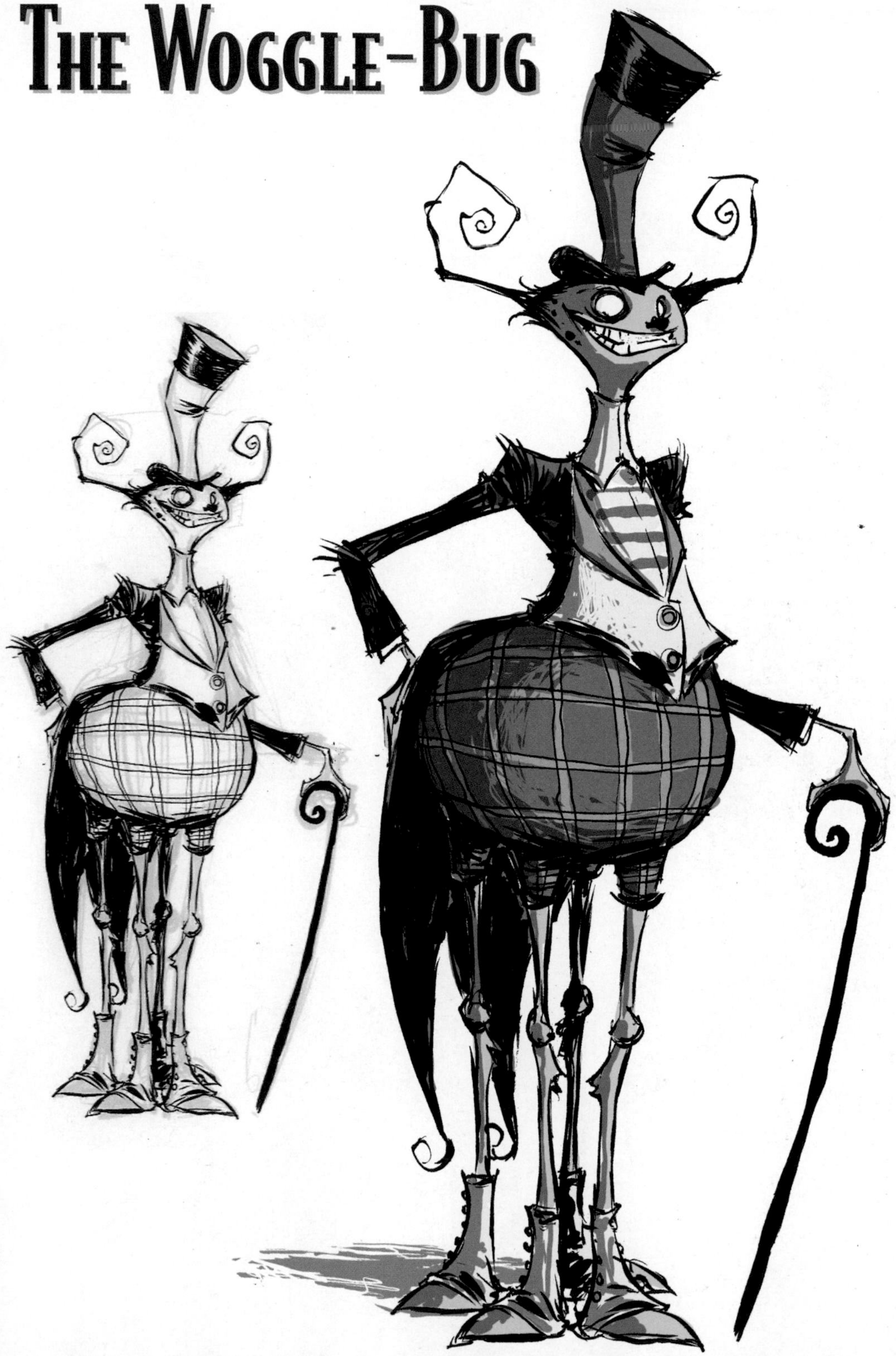

ISSUE ONE COVER PROCESS

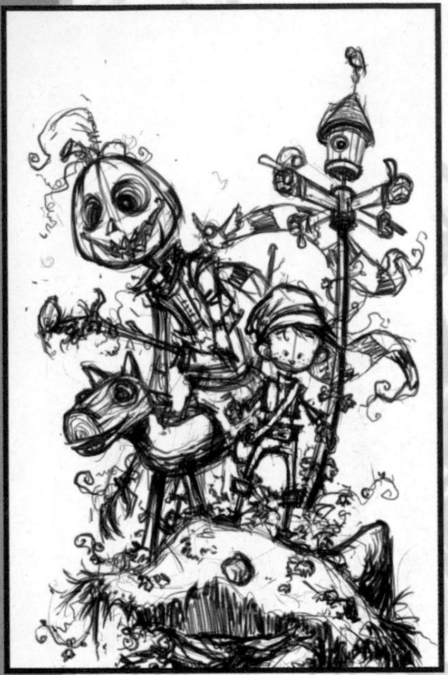

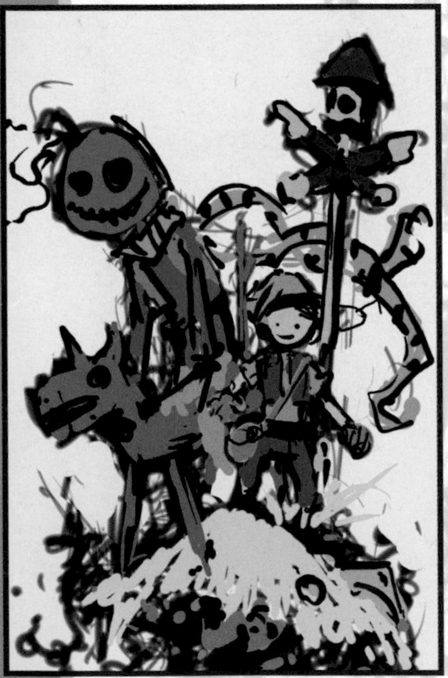

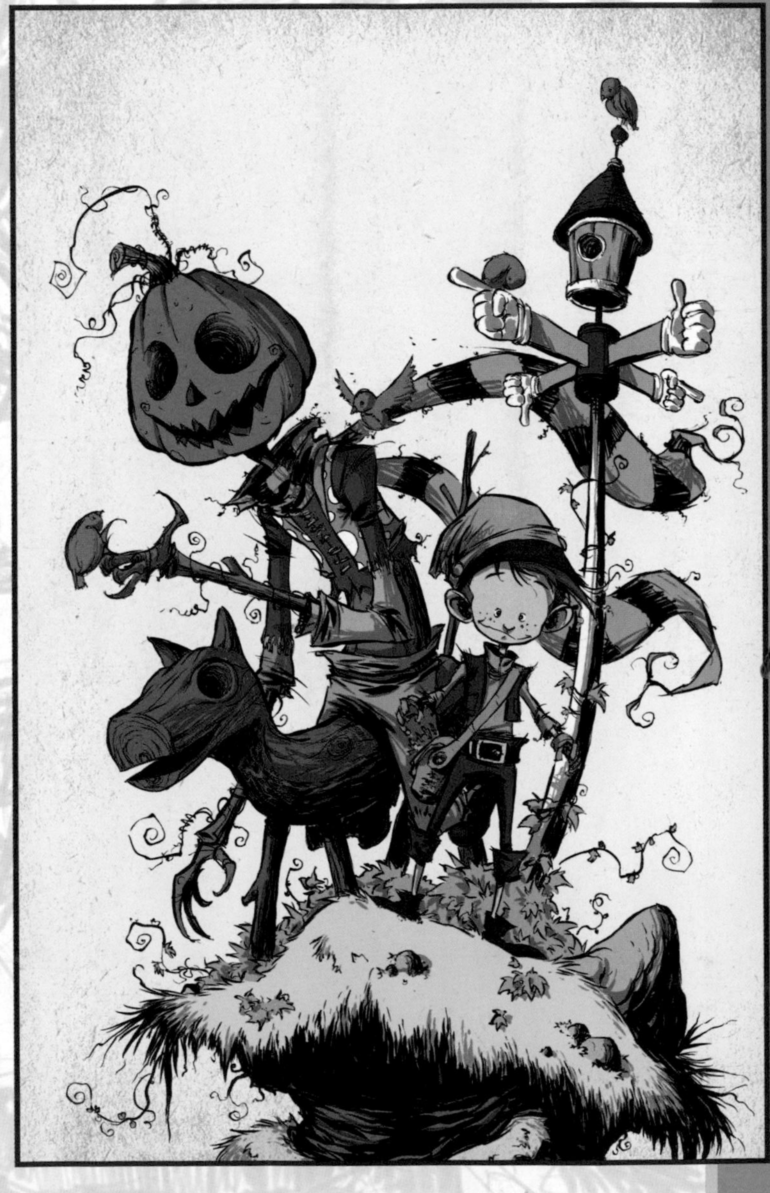

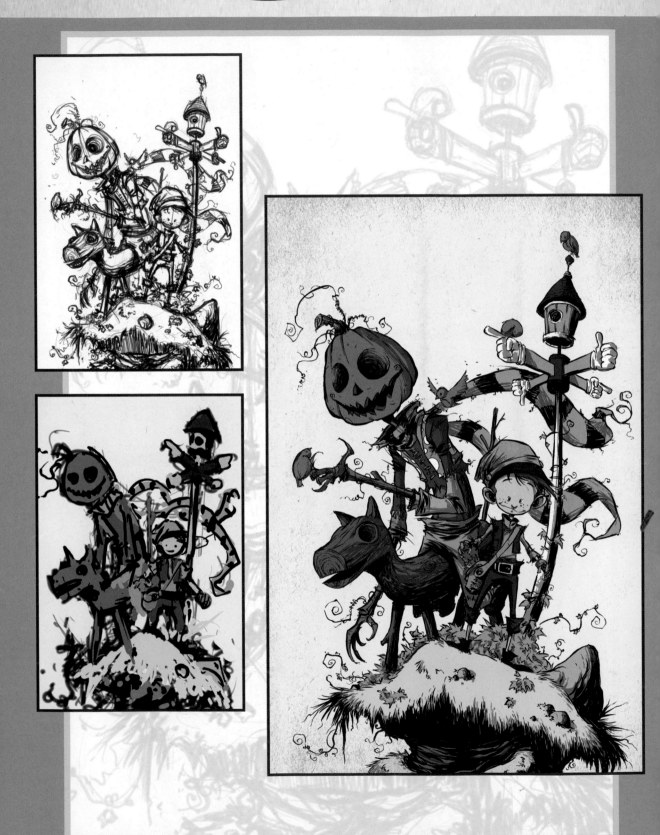